"*Deepening Democracy in Post-Neoliberal Bolivia and Venezuela* is an outstandingly researched, much welcome advance on what it means to 'deepen democracy' and the conditions that might help to achieve it, moving us beyond what has become a sterile debate over liberal democracy and radically progressive reformist politics."

Eduardo Silva, *Lydian Chair of Political Science, Tulane University, USA*

"Brilliantly researched, this is a major contribution to academic understanding to the crisis of democracy in Latin America and the tensions between markets, on the one hand, and demands for dignity and citizenship, on the other. A detailed study of anti-system outsider government in Venezuela and Bolivia, it is a valuable contribution to the comparative political economy of the left, and a must-read for anyone interested in contemporary debates about democratisation and populism."

Jean Grugel, *Co-Director of Interdisciplinary Global Development Centre (IGDC), University of York, UK*

"John Brown's debut monograph breaks new ground in the unfolding debate around the relationship between progressive governments and social movements in Latin America with a theoretically informed dense ethnography of Bolivia and Venezuela. It will be indispensable to students of Latin America and of comparative politics more generally. Recommended."

Ronaldo Munck, *Dublin City University, Ireland*

Deepening Democracy in Post-Neoliberal Bolivia and Venezuela

This book provides a timely and nuanced analysis of the successes and shortcoming of efforts to move beyond market democracy in Bolivia and Venezuela.

A twin crisis of democratic representation and socio-economic precarity created space for anti-system outsiders to emerge on the left flank of traditional party-systems in Bolivia and Venezuela, paving the way for a "post-neoliberal" democratization process. Over the course of the projects headed by Evo Morales in Bolivia and Hugo Chávez and his successor Nicolás Maduro in Venezuela, however, power struggles emerged between a recalcitrant elite, the left-led government, and organized popular sectors. These tensions shaped the pathways that processes followed, with simultaneous democratization and de-democratization occurring whereby a partial deepening and extending of democratic quality for popular sectors was accompanied by the bending of liberal norms. Comparing the varying balance and forms of power between competing actors, this book offers a novel and rich explanation of the partial and stuttering efforts to advance a post-neoliberal democracy in Bolivia and Venezuela.

Bringing important insights on the reasons for the emergence of anti-system leaders and parties, the impact that they have on the quality of democracy, and how progressive governments interact with social movements, this book will be of interest to researchers studying Latin America, as well as those specializing in development and political science more broadly.

John Brown is a lecturer at the Centre for the Study of Politics, Maynooth University, Ireland.

Routledge Studies in Latin American Development

The series features innovative and original research on Latin American development from scholars both within and outside of Latin America. It particularly promotes comparative and interdisciplinary research targeted at a global readership.

In terms of theory and method, rather than basing itself on any one orthodoxy, the series draws broadly on the tool kit of the social sciences in general, emphasizing comparison, the analysis of the structure and processes, and the application of qualitative and quantitative methods.

Bolivia at the Crossroads
Politics, Economy, and Environment in a Time of Crisis
Edited by Soledad Valdivia Rivera

Legal Experiments for Development in Latin America
Modernization, Revolution and Social Justice
Helena Alviar García

Brazilian Elites and their Philanthropy
Wealth at the Service of Development
Jessica Sklair

Deepening Democracy in Post-Neoliberal Bolivia and Venezuela
Advances and Setbacks
John Brown

Social Revolt in Chile
Triggering Factors and Possible Outcomes
Edited by Carlos Peña and Patricio Silva

For more information about this series, please visit www.routledge.com/Routledge-Studies-in-Latin-American-Development/book-series/RSLADc

Deepening Democracy in Post-Neoliberal Bolivia and Venezuela

Advances and Setbacks

John Brown

Routledge
Taylor & Francis Group
LONDON AND NEW YORK

First published 2022
by Routledge
2 Park Square, Milton Park, Abingdon, Oxon OX14 4RN

and by Routledge
605 Third Avenue, New York, NY 10158

Routledge is an imprint of the Taylor & Francis Group, an informa business

British Library Cataloguing-in-Publication Data
A catalogue record for this book is available from the British Library

Library of Congress Cataloging-in-Publication Data
Names: Brown, John, author.
Title: Deepening democracy in post-neoliberal Bolivia and Venezuela : advances and setbacks / John Brown.
Description: Abingdon, Oxon ; New York, NY : Routledge, 2022. | Series: Routledge studies in Latin American development | Includes bibliographical references and index.
Identifiers: LCCN 2021044968 (print) | LCCN 2021044969 (ebook) | ISBN 9781032201481 (hardback) | ISBN 9781032201504 (paperback) | ISBN 9781003262466 (ebook)
Subjects: LCSH: Bolivia—Politics and government—2006- | Venezuela—Politics and government—1999- | Bolivia—Economic conditions—21st century. | Venezuela—Economic conditions—21st century. | Democratization—Bolivia. | Democratization—Venezuela. | Morales Ayma, Evo, 1959- | Chávez Frías, Hugo. | Maduro, Nicolás, 1962-
Classification: LCC JL2231 .B76 2022 (print) | LCC JL2231 (ebook) | DDC 320.98—dc23/eng/20211018
LC record available at https://lccn.loc.gov/2021044968
LC ebook record available at https://lccn.loc.gov/2021044969

ISBN: 978-1-032-20148-1 (hbk)
ISBN: 978-1-032-20150-4 (pbk)
ISBN: 978-1-003-26246-6 (ebk)

DOI: 10.4324/9781003262466

Typeset in Bembo
by codeMantra

Contents

Acknowledgements and Dedications

I wish to thank the Irish Research Council for continued support over the entire process of researching and writing this book. To Barry, thank you for all of your calming words and encouragement. I would not be doing what I am doing without you. To Eduardo, thank you for your kindness and guidance since we first met. To the amazing people I have been lucky enough to meet in Bolivia and Venezuela whose passion and resilience inspired this project, I offer my deepest thanks.

To Mam, Dad, and Jenny, it is your support over the past number of years and your never-ending encouragement to explore the world and to find what makes me happy that has brought me here.

To Caro, for your support, feedback, passion, and belief in me when I was tired, thank you.

This book would not have been possible without the support of doctoral and postdoctoral funding from the Irish Research Council.

Introduction

The crisis of market democracy and the emergence of anti-system outsiders

Depending on who you ask about the democratization processes headed by Evo Morales in Bolivia and Hugo Chávez in Venezuela, you will get an array of polarized and complex answers regarding their impacts on democratic quality. Critics from the liberal school of democracy decry that the leaders were illiberal populists who damaged the very fabric of democracy by boosting the power of the president over other branches of government, by limiting private property rights, and by restricting opposition media organizations. Less orthodox analysts highlight that executive powers were boosted so as to overcome the power of entrenched economic and media elites who sought to limit the scope of the leftist presidents to govern from the left. While the processes have fostered polarizing debates between liberal and radical scholars, contrasting analyses have not been confined to academia.

During my fieldwork in Bolivia and Venezuela, popular sector appraisals of the processes highlighted both the advances and shortcomings of the processes. Supporters of the presidents from poor neighborhoods in both countries told me that democracy did not exist for them before the elections of Morales and Chávez.[1] For example, during a meeting of a community council in the Petare *barrio* of Caracas, a community organizer described to me that

> before Chávez, when I was younger and saw someone talking about the constitution we turned off the television because we felt that politics did not matter for us, it was only for 'them' … the rich. When Chávez came he asked us 'Do you know what this constitution says?' He encouraged us to ask questions.

Aside from being encouraged to participate in democratic politics, people regularly emphasized to me that for the first time in their lives they could call an elected government "their government" because policies actually sought to alleviate some of the worst excesses of poverty and exclusion that they experienced on a daily basis. Walking around low-income neighborhoods in Caracas, Venezuela and El Alto, Bolivia, residents showed me how state funding had supported the development of new housing projects, schools,

DOI: 10.4324/9781003262466-1

health services, and markets selling subsidized foods. Residents told me that previous governments had literally forgotten about them and left them isolated in the crumbling outskirts of cities. Under Morales and Chávez, new infrastructure projects sought to re-connect these forgotten sectors of society to urban centers. Indeed, on my daily trips on the new highway and cable-car system connecting El Alto to La Paz, mini-bus drivers and passengers told me that "Evo is one of us … He cares about us," "he listens to us." Likewise, while watching a game of basketball in Petare, Caracas, on a court built using state funds, a youth worker pointed up toward the highest reaches of the *barrio* where a cable-car system was under construction. The youth worker explained that the poorest residents of the *barrio* lived in the highest zones as the journey down the steep-sided valley was long and difficult. When the cable car is completed, he noted, "we will be connected, we will be part of Caracas, we will be part of Venezuela."

Popular sector support for the projects, however, was never uncritical. There were concerns over the presidents' moderating of reform processes in the face of opposition, while some popular sector organizers suggested that space for grassroots critique of the presidents and their parties was too limited. In Venezuela, an ardent Chavista (supporter of the process headed by Hugo Chávez) complained to me that when their local communal council and commune representatives sought to raise concerns regarding the speed and direction of the process with members of the new left-party, they were ignored and that a "bureaucracy of the Right" had been "replaced by a bureaucracy of the Left." Issues of a lack of space for critique were also prevalent in Bolivia. As the coordinator of Defense Committee for La Paz (CODELPA) stressed to me, Morales and his party "tell our popular organizations that 'if you support me, I will finance you, I will give you power'. They (popular organizations) have been co-opted, for me, they have been extorted."

Liberal academic analyses describe the processes as examples of illiberal de-democratization; radical scholars and supporters of the processes in Bolivia and Venezuela describe how popular voices have been incorporated into democratic politics for the first time; and some popular organization members suggest that while new voices may have been incorporated, critical popular voices were not. How is one to interpret such paradoxical interpretations of the reform processes in Bolivia and Venezuela? Were Chávez and Morales examples of authoritarian populists whose lack of respect for the norms and institutions of democracy placed democratic stability in doubt? Or were they radical democratizers who responded to calls from long-excluded sectors of society for political and socio-economic inclusion? Did left-wing governments seek to curb critical voices coming from sectors of their popular support base? Is it possible that democratic quality simultaneously weakened in some areas while strengthening in others? If so, what explains the directions processes took? This book sheds light on these questions by analyzing what happens to democratization processes when left-governments find themselves squeezed between popular sectors demanding political and socio-economic incorporation and a powerful opposition who seek to protect the status quo. In doing so, though examining two Andean cases in detail, the book's analysis is in effect responding to what is arguably the most important global phenomenon at present, namely the crisis of democracy.

Democracy in crisis

There is growing recognition, both in academic literature and in popular commentary, across the political spectrum from Liberals, Conservatives to Marxists, that the contemporary dominant model of democracy faces a crisis. There is, however, a debate as to how this crisis of democracy should be understood and responded to. The dominant narrative has focused on the illiberal behaviors of "populist" leaders whose discursive styles and lack of respect for liberal norms and institutions have threatened democratic stability.[2] The arguments suggest that if opportunistic populists are not kept from power, there is a risk of democratic backsliding leading to the emergence of hybrid, competitive authoritarian regimes in which democratic institutions are politicized and used by populists to skew the playing field to such an extent that an opposition's capacity to compete is seriously compromised.[3]

While mainstream analyses raise salient issues regarding the dangers of bending liberal norms, there are several issues with such appraisals. First, and most fundamentally, the symptoms of the crisis of democracy are conflated with the causes of the crisis of democracy. That is, by identifying populism as the major threat to democratic rule, the underlying causes that foster support for outsiders receive far less attention. From this, a second issue emerges whereby "populists" of all ideological stripes are understood as threats to democracy, irrespective of what it is that they seek to do when elected to office, or what forces shape their behaviors following election. Populism has become a catch-all term to describe—and in most cases denigrate—any challenger to the political status quo irrespective of fundamental differences between "populists" in terms of their stances on socio-economic, political, and identity issues. As such, rather than using a populist framing, the terms outsiders and anti-system parties are used here to describe leaders/parties who come from outside the traditional mainstream party system, who call into question the functioning of democracy, and who raise concerns regarding elite capture of institutions.[4]

Outsider, anti-system leaders and parties should be understood as responses to neoliberalization processes which fostered de-democratization processes. In the 1970s, Crozier, Huntington, and Watanuki (1975) wrote a highly influential report, *The Crisis of Democracy*, for the Trilateral Commission. The report began with a question: "Is political democracy, as it exists today, a viable form of government?"[5] The authors described a scenario (particularly in the United States, Western Europe, and Japan) whereby democracy itself had created its own crisis by fostering an overload of demands for increased participation, higher social security payments and a wider social security net, and better economic welfare. Citizens were said to be demanding "too much democracy" for the state to deliver, while an erosion of authority and governability was due to "over-participation." As such the report stated that the "crisis" of democracy was a result of the over-permissiveness of democracy itself.[6]

The report presented the challenge of how to reconcile democratic politics, which is built on the premise of equality, with market economics, which is centered on inequality.[7] With ideological origins in the liberal Weber-Schumpeter model of democracy,[8] proponents of a neoliberal-infused democracy believed that both political and economic life should be a matter of individual freedom and initiative. A free market society with a minimal state is the goal.[9] While neoliberalism is a contested concept, fundamentally it is an ideology "founded on an idealized vision of market rule and liberal freedoms, combining a utilitarian conception of market rationality and competitive individualism with deep antipathies to social redistribution and solidarity."[10] Projects of neoliberalization are not simply about a withdrawal of the state but are instead concerned with its capture and reuse. Neoliberalization processes thus entail both rollback politics of deregulation and dismantlement, and rollout politics of pro-corporate and market-conforming governance. Rollback and rollout neoliberalization processes "sought to create a political economy and social order where public policy is premised upon the dominance of the investor" and where dominant economic forces are insulated from democratic rule and popular accountability.[11] Monetarist economic policies are taken out of public debate and enshrined in binding supranational treaties, while the extent of policy is confined within "acceptable" limits set by transnational trading agreements, central banking mechanisms, and bureaucratic expertise.[12] Democracy in the neoliberal era thus became a technocratic affair with experts in non-majoritarian institutions, including independent central banks, playing an increasingly dominant role.[13] The rules of the game were designed to "'lock in' commitments to neo-liberalism and to 'lock out' other potential political economy alternatives."[14]

Concerns of socioeconomic citizenship and inequality were reduced to afterthoughts to the overarching drive to provide "good" investment environments. Labor became "flexible," meaning precarious. Austerity and social-welfare retrenchment became the norm. Individual risk was increased as socialization of risk was decreased, while neoliberal policy design allowed inequality to reach unprecedented levels.[15] Rising economic inequality is translated back onto rising political inequality in a vicious feedback cycle, as the owners of wealth increasingly set the rules of the game that promote their own interests.[16] This extremely narrow (low-quality political citizenship) and shallow (low-quality socio-economic citizenship) form of democracy underpinned by neoliberal rationale may be defined as "market democracy" in which the state's role is to guarantee the protection of the interests of transnational and domestic capital, irrespective of whether such interests run contrary to those of domestic citizens. This market model of democracy was promoted as "the only game in town" by both center-right and center-left parties. Unsurprisingly, the de-politicization of politics under market democracy, and its embrace by political parties on both the right and the left, meant that democracy became "devalued" as a political currency.[17] The neoliberal response to the 1970s "crisis of *too much* democracy" engendered a crisis of *too little* democracy today.

The general trend of a (self-reinforcing) narrowing and shallowing of democracy, and the congealment of parties and political leaders around marketized citizenship models, fostered the development of unstable democratic equilibria with traditional party systems feeling the strain in Europe, North America, and Latin America. Where the interests of the wealthiest sectors of society are organized into politics, while issues concerning popular classes are increasingly organized out, democracy becomes unstable. Where party–voter distances widen, while party–party differences narrow, popular indifference and distrust of parties and political institutions more generally grows.[18] This combination of mistrust in the political system alongside anomie and withdrawal from participation opened space for a movement of opposition that could threaten "democracy as we know it."[19] As parties and politicians become more detached from their traditional social bases, while inequality and socioeconomic precarity become entrenched, democracy is viewed by excluded sectors as a façade for the maintenance of elite privilege, and space for anti-system outsiders widens. Appealing to a sense of personal danger and a shared sense of political exclusion, such candidates may, not wholly inaccurately, portray the political class as having failed, and that it will go on failing, effectively barring citizens from any realistic prospect of a better life.[20]

Hence, while mainstream analyses locate "populism" as the threat to democracy, they confuse the symptoms of the crisis of democracy with its underlying causes. By painting all outsiders as threats to democracy, including anti-system leaders or parties that seek to respond to the underlying causes of the crisis of democracy, mainstream accounts of "populists" miss the very crux of the matter. This is not to suggest that all outsiders offer a genuine response to the narrowing of and shallowing of democratic quality over the course of neoliberalization processes. They do not. But neither should we fall into the trap of assuming that all outsiders are threats to democracy.

Anti-system outsiders have taken clearly distinctive forms[21] across Europe and the Americas, with conservative, regressive-reactionary outsiders such as Marine Le Pen and the National Front in France, Viktor Orbán and Fidesz in Hungary, and Donald Trump and the Republican Party in the United States "supporting trade protectionism and forms of 'welfare chauvinism'—that is, generous welfare states that concentrate their benefits on 'authentic' members of the ethno-national community, to the partial or complete exclusion of immigrant and minority populations."[22] Nativist, right-wing regressive outsiders "have thrived in northern and central European countries with relatively unified labor markets and universalistic welfare states under pressure from the forces of market globalization."[23] While space for such outsiders grew as a result of the narrowing and shallowing of democratic quality in the neoliberal era, their anti-market positions are not always clear. Indeed, many adopt "positions typical of the pro-market right, such as lower taxation, strong defense of private property and sympathy for business."[24] As such, while these anti-system outsiders critique some features of globalization and challenge the mainstream center-left and center-right parties who converged around neoliberalization processes, they offer little in the way of a clearly demarcated critique of the core underlying factors that fostered the crisis of democracy—and their own elections—in the first place.

In cases where financial crises were followed by free-market austerity and structural adjustments, and "where the traditional labor-based or leftist parties played a major role in the imposition of neoliberal austerity and adjustment programs, thus converging with the programmatic platforms of their more conservative rivals," mass social and electoral protest paved the way for the election of progressive outsider parties and candidates.[25] Moreover, these progressive outsiders emerged in countries where labor markets are highly dualistic and welfare states are segmented,[26] resulting in large sections of society being excluded from formal sector employment and the social protections that go with these jobs such as social security, health insurance, and unemployment insurance.[27] Outsiders in these cases critiqued mainstream party systems and promised voters redistributive policies and social protections from market insecurities, thereby aiming to provide both political and socio-economic incorporation for previously excluded sectors of society.[28] For example, SYRIZA in Greece and Podemos in Spain called into question the neoliberal model of capitalism and its unfettered markets. The leaders of these parties rejected austerity and supported "a shift in economic policy and regulation away from the preference for financial interests and in favor of a redistribution of wealth and income towards the non-wealthy majority in society."[29] While SYRIZA and Podemos politicians were elected to power and sought to deliver on electoral promises, their capacity to challenge the market model of democracy and its accompanying citizenship regime was curbed due to pressure from powerful creditor EU member states as well as threats of capital flight and disinvestment.[30]

With similarities in the underlying conditions that fostered the emergence of outsiders in Greece and Spain, in several Latin American cases progressive anti-system outsiders were elected to office where they remained in power for extended periods of time. Moreover, in comparison to their European counterparts, these governments made more radical efforts to challenge the market model of democracy and to incorporate excluded sectors via the creation of new spaces of political participation and socio-economic inclusion. While the more aggressive efforts to challenge market democracy ensured the outsider-led processes in Latin America retained greater popular support than their European counterparts, by their very nature the processes challenged the status quo and triggered opposition. In the struggles between the anti-system governments and opposition, both sides adopted institutional and extra-institutional tactics to advance their agendas. As such, the region's cases merit deeper investigation so as to uncover broader lessons regarding if and how progressive anti-system leaders/parties can respond to the crisis of market democracy that has engulfed much of the globe, what factors enable or restrict them from doing so, and what the longer-term impacts on democratic quality and stability of outsider-led processes may be.

Latin America's anti-system outsiders

Anti-system outsiders emerged in cases where labor-based and center-left parties were at the forefront of advancing neoliberal policies, a configuration found in Bolivia, Ecuador, and Venezuela.[31] Neoliberal policies were adopted in a bait-and-switch manner whereby center-left candidates reneged on pre-election promises not to adopt market-friendly reforms.

The adoption of neoliberal policies by center-left parties caused party systems to converge around variants of market orthodoxy, programmatically de-aligning partisan competition and channeling societal opposition into extra-systemic forms of social and electoral protest, thereby opening vacant political space for outsiders on the left flank of mainstream parties.[32] The underdeveloped nature of social citizenship and the dualistic labor market whereby the vast majority of workers are employed in the informal sector sees a divide in society between those with a place in organized, formal society, and those without.[33] As such, the anti-system nature of Latin America's outsiders refers to challenging political and economic elites whose insider status is founded on the exclusion of other sectors of the national community.[34] Reflecting protester sentiment, the electoral campaigns of progressive anti-system candidates such as Hugo Chávez in Venezuela and Evo Morales in Bolivia engaged in strident critiques of mainstream party systems, overtly critiqued neoliberalism and global capitalism, challenged domestic and transnational economic elite control of wealth and resources and called for a strong state that guaranteed social citizenship for all sectors of society. They also promised to deepen political participation via plebiscitary measures to convoke constituent assemblies and re-found national democratic regimes. Moreover, given Latin America's position as a post-colonial developing region and the sentiment amongst protesters that the United States and the International Monetary Fund were seeking to curb national sovereignty by imposing structural adjustments on borrowing governments, popular sectors and outsider-candidates adopted a progressive-internationalist stance that not only sought to curb the influence of unelected external (f)actors such as foreign capital and international financial institutions, but also advocated international solidarity with regional socialist/progressive parties and leaders. Anti-system outsiders thus engaged in a strident critique of market democracy and its neoliberal underpinnings, calling instead for a post-neoliberal model of democracy that was more attentive to the needs of the majority-popular sectors of society rather than investors, traditional elites, and transnational capital.

Echoing the broader "populist" analyses of outsider-candidates mentioned above, scholars from the liberal tradition have described how Chávez and Morales threatened democracy by challenging liberal norms.[35] For example, Weyland outlines the ways these leaders eroded institutional checks and balances and marginalized the opposition through "discriminatory legalism."[36] Likewise, Levitsky and Loxton[37] describe these cases as "competitive authoritarian" whereby democratic institutions exist and are used as the primary routes to power, but incumbents then abuse state powers to skew electoral competition in their favor to such an extent that an opposition's ability to compete is seriously compromised. Leaders in these cases were said to rely on "populist rhetoric" to build their political hegemony before riding roughshod over democratic norms by boosting the power of the executive. The Andean cases have become a sort of parable in mainstream accounts and the media regarding the dangers of "populism," with liberal scholars warning what awaits the "developed" democracies if outsiders are not kept from power. Levitsky and Ziblatt's "How Democracies Die" is a prime example. The authors mention Chávez a number of times, highlighting that it was in fact his "populism" that triggered an opposition-led coup, that he moved toward authoritarianism by delaying an election until oil prices rose, that he sought to pack the courts with loyalists, that he closed a newspaper, eliminated presidential term limits, arrested opposition media and political figures, and won elections that were "free" but not "fair" because of his influence over the media and the machinery of government. However, as Hellinger[38] highlights, Levitsky and Ziblatt present a narrative that selectively or wrongly paints a portrait of Chávez "to serve an argument not only against socialism but against progressive populism." The problems with such analyses are that they do not sufficiently couch executive behaviors within empirical realities, ignore opposition destabilization tactics, fail to account for the contested nature of democracy in the continent, and ultimately only capture a part of the story. Fundamentally, these analyses elide detailed discussion as to *why* left-presidents behaved in illiberal ways as well as *what* it is that they actually sought to do with boosted presidential powers.

While liberal scholars have decried the "hyper-presidential" nature of the "radical" left cases, anti-system outsiders in the Andes emphasized that entrenched political elites and regional powers blocked programs for change, and hence argued for a strong president who relied on "plebiscitarian appeals for popular support" so as to "counter the bias toward the status quo."[39] Hence, while liberal analysts rightly raise concerns regarding the stability of democracy where presidents accrue power in the office of the executive, progressive-outsiders and their support base highlight that a *stable* democracy that adheres to liberal norms does not automatically equate with a *quality* democracy. Indeed, the quest for "democratic stability" as a response to the "crisis of too much democracy" meant that for popular sectors "stable" democracies had become an incubator for the maintenance of political and economic exclusion, and hence, a new conception of democratic inclusion was required, even if this entailed challenging the boundaries of liberal democratic norms. Once again, this points to the logical fallacy of much of the academic theorizing on "illiberal populists" in Latin America, and beyond. It is precisely because "stable democracy" in the market era came to mean low-quality democracy that outsiders emerged. While conservatives argued for a neoliberal response to the "over permissiveness" of democracy and to foster greater stability, the model they advocated fostered such rampant inequality, precarity, and limited capacity for popular sectors to influence the political agenda that it could not remain stable in the long run. Once a trigger in the form of an economic crisis hit, the unstable democratic equilibrium that had been teetering collapsed and anti-system outsiders emerged to act as correctives to the underlying fault lines. However, whether such outsiders were able to respond to popular critiques of the market model of democracy was greatly influenced by resistance efforts from those who opposed the advancement of a post-neoliberal model.

As Ellner[40] stresses, the left-led governments in Latin America confronted powerful oppositions with clashes emerging regarding distinct visions of society and democracy. From the outset, opposition-blocs that adhered to strict neoliberal rationale rejected the legitimacy of progressive-outsiders' reform projects which supported, to greater or lesser degrees, nationalistic economic goals, regional integration to act as a counterbalance to US influence, ambitious social programs, non-elite input into decision-making processes and an increased role for the state in the economy. Moreover, opposition-blocs were backed, at times openly and at times more covertly, by North American and European politicians and state agencies. Opposition-blocs in the political sphere, who had been in office before the election of the progressive-outsiders, had traditionally held close linkages to, and supported the agendas of, privileged sectors including business groups, landowners, media owners, and church hierarchies. That is, an elite or oligarchic class existed.[41] Oligarchy combines economic and political power, and this power may be exercised formally or informally to ensure that public institutions serve private interests. In Latin America, oligarchy has tended to be organized within business families, political families, and mafias.[42] It is

> the political oligarchies that do most to constrain the reach of democratic politics … The radical economic and social extremes of Latin America do not simply describe a continuum from very poor to very rich but rather reveal a pattern of oligarchic interest and control.[43]

Oligarchic actors allied to powerful economic interests have traditionally targeted the executive to capture benefits that flow as patronage and privilege, capturing political parties and the democratic system to defend the status quo.[44] During the market democracy era when inequality increased, socio-economic well-being and security declined, and mainstream political parties offered no alternative to the neoliberal rationale, these political and economic elites became the central focus of popular sector animus. Echoing and re-enforcing popular sector concerns, progressive-outsiders represented a challenge to oligarchic and corporate interests, with calls for an overhaul of the distribution of political and economic power. Indeed, the point of departure for analyzing the Pink Tide of elections of leftist presidents in Latin America in the past two decades must center on the clash between non-hegemonic social groups and the old elites.[45]

Re-conceptualizing left-led democratization in Latin America (and beyond): the challenges of escaping the confines of market democracy

To respond to the shortcomings of liberal analyses of progressive outsider-led processes and the calls from heterodox scholars for a more rigorous appraisal of the clashes between competing social blocs, this book advances a novel conceptualization of democracy and a flexible framework that move beyond a narrow institutionalist focus. In doing so, the book develops nuanced analytical tools that allow for more accurate insights into the messy realities of struggles to advance a post-neoliberal democratization process.

While "competitive authoritarianism" speaks to the notion of hybrid regimes, a centralization continuum is advanced here that runs from "progressive centralization" through "regressive centralization" to "authoritarian centralization." Centralization in progressive centralization relates to a strengthening of executive power. However, rather than automatically depicting such boosting of executive power as being a power-grab for personalistic gains, as Weyland[46] argues, in some scenarios executive power *may* be used "progressively" to bypass opposition forces who limit the possibility to extend democracy to long-excluded popular sectors, while at the same time executive power is tethered to new, deepened spaces of popular sector participation who shape the actions of the president. The concept of progressive centralization allows us to evaluate democracy on three continuums; respect for liberal norms and use of executive powers; deepening democracy by boosting popular participation in decision-making processes; and extending democracy via boosting popular sector social citizenship and challenging entrenched inequality. Regressive centralization, meanwhile, captures the possibilities that executive power is boosted not only to curb the power of elite opponents but also to side-line or co-opt popular organizations that critique the behaviors of the ruling left-party or leader. At the same time, however, bottom-up access for less critical popular sectors may be retained while the quality of social citizenship is advanced. Centralization may become authoritarian when the executive authorizes state forces or militia to physically repress both opposition and contestatory popular sectors and ignores the outcomes of elections.[47]

While accounts of the Andean cases couched in the liberal tradition highlight the use of executive powers to curb the power of opponents of wealth redistribution as authoritarian behavior, in the most unequal region in the world strict respect for liberal norms may mean that radical challenges to inequality remain off the table. As Grugel and Riggirozzi[48] stress, there remains a fundamental question over

> whether it is possible to reach a cross-party or inter-elite consensus over some measure of social and economic redistribution or, whether on the contrary, an entrenchment of socio-economic privilege is still the price that must be paid for liberal democracy.

Such issues resonate outside the Latin American region. Indeed, this is precisely the situation in Europe and North America where center-left parties have abandoned any pretense of adhering to a project that would curb the spiraling inequality fostered by neoliberal globalization. These parties have succumbed to Margaret Thatcher's dictum that there is no alternative.

The conceptualization of democratic quality and democratization advanced here allows for engagement with the deep tensions inherent to any process that seeks to demonstrate that another world is possible, that is, where a progressive anti-system outsider is elected on a mandate to respond to the shortcomings of market democracy. Moreover, the notion of progressive centralization is useful if an analysis of progressive outsider-opposition contestation is to incorporate an extra-institutional sphere. While much has been written about progressive-outsiders' abuse of liberal institutions, there is a lack of analysis of the extra-institutional tactics used by opposition-blocs who seek to impede left-led processes that aim to redistribute political and socio-economic power. Indeed, this points to the more general need for a framework capable of highlighting why processes move in a given direction.

While left-led governments faced opposition-blocs who demanded pro-market orthodoxy and a protection of pre-existing political/economic power distribution, they simultaneously faced pressure from organized popular sectors via social movements, unions, and neighborhood organizations amongst others for greater participation and improved living conditions.[49] If traditional elite sectors advocate a market model of democracy while popular sectors call for more communitarian participative–substantive forms, how are we to understand the pathways and outcomes of processes headed by progressive-outsiders? To evaluate which social bloc left-governments respond to, why, and what tactics they use to achieve their goals, a relational framework that accounts for the power of left-parties in office, oppositional forces, and popular sectors is developed in this book. That is, to gain insight into the advances and setbacks of left-led efforts to escape the confines of market democracy and to respond to popular demands for boosted political and socio-economic incorporation, the book calls for analysis of oppositional power vis-à-vis left-governments as well as left-government—organized-popular base relations. Moreover, what *form* the powers of competing blocs take is addressed because the available sources of power to one bloc, and how they instrumentalize them, in turn shape the sources of power available to their adversaries and how they utilize them, which in turn shapes how processes impact on the quality of liberal, participatory, and substantive components of democratic quality. Though the framework is used in this book to evaluate Latin American cases, it is flexible and can be adapted to analyze differing contextual realities.

While mainstream scholars balk at the uncomfortable possibility that popular sector incorporation is boosted at the same time that the liberal rights of opposition elites are restricted, this, unfortunately, is closer to the realities in Latin America. Unlike normative accounts that hold liberal democracy to be the beginning and the end of debates regarding the outsider-led processes, the aim here is not to hold one model above all others but rather to examine empirical realities and to bring popular sector opinions into discussions when assessing democratic quality. Grading a country as democratic or undemocratic by simply check-marking whether a country meets Dahl's characteristics of a polyarchy[50] elides such discussions of democratic quality from the perspective of vulnerable sectors, as well as the potential that opposition-blocs do not play by the rules. Therefore, such "analyses" drafted from offices in Europe and North America miss the fundamentally contested nature of democracy in the region, which is in fact the crux of the matter. The case study chapters of this book seek to respond to such shortcomings.

While liberal analyses offer only part of the story of outsider-led processes, there is also an issue in some heterodox theorizing regarding the potential for anti-system progressives to respond to the crisis of market democracy. For example, Chantal Mouffe[51] has cogently outlined how the "consensus of the center" of parties around a market model of democracy has fostered a post-democratic scenario, and she calls for a "left populism" in response. There is an issue, however, that remains under-theorized in her work regarding how to respond to the crisis of market democracy. The problem rests in the lack of discussion of what may actually happen if and when a "left-populist" is elected to office. As the power framework briefly discussed above suggests, it is not sufficient to assume that left-governments will always govern from the left—that is, in the name of popular sectors. If an opposition-bloc's power over the governing left is extremely high, and the government moderates policies in response, tensions between the left-party and the popular base may emerge. This in turn raises questions regarding whether popular sectors are willing to confront "their" parties, are capable of having their voices heard, what tactics they use to hold the government to account and, crucially, how left-governments respond to popular sector critique. That is, party-base relations must be a central component of enquiry. The framework and analysis in this book sheds light on such matters, advancing our understandings of how processes headed by progressive-outsiders aimed at escaping the confines of market democracy may advance, stall, or reverse altogether.

In summation, the central issues this book seeks to deal with relate to why progressive-outsider candidates are elected, what impact they have on the quality of democracy not only in liberal terms but also in more participative, substantive criteria, and what the longer-term impacts of such projects may be in terms of popular sector organizational power and the nature of the party system. Moreover, rather than a simple descriptive evaluation of outcomes, the book addresses the key issue of *why* projects advance as they do.

While issues surrounding the crisis of market democracy are universal, the case study chapters of this book focus on the Bolivian and Venezuelan processes. A contextualized comparison[52] of Bolivia and Venezuela is well suited to uncovering emergent tensions in left-led efforts to challenge the political and economic exclusion popular sectors experienced in the market democracy era. In both cases, neoliberal reforms were imposed by labor-based or center-left parties, thereby leaving opponents of processes without effective representation in established parties.[53] Both cases witnessed recurring cycles of anti-neoliberal protest[54] and "societal claims were mobilized outside and against established party systems, forcing traditional parties to share the political stage with new popular contenders."[55] These progressive-outsiders, Hugo Chávez in Venezuela and Evo Morales in Bolivia, were elected on a mandate to "carry out radical change in both political institutions and economic policies."[56] Newly elected presidents established constituent assemblies to respond to popular concerns and heterodox economic policies were, to varying degrees, adopted in both cases.[57] Traditional elite groups used an array of tactics to limit the left-led processes, ruling parties and leaders boosted executive powers, and tensions between the party and sectors of the organized popular base emerged. As such, while these cases are often analyzed via the mainstream competitive authoritarian lens, given that in both cases illiberal behaviors were accompanied by efforts to deepen and extend democratic quality for popular sectors and that opposition-blocs used institutional and extra-institutional tactics to hinder the processes, the cases are in fact key sites to evaluate via the progressive/regressive/authoritarian centralization lens and the relative power framework. Moreover, given the emergence of party-base tensions over the course of the processes, the cases are ideal sites to examine how leftist forces from above and below interact and how such relations may shape the direction and outcomes of post-neoliberal processes.

Overview of the book

In Chapter 1, I discuss the ways that progressive, outsider-led post-neoliberal democratization processes may impact on democratic quality and the novel progressive/regressive/authoritarian centralization continuum is developed. Next, I outline the historical analytic framework. The framework calls for analysis of factors present before the elections of outsiders that may influence not only the type of outsider that is elected, but that may also feedback onto the processes following election such as the histories of popular sector mobilization and the early relationships between progressive-outsiders and grassroots protesters. While antecedent factors matter for the directions that processes take, the framework calls for analysis of how historical factors interact with emergent relative power struggles between the left-led government, opposition-blocs, and popular sector organizations, shaping the pathways and outcomes of progressive-outsider-led processes.

In Chapters 2 and 5, I analyze the antecedent eras to the election of progressive-outsiders in the Venezuelan and Bolivian cases. The chapters outline how crises of democracy in both cases fostered unstable democratic equilibria in which the legitimacy of mainstream parties was eroded. However, as the chapters detail, there were variances between the cases in terms of the histories of popular sector organizing which in turn influenced the nature of anti-neoliberal protest and the linkages between outsiders and the base. In Venezuela, ad hoc eruptions of popular anger were common, but protests were generally uncoordinated with no popular organization or movement playing a unifying role. In this scenario, Hugo Chávez and his electoral vehicle, the *Movimiento V República* (Fifth Republic Movement- MVR), emerged independently of popular movements, playing a vanguardist-type role that represented myriad popular grievances. In Bolivia, there is a long history of popular sector organization and the anti-neoliberal protests built on decades of coordinated mobilization. In this scenario, Evo Morales emerged organically from the anti-neoliberal protests at the head of a movement-based party, the *Movimiento al Socialismo* (Movement toward Socialism(MAS)).

In Chapters 3 and 4, I trace the evolution of Venezuela's outsider-led process under Hugo Chávez highlighting how it evolved from a period of progressive centralization to regressive centralization and, under Chávez' successor Nicolás Maduro, to authoritarian centralization. To contextualize this evolution, I analyze the changing relative balance of powers between the left-led government and an oppositional-bloc comprising domestic and transnational forces, both of whom used an array of institutional and extra-institutional tactics to achieve their agendas/limit their opponents. Moreover, the chapters discuss how a general lack of popular sector autonomy from the newly created left-party meant that bottom-up critique of illiberal behaviors by party-officials was limited. However, despite the slide toward authoritarian centralization, I discuss how the party's organizational structure and the local spaces of popular sector organizing forged during the process may survive a transition in party leadership, indicating that a full return to market democracy is unlikely.

Chapters 6 and 7 discuss how the Bolivian process moved through a period of progressive centralization toward regressive centralization. Despite initial successes in boosting popular sector incorporation, I discuss how Morales sought to weaken the power of contestatory organizations. Such party-base tensions arose due to the government's incapacity to overcome the opposition-bloc's resistance to more radical elements of the post-neoliberal project. When Morales sought to change the constitution to allow repeated re-election, he was ousted in a right-wing coup. While some sectors of the MAS base took to the streets in support of Morales, others remained quiet, and others still participated in anti-Morales protests, thereby helping prevent a drift from regressive centralization to authoritarian centralization. The chapters conclude with a discussion of the longer-term legacies of Bolivia's outsider-led post-neoliberal process, suggesting they will be defined by the capacity of organized popular sectors to re-group and overcome internal divisions fostered by the MAS, to reclaim and strengthen participatory spaces opened under Morales' leadership, and, via these spaces, to defend and advance the socio-economic gains achieved during the process.

In Chapter 8, I compare and contrast the two cases, emphasizing how varying formulations of relative powers and transnational leverage shaped the kind of opposition-government tensions that emerged, which in turn shaped and were shaped by party-base tensions. The chapter also discusses the sticky issue of the simultaneous de-democratizing and democratizing features of both processes whereby illiberal executive actions in response to oppositional tactics (institutional and extra-institutional) were accompanied by efforts to boost popular incorporation. When the projects diverged from popular demands due to the power of opposition-blocs, and when the processes drifted toward regressive centralization (Bolivia) and even authoritarian centralization (Venezuela), party-base tensions emerged. However, the chapter notes that the extent of these tensions and the capacity of the base to hold the left-governments to account varied between the cases due to the differences in histories of mobilization, the nature of how the outsider-party was formed, and how popular sectors were incorporated over the duration of the processes.

Finally, in the Conclusion, I discuss the more general lessons from the case studies regarding the crisis of democracy facing society today. I reflect on the need for left-parties to offer a genuine alternative to market democracy to prevent the nativist-right from capturing popular discontent with democracy. Furthermore, I emphasize the importance of popular sector organizations and movements in the struggle to overcome the crisis of market democracy. As the Andean cases highlight, if a progressive leader is elected to power, the popular base must maintain critical support. They should engage in defensive mobilization when neoliberal proponents seek to limit progressive reforms or topple the democratization process, while at the same time retaining sufficient autonomy to engage in offensive mobilization if and when the party veers from a progressive path and where leaders abuse executive power.

Notes

1 Based on fieldwork interviews in both countries in 2016 and 2017 as well as electronic contacts in 2018–21. See Chapter 1 for details.

2 For example, see Steven Levitsky and Daniel Ziblatt, *How Democracies Die* (New York: Crown, 2018); Yascha Mounk, *The People vs. Democracy. Why Our Freedom Is in Danger and How to Save It* (Cambridge, MA: Harvard University Press, 2018).

3 For a discussion of hybrid regimes and competitive authoritarianism, see Steven Levitsky and Lucan Way, *Competitive Authoritarianism: Hybrid Regimes after the Cold War* (Cambridge: Cambridge University Press, 2010).

4 There is an enormous literature regarding the terms "populism" and "populist" and while there are distinctions between right- and left-forms or exclusionary- and

inclusionary forms in academia, several issues with the concept persist. The term remains conceptually loose and is used so widely in the media and by politicians in a variety of incompatible ways that the concept has been stretched. Indeed, analyses of populism and populist leaders are often underpinned by an unacknowledged bias toward liberal democracy. Despite there being many populisms, in the public conscience, the term populism has become associated primarily with right-wing leaders like Donald Trump. The terms "outsider" and "anti-system" avoid the normative bias underpinning common, and often-times academic, usage of the concept of populism. For an excellent analysis on the (mis)use of the concept of populism, see Barry Cannon, "Must We Talk about Populism? Interrogating Populism's Conceptual Utility in a Context of Crisis," *New Political Science* 40, no. 3 (2018): 477–96.

5 Michael Crozier, Samuel P. Huntington and Joji Watanuki, *The Crisis of Democracy: Report on the Governability of Democracies to the Trilateral Commission* (New York: New York University Press, 1975).

6 For a discussion, see Wolfgang Merkel, "Democracies and their Crises Reconsidered," *WZB Democracy Blog*, (May 29th, 2015).

7 Jorge Nef and Bernd Reiter, *The Democratic Challenge: Rethinking Democracy and Democratization* (London: Palgrave Macmillan, 2009): 138.

8 Alison Ayers and Alfredo Saad-Filho, "Democracy against Neoliberalism: Paradoxes, Limitations, Transcendence," *Critical Sociology* 41, no. 4–5 (2015): 598.

9 See for example Friedrich Hayek, *The Constitution of Liberty* (London: Routledge, 1960); Friedrich Hayek, *The Road to Serfdom* (London: Routledge, 1976); Robert Nozick, *Anarchy, State and Utopia* (Oxford: Blackwell, 1974).

10 Jamie Peck, Neil Brenner and Nik Theodore, "Actually Existing Neoliberalism," in Damien Cahill, Melinda Cooper, and Marijn Konings (eds), *The SAGE Handbook of Neoliberalism* (London: Sage, 2018): 6.

11 Stephen Gill, "New Constitutionalism, Democratization and Global Political Economy," *Global Change, Peace and Security* 10, no. 1 (1998): 23.

12 Nef and Reiter, *The Democratic Challenge*, 139.

13 Peter Mair, *Ruling the Void: The Hollowing of Western Democracy* (New York: Verso, 2013).

14 Gill, "New Constitutionalism," 79.

15 Thomas Piketty, *Capital in the Twenty-First Century* (Cambridge, MA: Harvard University Press, 2014).

16 See for example Larry Bartels, *Unequal Democracy: The Political Economy of the New Gilded Age* (Princeton, NJ: Princeton University Press, 2018); Merike Blofield (ed.), *The Great Gap: Inequality and the Politics of Redistribution in Latin America* (Pennsylvania: Pennsylvania State Press, 2011).

17 Ronaldo Munck, "Neoliberalism and Politics, and the Politics of Neoliberalism," in Alfredo Saad-Filho and Deborah Johnston (eds), *Neoliberalism: A Critical Reader* (London: Pluto Press, 2005): 60.

18 Mair, *Ruling the Void*.

19 Philippe Schmitter, "'Real-existing' Democracy and Its Discontents: Sources, Conditions, Causes, Symptoms, and Prospects," *Chinese Political Science Review* 4, no. 2 (2019): 152.

20 John Dunn, "The Challenge of Populism: Why Populist Politics Spreads in the World," *Populism* 2 no. 1 (2019): 56.

21 It is beyond the scope of this introduction to detail in full the varying contextual factors that shape what type of outsider emerges. For analyses see Jonathan Hopkin, *Anti-System Politics: The Crisis of Market Liberalism in Rich Democracies* (Oxford: Oxford University Press, 2020); Jonathan Hopkin and Mark Blyth, "The Global Economics of European Populism: Growth Regimes and Party System Change in Europe," *Government and Opposition* 54, no. 2 (2019): 193–225; and

Kenneth Roberts, "Crises of Representation and Populist Challenges to Liberal Democracy," *Chinese Political Science Review* 4, no. 2 (2019): 188–99.
22 Roberts, "Crises of Representation," 197.
23 Ibid., 198.
24 Hopkin and Blyth, "The Global Economics of European Populism," 209.
25 Roberts, "Crises of Representation," 197.
26 Hopkin and Blyth, "The Global Economics of European Populism;" Hopkin, *Anti-System Politics*; Roberts "Crises of Representation;" Kenneth Roberts, *Changing Course: Party Systems in Latin America's Neoliberal Era* (New York: Cambridge University Press, 2015).
27 For a study of the European context see Hanspeter Pappas and Takis S. Kriesi (eds), *European Populism in the Shadow of the Great Recession* (Colchester: ECPR Press, 2015). For the Latin American scenario see Roberts, *Changing Course.*
28 See Eduardo Silva and Federico Rossi (eds.), *Reshaping the Political Arena in Latin America: From Resisting Neoliberalism to the Second Incorporation* (Pittsburgh: University of Pittsburgh Press, 2018); Roberts, "Crises of Representation."
29 Hopkin and Blyth, "The Global Economics of European Populism," 208.
30 I return to this issue in the conclusion to the book where I outline future avenues of cross-regional comparison.
31 Roberts, *Changing Course.*
32 Ibid.
33 David Smilde, "Introduction: Participation, Politics and Culture – Emerging fragments of Venezuela's Bolivarian Democracy," in David Smilde and Daniel Hellinger (eds), *Venezuela's Bolivarian Democracy: Participation, Politics, and Culture under Chávez* (Durham, NC and London: Duke University Press, 2011).
34 Kenneth Roberts, "Bipolar Disorders: Varieties of Capitalism and Populist Outflanking on the Left and Right," *Polity* 54, no. 4 (2019): 641–653.
35 See for example Jorge G. Castañeda, "Latin America's Left Turn," *Foreign Affairs* 65, no. 3 (2006): 28–43; Kurt Weyland, "Latin America's Authoritarian Drift: The Threat from the Populist Left," *Journal of Democracy* 24, no. 3 (2013): 18–32.
36 Weyland, "Latin America's Authoritarian Drift."
37 Steven Levitsky and James Loxton, "Populism and Competitive Authoritarianism in the Andes," *Democratization* 20, no. 1 (2013): 107–36.
38 Daniel Hellinger, "Bolivarian Democracy from Five Perspectives," *Latin American Perspectives* 47, no. 4 (2020): 247.
39 Gerardo Munck, "Building Democracy… Which Democracy? Ideology and Models of Democracy in Post-Transition Latin America," *Government and Opposition* 50, no. 3 (2015): 374.
40 Steve Ellner (ed.), *Latin America's Pink Tide: Breakthroughs and Shortcomings* (Maryland and London: Rowman and Littlefield, 2020): 1.
41 Joe Foweraker, *Polity: Demystifying Democracy in Latin America and Beyond* (Boulder, CO: Lynne Rienner, 2018).
42 Ibid., 2–3.
43 Ibid., 91.
44 Ibid., 100.
45 Ellner, *Latin America's Pink Tide*, 15–16.
46 Weyland, "Latin America's Authoritarian Drift."
47 These concepts are discussed at greater length in the following chapter.
48 Jean Grugel and Pía Riggirozzi, "Neoliberal Disruption and Neoliberalism's Afterlife: What is left of Post-neoliberalism," *Critical Social Policy* 38, no. 3 (2018): 561.
49 John Brown, "Party-base Linkages and Contestatory Mobilization in Bolivia's El Alto: Subduing the Ciudad Rebelde," *Latin American Perspectives* 47, no. 4 (2020): 40–57; Barry Cannon and Peadar Kirby (eds.), *Civil Society and the State in Left-led Latin America* (London, New York: Zed Books, 2012).

50 Robert Dahl, *Democracy and Its Critics* (New Haven, CT: Yale University Press, 1989).
51 Chantal Mouffe, *For a Left Populism* (New York: Verso Books, 2018).
52 Richard Locke and Kathleen Thelen, "Apples and Oranges Revisited: Contextualized Comparisons and the Study of Comparative Labor Politics," *Politics & Society* 23, no. 3 (1995): 337–67.
53 Roberts, *Changing Course.*
54 Eduardo Silva, *Challenging Neoliberalism in Latin America* (New York: Cambridge University Press, 2009).
55 Roberts, *Changing Course*, 5.
56 Steven Levitsky and Kenneth Roberts "Introduction: Latin America's 'Left Turn': A Framework for Analysis," in Steven Levitsky and Kenneth Roberts (eds.), *The Resurgence of the Latin American Left* (Baltimore, MD: Johns Hopkins University Press, 2011): 19.
57 Eduardo Silva, "Reorganizing Popular Sector Incorporation: Propositions from Bolivia, Ecuador, and Venezuela," *Politics & Society* 45, no. 1 (2017): 93.

1 Re-conceptualizing democratization in progressive-outsider cases

Chapter overview

The elections of progressive outsiders Evo Morales in Bolivia and Hugo Chávez in Venezuela represented a point of inflection in both countries that opened post-neoliberal (de)democratization processes. Both were elected on mandates to challenge the confines of market democracy and foster a more inclusionary citizenship regime for long—excluded popular sectors in both political and socio-economic terms. The projects had mixed results in terms of their impacts on democratic quality with simultaneous democratization and de-democratization occurring. In Venezuela, the quality of popular sector political and socio-economic incorporation was initially radically boosted, a new left-wing party was forged, while at the same time the use of executive powers increased. Over time, tensions between the ruling left-party and critical sectors of the base emerged. However, such critique was generally side-lined. The process moved in an authoritarian direction as election results were ignored, state forces were used to repress both opposition supporters and former popular sector allies, while the ruling left-party entrenched itself in power with the backing of the military. However, despite such authoritarian behavior, the left-wing party formed during the process retains support from a significant sector of the popular base and has a strong organizational capacity relative to all other parties in the country. However, as the party leadership has also sanctioned repressive measures against contestatory sectors of the popular base, has been implicated in massive corruption scandals while the economy has collapsed, and has flagrantly broken with all liberal standards including respect for electoral outcomes, it remains to be seen to what extent the party's organizational structure will survive if and when the party lose/are forced from office.

Like the Venezuelan case, in Bolivia, a new left-wing party was established and the quality of political and socio-economic incorporation for popular sectors was initially boosted. Presidential powers also expanded. Tensions between the left-party and sectors of the popular base emerged, while other sectors retained direct access to the executive and decision-making channels. There were top-down efforts to curb grassroots critique of the left party and

DOI: 10.4324/9781003262466-2

the president, with schisms promoted in some popular organizations. Efforts to change the constitution to allow the president to run for office again triggered protests from both middle classes and some popular sector organizations. With the president forced from office, popular sectors demonstrated massive electoral support for the candidate of the left-wing party established at the outset of the process, indicating a progressive long-term, institutionalized shift in the party system.

To shed light on the paradoxical processes and to help us understand the similarities and divergences between the cases, this chapter develops a novel conceptualization and framework for evaluating progressive outsider-led democratization processes. As argued earlier, while some critics describe the projects as illiberal, authoritarian processes that simply damaged the quality of democracy, such accounts capture only part of the empirical realities. There is a failure to locate the processes in wider empirical contexts that account for popular conceptualizations of democracy and citizenship. As Foweraker[1] stresses, any comparisons or discussions of democratic performance can only be meaningful if they are placed in their proper political context. Variations in performance "necessarily flow from the constraints imposed on democratic government by oligarchic powers and prerogatives."[2] Moreover, while oligarchic powers influence how left-governments govern, left-leaders have also been squeezed from below by popular forces demanding a move toward a post-neoliberal, participative-substantive model of democracy. As such, any effort to understand the pathways and outcomes of the left-led processes must eschew simple causal analysis and account for the ways that multiple actors with multiple sources of power seek to advance their prerogatives while hindering those of opponents.

In the following section, I discuss data collection techniques used to support the analysis of the two cases. Then, the outcomes of interest of this study—namely the impacts on democratic quality and the legacies of outsider-led processes—are conceptualized and instrumentalized. Next, a framework that calls for analysis of historical and emergent causes that shaped the direction and outcomes of the processes is developed. The final section of the chapter outlines research design.

Data collection: bringing popular voices back in

To support my case studies, I carried out research in the field in Venezuela in 2016 and in Bolivia in 2017. In 2019, 2020, and 2021, I carried out electronic interviews to support earlier data collection. I conducted over 80 in-depth interviews with members of urban popular organizations and union leaders. Interviews were semi-structured with open-ended questions allowing respondents freedom to detail their experiences. These interviews provide the basis for my analysis of popular sector interpretations of the successes and issues of the processes, whether bottom-up critique of processes was fostered or blocked, what happened if and when parties diverged from popular demands, how party-officials sought to meddle in popular organizations, why popular sector organizations engaged in defensive mobilization in support of the party or offensive contestatory mobilization against the party, and what the long-term impacts of the left-led processes on the quality of popular sector incorporation were. These interviews are supported by interviews with party members, journalists, and researchers to tease out why processes advanced as they did.

The reason for focusing data collection on popular sector organizations is simple; these organizations' members were the most consistently excluded group—both politically and economically—under market democracy and as such it has been these groups who most actively called for a more inclusionary citizenship model. Such popular organization members are the key actors capable of stating whether or not democratic quality has been boosted and to what extent changes have become embedded. Moreover, these popular organizations have played, to varying degrees, central roles in shaping the directions of the processes. They are not simply passive recipients of government handouts, as some crude, ill-informed mainstream analyses suggest. Indeed, examining the varying capacity of popular organizations to influence parties and policymaking should be a core component of any analysis of the outsider-led processes. While historical analysis of the cases is developed by using secondary resources, it would not have been possible to gain nuanced answers to questions regarding the democratization processes without face-to-face interactions with popular actors. Respondents emphasized that they had very rarely been offered the opportunity to voice their opinions on the processes and resented the fact that their experiences were often written about by media and academic sources who had not actually sought the viewpoints of local popular actors.

In Venezuela, primary research focused on two core groups; urban popular organizations that came into existence after the election of Hugo Chávez, and organizations that pre-date Chavez's election that had a history of organizing around ideas of inclusionary models of democracy. In Bolivia, primary research focused on urban popular groups with long histories of mobilization calling for radical substantive democratization. The analysis centered on groups who retained support for Evo Morales and on groups who initially backed the president but who withdrew support over the course of the process. All four groups, two in Venezuela and two in Bolivia, comprise popular actors who support the building of a post-neoliberal democracy. However, variances in organizational history as well as party-base relationships allow for both cross-case and internal comparisons.

In Venezuela, data collection focused on two sites in the capital city of Caracas, the José Felix Rivas *barrio* in Petare and the parish of El 23 de Enero. About 88 percent of Venezuelans live in urban environments[3] so focusing on the city of Caracas is not unrepresentative of the country in general. José Felix Rivas is located in the popular parish of Petare, in the densely populated municipality of Sucre, eastern Caracas. Petare is a sprawling zone that, in general did not have a strong history of well organized, collective mobilization before the election of Hugo Chávez. However, numerous spaces of popular organization emerged following Chávez' election. The site is representative of popular urban areas across the country due to its similar indicators for income, employment, education, and housing levels.[4] The popular zone of 23 de Enero is located in the Libertador municipality in the Capital District of western Caracas. The name 23 de Enero (23 January) references the date in 1958 when the Venezuelan dictator Marcos Pérez Jiménez was overthrown. The barrio is seen by residents as the heart of Chavismo. The Hugo Chávez-led coup attempt of 1992 was headquartered in the Cuartel de la Montaña building in 23 de Enero, while this same building now houses the mausoleum to Chávez; 23 de Enero has a long history of popular protest and left-wing guerrilla urban warfare demanding that the state deliver services to the urban poor.

In Bolivia, analysis centered on the popular indigenous city of El Alto. While Evo Morales and his *Movimiento al Socialismo* (MAS) party emerged from a resistance movement of coca producers—the *cocaleros*—and relocated miners in the Chapare province, and actors and organizations based in this province make up the original core constituency of the MAS, primary data collection does not focus on such actors.[5] Primary data collection instead focused on the experiences of urban popular organization members in El Alto for several reasons. This book seeks to offer a critical-progressive analysis. That is, rather than simply offering a fawning support of the processes that is blinkered to any shortcomings, while avoiding narrow-minded ideologically guided attacks on the processes that seek to delegitimize any attempt at building an alternative to market democracy, the approach taken here seeks to critically evaluate both the successes and shortcomings of efforts to construct a post-neoliberal democracy. Given the nature of the relationship between the MAS, Morales, and the organic base, it was less likely that primary data collection in the Chapare would have identified such critical evaluations of the post-neoliberal process or that such actors would mobilize against the president and the party. As such, analysis instead focused on the experiences of popular sectors in El Alto, the *Ciudad Rebelde* (Rebellious City).[6] To support the interviews with *Alteños'* (people from El Alto), I interviewed numerous popular organization members in the capital La Paz, as well as organizers of national-level bodies.

Popular organizations in El Alto were at the heart of anti-neoliberal protests that paved the way for the election of progressive outsider Evo Morales, and these organizations have a long history of calling for a radical deepening of democratic quality. Indeed, attitudes in El Alto are perceived to be a barometer of the sentiment in the country as a whole. By comparing and contrasting the experiences and opinions of *Alteños* who continued to support the MAS and Morales with those who desisted in doing so, a nuanced understanding of the strategies, successes, failures, and legacies of Bolivia's post-neoliberal democratization process can be gleaned.

To support my analysis of the processes in both cases, official party documents, popular organization documents, and newspapers were collected and analyzed. I also attended numerous meetings of popular organizations and attended protests. Attending protests and organization meetings and being seen on a regular basis by local actors helped to establish my trustworthiness, while also giving me an opportunity to observe how actors speak to each other in a natural setting. Such occasions also allowed me to engage in more informal conversations helping me to gain a deeper comprehension of realities than would have been possible via formal interviews alone. In both countries, I was taken on tours of the locality, presenting me the opportunity to engage in informal discussions regarding the historical development of the sites. For example, in El Alto, I was brought to the outskirts of the city for lunch with one interviewee's family before we walked around the neighborhood. This allowed me to witness first-hand the poverty levels in the city and the lack of development in terms of roadways and gas and water connections. While in El 23 de Enero in Venezuela, I met a woman selling cigarettes and newspapers from a kiosk. She brought me to a shrine she had set up for the deceased former president Hugo Chávez, stating that she goes there to thank Chávez every day for the gift of freedom he gave her. Such interactions help to comprehend just how Chávez was and is perceived as a savior and saint by some sectors, which then helps to contextualize responses by popular actors during interviews. I was also invited to breakfasts, lunches, and dinners with families in both case countries. Such interactions, including with the parents of interviewees, allowed me to gain further insight into the historical grievances of the popular actors, thereby helping me to frame the post-neoliberal processes. Taking public transport every day across the cities also allowed me to grasp the astonishing scale of inequality between the rich and poor in both countries. Engaging in informal conversations with bus drivers or metro passengers offered me further scope to grasp the general sentiment in both countries regarding the successes and shortcomings of the processes.

Outcomes of interest

Given that democracy is an essentially contested concept it is important to begin by identifying what the term implies in this book. The democratization literature identifies hundreds of democracies "with adjectives."[7] Disputes and differing adjectives placed in front of democracy are really about *how much* democracy is desirable or practicable.[8] As such democracy may be understood as existing on a continuum of "how much democracy exists in reality." As the central concerns of this book relate to examining the democratization (and de-democratization) processes headed by leftist leaders elected on mandates to challenge the exclusionary model of market democracy, the baseline against which to measure the developments or lack thereof, is the thin citizenship regime associated with market democracy. Thicker participatory, substantive citizenship regimes which respond to popular sector conceptions and which informed the protest waves that opened the space for outsider-left candidates' elections lie at the opposite end of the continuum. Democratic quality then is not a dichotomous variable that either does or does not exist. While "ideal" types can be conceptualized at each pole of the continuum, empirical realities will fall somewhere along the continuum between each pole.

Narrow and shallow democratic quality: a market model of democracy

The market model of democracy can be understood as an extremely thin liberal democracy underpinned by neoliberal rationale whereby public policy is premised upon the dominance of the investor and economic elite interests (domestic and transnational), irrespective of how such policy matrices impact on popular sector political and socio-economic citizenship. Market democracy "explicitly isolates the political from the socioeconomic sphere and restricts democracy to the political sphere."[9] Citizenship is commodified whereby goods such as education, health, housing, welfare, and water are to be purchased on the market.[10] Rather than the state guaranteeing quality social citizenship, "subjects" are treated as individual entrepreneurs in every aspect of life, responsible for their own well-being, and citizenship is reduced to success in this entrepreneurship.[11]

In sum, market democracy entails a shallow and narrow form of political and social citizenship. It is shallow because it fosters unaccountable, technocratic decision-making procedures dominated by capital and aligned supranational bodies. Indeed, the central objective of a market democracy is to foster an ideal environment for FDI and domestic capital. At the same time that the interests of capital are organized in and protected from democratic input, the interests of labor and popular sectors must be organized out so as to allow for capital accumulation. Privatization of public assets, cuts to taxation and welfare spending, labor flexibilization, and deregulation of business and financial sectors are thus core features. Policies aimed at tackling inequality are not features of "ideal" market democracies.

Deep and extended democratic quality: a "post-neoliberal" democracy

While an "ideal-type" narrow and shallow market democracy occupies one pole of the democratic quality continuum, a "post-neoliberal" model occupies the other pole. Roberts suggests that robust democratization involves two components; a deepening and an extending.[12] The logic of deepening involves intensifying popular sovereignty in the political sphere. Such deepening entails increasing popular self-determination by means of more direct participation in decision making processes and/or more effective mechanisms for holding elected representatives and public officials accountable to their constituents.[13] While liberal theorists see democracy as a set of rules, procedures and institutions, "thick theorists" on the other hand see democracy as a process that must be continually reproduced, a "way of regulating power relations in such a way as to maximize the opportunities for individuals to influence the conditions in which they live, to participate in and influence debates about the key decisions which affect society."[14] Democracy should facilitate the active involvement of the citizenry, reach political consensus through dialogue, devise and implement public policies that foster a productive economy and a healthy society, and ensure that all citizens benefit from the nation's wealth.[15]

A deep democracy, then, seeks to redistribute political power away from economic elites and traditional political elites toward popular sectors. It is associated with, though not limited to, a re-politicization of politics more broadly by restricting technocratic control over issues regarding economic, health, and welfare policies; boosting spaces for popular deliberative participation; re-call referenda; and strengthening unions. Following Etchemendy,[16] who outlines how governments can engage working-class organizations, deepened democracies will see governments (a) granting state positions to militants or leaders of labor unions or territorial-social movements (TSMs)[17]; (b) fostering the involvement of labor unions and TSMs in the design and implementation of (generally social and/or labor) policies that benefit popular organizations or their constituencies; and (c) promoting or actively tolerating collective action on the part of unions and/or TSMs.

An extensive democracy meanwhile entails attempting to redress social and economic inequalities so as to prevent economic power from skewing the articulation of popular interests and blocking the exercise of popular sovereignty. Social equality is not simply a substantive outcome that is external to the functioning of democracy, but is also a prerequisite for equal access and unbiased democratic contestation, and is thus a vital indicator of procedural fairness.[18] This substantive understanding therefore envisions democracy as a transformative project that addresses the social and economic inequalities of society. It is about boosting the quality of state guarantees for social citizenship for all citizens irrespective of capacity to pay in areas including education, food, health, housing, and information. Progressive taxation, high corporation taxes, universal pensions, wealth and inheritance taxes, judicial support for workplace democracy, communal land ownership schemes, and nationalization of key sectors of the economy are some components of an extended democracy.

The notion of a democratization process that deepens and extends democratic quality resonates with Silva and Rossi's[19] concept of popular sector (re)incorporation. Incorporation for these authors involves the expansion of substantive rights "in ways that the expressed interests of major, politically significant new and old popular sector organizations find, at minimum, programmatic expression in left governments."[20] Moreover, incorporation relates to the "concrete institutional mechanisms that link popular organizations to the political arena and policy-making."[21] Deepening and extending democracy as a response to popular sector disincorporation during the market era of democracy thus entails fostering or accommodating new spaces of popular sector inclusion in decision making-processes so as to allow popular concerns to shape, or at least influence, the agenda of governing parties, legislatures and executives. The nature of this deepening of popular participation, that is the form that popular interest intermediation takes, may vary. Silva[22] theorizes segmented popular interest intermediation regimes whereby governments have differentiated responses to differing popular sectors. Unions or socio-territorially organized segments may dominate participation. Moreover, in segmented intermediation regimes elements of corporatism and clientelism may exist alongside top-down state managerialism whereby policy is developed to respond to traditional popular sector concerns, but without bottom-up participation in the policy process. Informal contestatory intermediation meanwhile sees governments propose policies, popular sector organizations then protest on the streets regarding proposed policies, government/party-popular organization negotiation follows, and governments then re-draft the policy.

Centralization

While democratic quality may be assessed along a shallow-deep continuum regarding the quality of popular sector political inclusion and a narrow-extensive continuum regarding the quality of social citizenship, as liberal critiques of left-led process have emphasized, democratic quality must also be assessed in terms of liberal/illiberal standards and, in particular, the centralization of power in the executive. Such centralization of decision-making power may encompass

> an increase in the size and resources of the executive branch, a curtailment of judicial autonomy, an assertion of decree power against legislative oversight or resistance, and a centralization of political control to the detriment of local and regional political authorities.[23]

While such centralization of power clearly challenges liberal norms, to fully conceptualize centralization and its impact on democratic quality requires evaluating it in relation to efforts to deepen and extend democracy. That is, beyond a simple description of the illiberal nature of centralization, it is necessary to ask why such centralization occurs and what executive power is used for.

As discussed in the introductory chapter, a continuum that runs from authoritarian centralization via regressive centralization to progressive centralization is advanced here. "Progressive centralization" sees a strengthening of executive power which is used to bypass elite opposition forces whose central aim is to limit the scope of left-led democratization processes. Elections are held and are free. However, state resources may be used to limit the capacity of opposition-blocs whose dominance over the media and the economy would allow them to skew the electoral playing field in their direction. At the same time, the executive remains open to, and is guided by, popular organizations who participate in new spaces of participation, thereby ensuring that the executive is responsive to popular concerns rather than personalistic projects. Progressive centralization occurs then where increased executive power is used to overcome elite opposition to redistributive projects, while it is simultaneously counterbalanced from below by popular power, thereby fostering a dual process of democratic extending and deepening for popular sectors, at the same time that respect for liberal norms declines.[24] If presidential powers are boosted so as to overcome opposition destabilization tactics and to adhere to programmatic demands that emerge from popular participatory spaces and that call for redress of embedded socio-economic exclusion, the term progressive centralization is more useful than competitive authoritarianism.

Regressive centralization occurs where executive power is used to confront the power of elite opponents to redistributive reforms, like the more progressive form detailed above. However, it is also used to side-line or co-opt popular organizations that critique the direction of the left-led processes. At the same time that regressive centralization is used to curb elite opposition powers as well as the contestatory capacity of critical popular sector organizations, some more "loyal" or less contestatory popular organizations may retain access to the executive to influence agendas and policymaking, while also receiving state funding for projects. Similar to "progressive centralization," elections are held and the outcomes respected, but state resources are used by the ruling party to counterbalance elite opposition powers. While under regressive centralization popular sector capacity to challenge executive decisions is weakened via clientelism and co-optation, when state powers are used to physically repress both elite opposition and contestatory popular sectors the term authoritarian centralization is more apt. Moreover, under authoritarian centralization the outcomes of elections that do not go the way of the ruling party are rejected/ignored. The use of police and army forces or state-sponsored militia to repress popular discontent and elite opposition-blocs and the failure to respect electoral outcomes is what differentiates authoritarian centralization from regressive centralization (see Table 1.1).

Incorporating an analysis of a centralization continuum with a continuum that runs from market democracy (narrow, shallow) to post-neoliberal democracy (deep, extended) allows us to account for the concerns of both liberal and participative-substantive scholars. That is, conceptualizing democratic quality in such a manner allows for us to concurrently conceive of a "diminished subtype" *and* "adjective-plus"[25] concept of democracy and to grasp empirical realities in which processes may contain simultaneous democratizing and de-democratizing features. For example, in a purely liberal account, the centralizing component of "progressive centralization" outlined above would lead to some sort of diminished-subtype concept such as "illiberal democracy." Conversely, from a more participative-substantive approach, the use

Table 1.1 Types of centralization (author's own elaboration)

	Progressive Centralization	*Regressive Centralization*	*Authoritarian Centralization*
Liberal democracy	• Elections generally free • Electoral outcomes respected • Use of decrees to bypass political opposition in legislature or judiciary • Limiting power of opposition-controlled mayoralties/local governments • Use of state resources to limit economic and media power of opposition-bloc	• Elections generally free • Electoral outcomes respected • Use of decrees to bypass political opposition in legislature or judiciary • Limiting power of opposition-controlled mayoralties/local governments • Use of state resources to limit economic and media power of opposition-bloc	• Elections generally unfree • Electoral outcomes not respected • Use of state forces of repression to side-line opposition • Use of state forces of repression against contestatory popular sectors
Deepened democracy	• Participatory spaces created and linked to executive, bottom-up shaping of agenda and influence in policymaking • Party or ministerial/state positions for union and movement leaders • Contestatory interest intermediation supported	• Top-down control of some participatory spaces, clientelism • Loyal or core sectors of popular base retain bottom-up influence on executive via participatory spaces • Co-opting of popular sector leaders in party or ministerial/state positions • Contestatory interest intermediation ignored/weakened via top-down meddling in organization leaderships	• Top-down control of participatory spaces, clientelism • Contestatory interest intermediation repressed
Extended democracy	• Boosted popular sector social citizenship (pensions, education, health, nutrition) • Pro-worker labor laws • Progressive taxation • Land reform/redistribution • Nationalizations of key sectors of economy	• Boosted popular sector social citizenship (pensions, education, health, nutrition) directed toward loyal sectors of base • Pro-worker labor laws for loyal sectors • Progressive taxation • Land reform/redistribution • Nationalizations of key sectors of economy	• Use of executive controlled scarce resources to guarantee allegiance of some popular sectors

of state powers to boost spaces of poplar sector incorporation would lead to an adjective-plus concept such as "radical-inclusionary democracy" or some such. The approach taken here allows us to account for both approaches at the same time, thereby enriching how we theorize democratization, in particular left-led outsider/populist cases, as well as helping us to overcome partial analyses of empirical cases which fail to grasp nuanced realities.

Long-term outcomes of left-led processes

Assessing whether the processes have/are likely to have long-term impacts requires evaluating the extent to which left-led processes have responded to the issues that fostered a crisis of legitimacy and an unstable democratic equilibrium in the first place. That is, it is necessary to identify if trust in the party-system and democracy more broadly has been restored amongst popular sectors; whether new spaces of participation have been institutionalized so that organized popular sectors have access to decision-making processes regardless of who is in office; and whether gains achieved in terms of boosted social citizenship are likely to be accepted by all political parties. Understanding the legacies of the left-led processes also requires evaluation of whether party-systems are more representative of the socio-economic cleavages that exist in society compared to the left-right consensus of the center during the market democracy era. As such, the analysis must address whether a well-organized and popularly legitimate political party capable of competing in elections on popularly mandated agendas exists. Underpinning all of these longer-term legacies—democratic legitimacy, new spaces of popular participation, institutionalization of social policies, and a more representative party-system—is the nature of popular sector mobilizational contestatory power. That is, without an autonomous, well-organized base of popular sector organizations capable of engaging in mass mobilizations to defend gains achieved during left-led processes, to push for further incorporation, and to hold elected officials to account—whether from left- or right-wing parties—any gains achieved during the left-led processes may be transitory. As such, a crucial outcome, which shapes our understandings of all other outcomes, is the impact that left-led processes have had on popular sector organizational and mobilizational power. In sum, whether popular sectors are more united or divided, autonomous or co-opted, and politicized or de-politicized following left-led processes are key variables that must be evaluated empirically.

Historical and emergent factor explanations

To analyze the emergence, pathways and outcomes of left-led democratization processes, a comparative historical analytic framework is developed that integrates structure, agency and institutions. As Collier and Collier[26] stress, a theoretical model should examine "antecedent conditions" which may "be part of the causal chain in a theoretical explanation… when they differentiate units undergoing" processes of change.[27] Historical causes refer to dynamics that occur in the early stages of processes and that may shape or feedback onto the processes at later stages.[28] That is, when seeking to explain and compare post-neoliberal democratization processes following the election of progressive-outsiders, it is important to examine factors before the elections that open space for the outsiders, that influence what type of outsider is elected, and that continue to influence the pathways processes follow after the elections.

While it is important to account for historical or antecedent factors, it is important not to fall into a similar trap as modernization theorists who assume a linear path to some pre-determined democratic outcome given a set of pre-existing conditions. That is, it is insufficient to simply compare the historical factors in two cases and assume that a given combination of antecedent conditions will produce a given democratic outcome. Rather, we must identify if and how factors present before the election of progressive outsiders to office feedback onto the process, influencing its pathways, while simultaneously accounting for multiple factors that emerge along the way and cause the process to spring forward, reverse, or change course altogether. In summation, while historical causes may foster weak forms of path dependency, evolving emergent factors may jolt the democratization processes in differing directions.

One may ask whether comparative analysis of cases undergoing similar processes (left-led post-neoliberal democratization processes), but with multiple emergent variables in a given context should be eschewed. For example, process-tracing theorists argue that in order to explain an outcome of interest *x*, we should compare cases on an independent variable *y*. While variations in historical causal factors may allow for such an approach, what are we to do in cases with multiple emergent or intervening variables? Despite the difficulties in outlining a causal mechanism that easily explains variations between cases, a flexible theoretical framework capable of evaluating similar processes in distinct contexts with multiple emergent variables can be developed. To do so, it is necessary to clearly theorize which emergent factors must be accounted for before then categorizing the multiple emergent variables so as to allow for typological theory-building.

As detailed below, the focus of study here is the nature of emergent relative power struggles between the ruling left-party, the organized popular base, and the (domestic and transnational) opposition-bloc. Within each broad categorization of emergent factors (ruling party power, popular power, and opposition-bloc power), a number of variables that can be instrumentalized are detailed, allowing for cross case comparison not only at the categorical level (e.g., strong ruling party power, low popular power, and low opposition-bloc power) but also in terms of the *nature* of power within each categorization (e.g., strong political power of ruling party vis-à-vis opposition-bloc, weak economic power of ruling party vis-à-vis opposition-bloc, and strong mobilizational power of popular base).

I do not wish to suggest that a generalizable causal mechanism can be gleaned from comparing two cases. However, if the theoretical framework is broad enough to capture the major elements of the historical context and allows for categorization of emergent variables then, via historical analysis of processes in cases with divergent outcomes, a comparative analysis can highlight which contextual factors are most important in terms of causing processes to advance, stall, or regress. That is, by transforming the specific explanations of each case into the concepts and variables of the general theoretical framework, specific historical explanations can be used to formulate theory.[29] More specifically, similarities or differences between cases in terms of historical causes and the forms that emergent power struggles take, how these historical and emergent factors influence each other, and how they shape the pathways and outcomes of left-led democratization processes can be identified, thereby allowing for not only rich case analysis but the advancement of democratization theory more generally. Moreover, within-case, periodized comparative analysis can be used for typological-theory development whereby the outcomes (democratic quality) and the factors that influenced outcomes can be analyzed and compared at several conjunctures in a given case.

Historical factors

To understand why outsider-left parties and leaders were elected to office on mandates to boost the political and economic inclusion of popular sectors requires evaluating the nature of existing democratic citizenship under market democracy, the form of popular protests against political and economic exclusion, and the why mainstream existing party-systems collapsed. Moreover, by evaluating the antecedent era, we can identify key actors and competing notions of democracy, thereby grounding analyses of post-election power struggles in empirical realities. Furthermore, while analysis of historical factors helps us to identify why progressive outsider presidents are elected as well as the rival camps that are likely to struggle for dominance following elections, the nature of party-base or leader-base relations in the antecedent stage may also be a key part of the explanation of the directions post-election aftermath processes follow.

The form of protest against political and economic exclusion under neoliberalism, that is, whether it is well coordinated by powerful grassroots movements or whether it is a spontaneous ad-hoc eruption, will influence the nature of leader-base relations both during the antecedent era and in the post-election processes. Co-ordinated protests where popular movements have high levels of organizational and mobilizational power are more likely to foster an organic relationship whereby a new leader and party emerge as the political expression of organized groups in civil society.[30] Conversely, in cases where protests are on a mass scale but are uncoordinated and where organizational power of the popular base is low, relations between popular protesters and the new leader and party will tend toward a vanguard relationship.[31] In such a scenario, a leader emerges independently of the unconnected protest movements but claims to represent their demands and concerns.

Processes that originate in more vanguardist-type leader-base relations are likely to continue on a path of top-down incorporation whereby the reform process is guided by elected officials with little input from organized popular sectors. State resources may be used to sponsor spaces of popular participation. However, if and when confrontations between party and base emerge regarding the direction of the process, cases that do not demonstrate historically well-organized autonomous organization in the antecedent stage are less likely to witness mass contestatory mobilization against the left-party. Such cases are also less likely to demonstrate capacity to resist party-influence over the spaces of participation. Furthermore, in processes that emerge from vanguardist-type origins, if the party-leadership move in illiberal directions, given the ties between party and base and the lack of mobilizational autonomy, popular sectors are unlikely to be able to act as a counterbalance to prevent a slide from progressive centralization through regressive centralization to wholesale authoritarian centralization.

Conversely, as Anria[32] emphasizes, parties that develop close links with social movements and civic organizations in their formative stages generate an inclination for greater grassroots input, allowing for incorporation to be directed from below while decreasing the likelihood that the party leadership diverge from popular demands. Those cases with strong histories of autonomous organization in the antecedent era and where popular organizations play founding roles in left-parties are thus more likely to witness popular critique of the governing party—not only where it diverges from popular demands for boosted political and socio-economic inclusion, but also where it creeps in an illiberal direction. That is, processes that originate in organic movement-party relations are more likely to see popular power act as a counterbalance to centralizing behaviors by party leaders in the executive, thereby decreasing the risks of a slide from progressive to regressive centralization and on to authoritarian centralization. However, the historical forms of protest and the nature of formative party-base relations do not foster strong path-dependent processes. That is, while historical origins matter, and feed on to the process following the election of leftist parties and presidents to office, emergent power struggles interact with these historical factors to shape the pathways that processes follow.

Emergent factors

Post-neoliberal democratization processes are likely to be heavily influenced by struggles between competing actors with competing visions of democracy. While left-led governments will face opposition-blocs who reject the notion of building a post-neoliberal democracy and defend the ideal of a market democracy, this does not mean that oppositional tactics will be restricted to use of liberal institutions. As Monedero[33] stresses, when popular parties with redistributive agendas win electoral majorities and gain, in principle, access to the governmental levers of power, they face a host of obstacles in implementing their campaign promises. In democracies,

> enormous pressures can be brought to bear upon radical administrations, whether at municipal, state or federal level. The mainstream media, the judiciary, the intelligence services, opposition parties may all come into play, with scandals whipped up out of trifles, judicial harassment, dirty tricks or political maneuvers—and this even before market pressures are taken into account.[34]

The actions of right-wing politicians who purportedly advocate liberal democracy are often shaped less by their support for the model of liberal democracy than by their opposition to the post-neoliberal model of popular democracy.[35] Left-leaders will thus be squeezed between popular demands for greater participation and improved living conditions, and domestic and transnational elite demands for pro-market orthodoxy as well as the protection of the interests of capital and its supporting and enabling elites.[36] To grasp the pathways and outcomes of left-led democratization processes, it is therefore necessary to identify the *relative power* of the left-led government, the popular base, and an oppositional-bloc comprising domestic and transnational actors opposed to challenging the neoliberal model. Jessop's[37] strategic-relational approach is useful in this regard.

Jessop[38] starts from the proposition that the state is a social relation that "reflects the changing balance of power among social forces."[39] Jessop continues:

> Putting states in their place like this does not exclude (indeed, it presupposes) specifically state-engendered and state-mediated processes. It does require, however, that they be related both to their broader social context and to the strategic choices and conduct of actors in and beyond states.[40]

State managers' selection of strategies, projects, and policies will influence the opportunities for groups to achieve their goals, and at the same time the balance of forces in society will influence the range of policy options available to state managers. While elected leftist politicians are key exercisers of state power, they act in relation to, and influence, a wider balance of social forces (the organized popular sectors and elites). Therefore, to study the relation between the left-led state, the organized-popular base, and economic elites, "we must consider how state powers are exercised and aligned (or not) with specific class interests in particular societies and conjunctures, and vice versa."[41] To do this, we must identify what increases the power of elites and the popular base to exert pressure on state managers and what increases state managers' capacity to influence the power of both groups.

Mann[42] suggests that the interrelations between four sources of social power—ideological, economic, military, and political—determine the relative power of actors. Left-governments and elite oppositional forces thus seek to contest control of these four sources of power which "engender the structural bases and resource capabilities upon which social order and domination rest."[43]

Examples of sources of political power that left-governments and elite opposition vie for include control of the judiciary, executive and legislature, political parties and coalitions of parties, and municipal and local governments. Indeed, following election on mandates to deepen and extend democracy, outsider-left candidates in Latin America confronted a congress, judiciary and other state agencies controlled by traditional parties.[44] Madrid, Hunter, and Weyland[45] stress that it was the backlash by traditional parties via institutions such as congress and courts against far-reaching socio-economic reforms that triggered a re-organization of legislative and judicial branches that saw executive power increased. While such accounts focus on the oppositional use of political power to limit radical democratization processes, opponents of post-neoliberal reforms do not only rely on parties and democratic institutions. That is, political power is not the only source of power that must be accounted for when analyzing left-led democratization processes.

Ideological power derives from "the capacity of ideas to shape policy options and principles of social organization."[46] Sources of ideological power include the domestic and foreign media, think-tanks, universities, and religious institutions. Ideological elites—that is, owners of media conglomerates, heads of churches, think-tank and research institute directors etcetera—may align with, or indeed form part of, the traditional dominant elite class who oppose the post-neoliberal democratization project and as such will seek to delegitimize and destabilize left-governments where possible. Misinformation campaigns and smear campaigns are likely tactics used by those who wield ideological power and who seek to shape public opinions regarding the left-led processes. Ideological powers can thus be used to attempt to sway voter behavior, to foster anti-government sentiment and foment protest, and to shape international perceptions of realities with concrete impacts regarding foreign governments' or businesses' willingness to engage in economic projects in the left-led countries. Left-governments sources of ideological power are likely to be far weaker than those of the opposition-bloc. While state-media is one source of ideological power for left-governments, use of political powers via executive decrees or legislative reforms may be used to try and limit the ideological powers of the opposition-bloc, for example via refusing to renew licenses of television stations or censoring highly critical newspapers.

Economic power depends on the "effective possession of economic resources."[47] Sources of economic power include control of the banking and commerce sectors, taxation, business and investment ownership, and natural resource control. Groups who can monopolize control over production, distribution, exchange, and consumption strengthen their structural and instrumental power. Building on earlier debates among theorists such as

Nicos Poulantzas, Ralph Miliband, and Fred Block, among others, Culpepper[48] states that structural power "results from the fact that firms and capital holders control the investment decisions on which the economy depends for growth." Where the structural power of economic elites is high, the range of policy options available to state managers who challenge the interests of capital is narrowed. That is, economic elites seek to use their sources of economic power to constrain progressive policies, thereby limiting the possibility of extending democracy.[49] Furthermore, as Robinson[50] notes, in a globalized setting, the neoliberal drive toward a "single unified field for global capitalism" has significantly boosted the structural power of transnational capitalists, thereby limiting the autonomy of state managers who face pressures to promote an environment friendly to transnational economic elite interests. While capital's power influences the range of policy options available to state managers, the structure of the capitalist system is one of mutual dependency between state managers and economic elites; capital depends on state managers' providing a regulatory environment conducive to generating profits.[51] Therefore, state managers are not wholly constrained by the power of capital and may strategically select policies that, in certain conjunctures, favor popular-class interests over those of capital.[52]

Military power is a coercive power that relies on the use of force and arms, and the military and police elites who monopolize it can obtain collective and distributive power.[53] While it could be argued that the military is controlled by the state and should therefore fall under the heading of political power, given the history of the military to act independently in Latin America, it is necessary to separate military from political power.[54] Military power is not confined to armies as governments and oppositional forces may use connections with gangs and paramilitaries to achieve their goals.

While domestic elites and left-governments may make use of their relative sources of ideological, economic, military and political powers to advance their agendas while restricting their opponents, it is important to emphasize the role of transnational forces that shape the environment in which post-neoliberal democratization processes develop. Globalization fundamentally challenges the notion that democratization is something which simply occurs in territorially bounded states.[55] The transnational wing of the opposition-bloc may comprise foreign states, regional bodies, supranational institutions, and transnational capital amongst others. The power of external actors over domestic state managers is influenced by the extent and form of "leverages" by forces who oppose the left-governments and the post-neoliberal process.[56] Oppositional leverage describes a governments' vulnerability to external pressure which may be exerted in "a variety of ways, including political conditionality and punitive sanctions, diplomatic pressure, and military intervention."[57] Weak states with underdeveloped economies are more vulnerable to external pressure than those with substantial economic power because they are more reliant on foreign investment; require insertion into global supply chains for exporting goods produced (often primary commodities) and for importing goods that are not produced locally (including medicines, foodstuffs, key components in producing exports etcetera); and are more likely to require lending from pro-market international financial institutions whose conditional lending curbs state autonomy. Transnational oppositional leverage may be reduced, however, where a country has economic, political, or military support from an alternative power, be that at the regional level or beyond.

Mann's IEMP approach is useful for comprehending Latin America's outsider-led processes given the nature of the region's elites.[58] Foweraker[59] states that oligarchies are prevalent in Latin American societies whereby families with ties to powerful political parties and the media seek to ensure that the agenda of policymaking does not harm their economic interests. In Latin America, "media are with few exceptions owned by and operated within vertical family firms controlled by concentrated economic elites that interact in a mutually beneficial way with political authorities."[60] The owners of the dominant media in the region "are part of broader economic elites that have benefitted from the status quo of inequality and tend to share a worldview that normalizes the current state of social relations."[61] In Schneider's[62] analysis of hierarchical capitalism in the region he describes the nature of big business groups, outlining that small numbers of huge business groups account for large shares of economic activity and that business groups are mostly owned and managed by families, often spanning several generations. Indeed, North and Clarke[63] state that socioeconomic development in Latin America continues to be "blocked and distorted...by the power and overwhelming influence of a small elite." The top decile of income earners in the region control more than 70 percent of all assets while the GINI coefficient for land distribution stood at .8 for South America, far above the global average.[64] Extreme inequalities in land and wealth distributions allow an elite class to have outsized influence on political decision-making because of the structural power that asset ownership confers on them vis-à-vis the state and civil society actors. These elites also dominate ownership of transnationals in areas such as mining, agro-industry, cement, food industries, and primary-commodity extraction, imbuing them with enormous power. During the antecedent era, mainstream parties represented the interests of these traditional domestic elite families (as well as international capital) who supported the market model of democracy. As such, when analyzing the left-led Andean cases, oppositional-blocs are conceptualized as elite-networks in political, ideological, economic, and even military spheres whose goal is to limit challenges to the status quo of political and economic power distribution.

The use of IEMP sources of power by left-governments and opposition-blocs influence how their opponents respond. That is, the choice of tactic by government or opposition (which is determined by the forms of power they can wield) in turn shapes the responses and tactics of their adversaries (which in turn are determined by the available sources of IEMP they can direct) in a dialectic process. As such, this relative power struggle greatly influences whether post-neoliberal democratization processes not only can advance in terms of deepening or extending the quality of citizenship for popular sectors but will also impact on left-leaders' use of centralized executive power to overcome powerful domestic and transnational opponents and respond to popular demands. The nature of such struggles will also influence popular sector support/acceptance of the bending of liberal norms via the boosting of executive powers. That is, in scenarios where opposition-blocs adopt an array of IEMP tactics to limit the capacity of elected left-governments to govern from the left, popular sectors are more likely to back the party even when they creep in an illiberal direction.

While left-governments and opposition-blocs push and pull in differing directions with direct impacts on the direction and outcomes of processes, these struggles cannot be understood outside of a wider analysis that accounts for the role of popular sector power. Powerful popular bases are more likely to counterbalance opposition-bloc demands on left-parties to moderate reforms processes; they are more capable of keeping left-parties internally democratic by preventing a top-down directing of processes that does not allow for bottom-up input into decision-making processes; and they may also act as a key emergency handbrake on centralized executive power sliding in an authoritarian manner. Powerful bases, while holding left-parties in office to a more radical agenda, in turn are likely to foster greater left-government—opposition struggles. Grasping these relative power balances is the crux of gaining an understanding into the "why" questions regarding the direction and outcomes of post-neoliberal democratization processes.

A key measure of the base's power is its capacity to engage in mobilization that is disruptive, on a mass scale, can last for long periods of time, and can frequently and rapidly convene. Mobilization capacity is dependent upon the organizational strength and unity of popular bases as well as their levels of autonomy from the left-party.[65] Autonomy from the party means that popular organization survival is not dependent on party funding and that organization leaders avoid co-optation whereby they enter the party structure or take a state position but become detached from and unresponsive to the grassroots base of their organization.

Where popular sectors are well organized and where organizations retain autonomy, mobilization capacity of the base is higher and it is more likely that they will be able to engage in informal contestatory interest intermediation—"routinized interactions where the government proposes a policy, affected popular sector organizations protest vigorously, negotiation ensues, and government abides by agreements."[66] Contestatory interest intermediation is in fact both an outcome of post-neoliberal incorporation projects *and* an intervening variable that shapes the direction of processes. That is, while contestatory interest intermediation signifies a deepening of democracy (a key outcome of the processes analyzed here), if contestatory intermediation emerges during a post-neoliberal democratization process it is likely to influence whether and how a process further evolves.

Whether contestatory interest intermediation is regularly used depends on the relationship between base and party, which in turn is influenced by left-government—opposition-bloc relations. A common agenda or universal enemy facing the base and the party is more conducive to an ally-type relationship, and therefore lower levels of contestatory mobilization may be expected. In ally relationships it is also more likely that there will be extensive and intensive linkages between base and party. Extensive linkages are "loose political ties based largely on an exchange of particularistic goods" including clientelist/selective side-payments and patronage pay-outs.[67] Intensive linkages include the integration of popular organizations into the formal bureaucratic party structure. Where intensive linkages are built, popular organizations are more likely to become deeply invested in the party and to prove dependable allies. The formation of linkages between base and party is important in that it offers an alternative to informal contestatory interest intermediation as a means of bottom-up influence on party decision making.[68]

However, where the power of opposition-blocs over left-parties in office is strong and the party adopts capital-friendly policies, an adversarial base-party relationship is more likely and contestatory intermediation will be more frequent. Party-leaderships in turn may seek to limit the space for successful intermediation. Furthermore, extensive and intensive linkages forged during ally-type state-society relations may actively disorganize the independent capacities of the popular base.[69] Extensive linkages may buy off movement leaders and reduce the likelihood of contestatory mobilization, even where party decisions impinge on the well-being of the popular organization's grassroots base, while intensive linkages are likely to weaken organizations' autonomy. Moreover, if left-party leaders are seen by ordinary members of social movements to be favoring capital over popular demands and the leadership of the popular organization fails to call for contestatory mobilization because of co-optation, tensions *within* the organization are likely. These tensions may fracture the unity and organizational strength of the base, thereby ensuring a smoother governance environment in which left-state managers seek to avoid radical challenges to the interests of capital. In other words, where popular organizations split, they are less capable of offensive mobilization to hold left-state managers to popular demands.

In sum, historical and emergent factors influence the emergence, pathways and outcomes of post-neoliberal democratization processes, shaping the forms and extent of democratic deepening and extending, as well as whether centralization occurs, how executive powers are used and whether such illiberal behavior retains popular legitimacy. These outcomes also determine the potential longer-term legacies of post-neoliberal processes. Whether the processes manage to respond to popular sector concerns that emerged in the antecedent stage will influence whether or not popular sector trust in the party-system and democracy more broadly is restored. Relatedly, the varied pathways will influence whether or not a legitimate, well-organized party capable of representing popular demands in the electoral arena is established, thereby representing a long-term legacy of a process. Fundamentally, the pathways that processes take will influence the nature of popular sector organizational and mobilizational power, which in turn will determine whether or not advances achieved in terms of deepening and extending democracy will be actively defended from below in the face of backsliding, whether a party of the left or right is in power. This then is the ultimate test regarding long-term legacies of post-neoliberal processes.

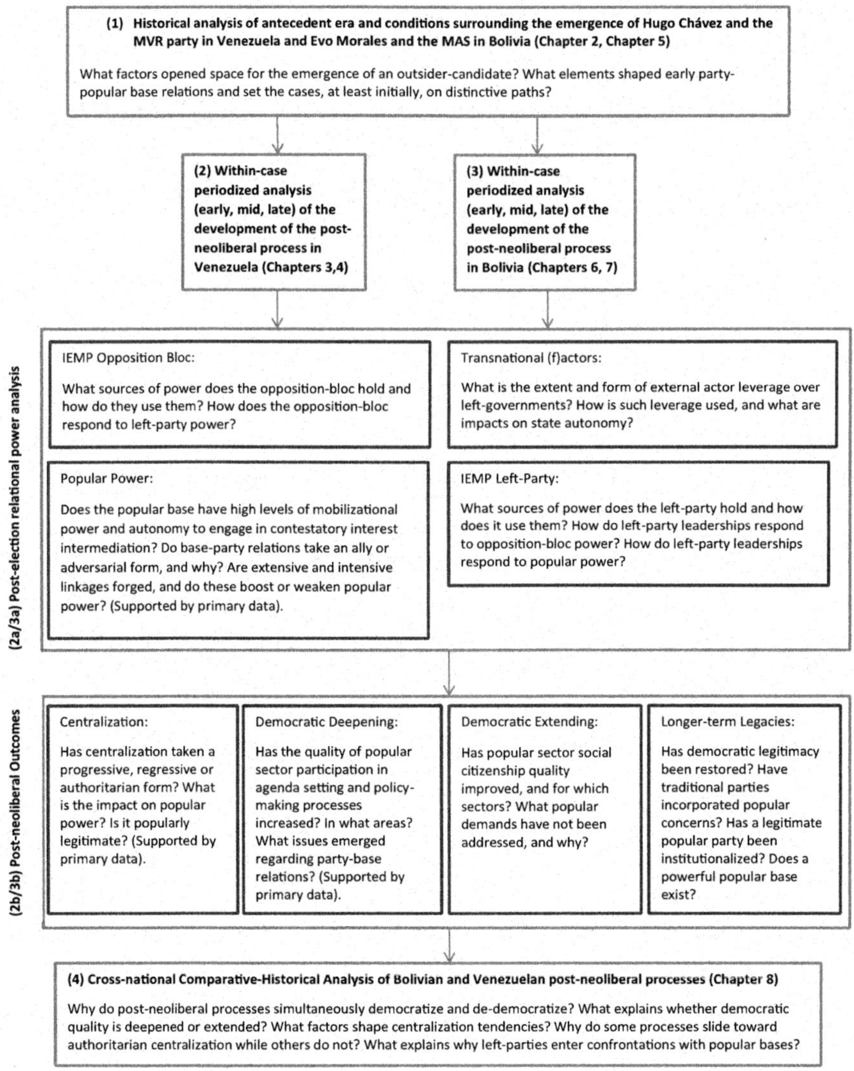

Figure 1.1 Research design.

Research design

I address the puzzle of why progressive-outsider parties and leaders emerge and why they foster simultaneous democratization and de-democratization processes by combining a within-case periodized research design with a cross-case comparative design. Figure 1.1 summarizes the research design. In Chapters 2 and 5 I analyze the historical factors that influenced the emergence of outsiders in Venezuela and Bolivia as well as the antecedent conditions regarding party-base relations that fed back onto the processes following the elections of Hugo Chávez and Evo Morales. Next, the struggles in Venezuela between left-governments, opposition-blocs, and popular sector organizations are analyzed and located within a wider transnational setting so as to evaluate how varying relative balances of power between actors, and the varying forms of power that each actor wields, shaped the directions the post-neoliberal process followed (Chapters 3 and 4). The relative power framework is then used to evaluate the Bolivian process and outcomes (Chapters 6 and 7). The processes and outcomes are then compared (Chapter 8) before broader lessons from the cases regarding responding to the crisis of market democracy are discussed (Conclusion).

Notes

1 Joe Foweraker, *Polity: Demystifying Democracy in Latin America and Beyond* (Boulder, CO: Lynne Rienner, 2018): 180.
2 Ibid.
3 World Bank figures, 2020, accessible at https://data.worldbank.org/indicator/SP.URB.TOTL.IN.ZS?locations=VE.
4 National Institute of Statistics, Venezuela, "XIV Censo Nacional de Población y Vivienda 2011," accesible at http://www.ine.gov.ve/documentos/Demografia/CensodePoblacionyVivienda/pdf/miranda.pdf.
5 This is not to suggest that analysis of how core-organizations interact with the party and process are ignored. Rather, secondary sources are used for such discussions.
6 Sian Lazar, "El Alto, Ciudad Rebelde: Organizational Bases for Revolt," *Bulletin of Latin American Research* 25, no. 2 (2006): 183–99.
7 David Collier and Steven Levitsky, "Democracy with Adjectives: Conceptual Innovation in Comparative Research," *World Politics* 49, no. 3 (1997): 430–51.
8 David Beetham, "Liberal Democracy and the Limits of Democratization," *Political Studies* 40, no. S1 (1992): 40.
9 William Robinson, "Promoting Polyarchy in Latin America: The Oxymoron of 'Market Democracy'," in Eric Hershberg and Fred Rosen (eds), *Latin America after Neoliberalism* (New York: The New Press, 2006): 100.
10 Emir Sader, *The New Mole: Paths of the Latin American Left* (London: Verso, 2011): 132.
11 Thomas Lemke, "'The Birth of Bio-politics': Michel Foucault's Lecture at the Collège de France on Neo-liberal Governmentality," *Economy and Society* 30, no. 2 (2001): 201.
12 Kenneth Roberts, *Deepening Democracy? The Modern Left and Social Movements in Chile and Peru* (Stanford, CA: Stanford University Press, 1998).

13 Ibid., 30.
14 Mary Kaldor and Ivan Vejvoda, "Democratization in Central and East European Countries," *International Affairs* 73, no. 1 (1997): 67.
15 Archon Fung and Erik Olin Wright, *Deepening Democracy: Institutional Innovations in Empowered Participatory Governance* (London: Verso, 2003): 5; see also Carole Pateman, *Participation and Democratic Theory* (Cambridge: Cambridge University Press, 1970) and Crawford Brough Macpherson, *The Life and Times of Liberal Democracy* (Oxford: Oxford University Press, 1977).
16 Sebastián Etchemendy, "The Politics of Popular Coalitions: Unions and Territorial Social Movements in Post-neoliberal Latin America (2000-15)," *Journal of Latin American Studies* 52, no. 1 (2019): 157–88.
17 As Etchemendy (Ibid.) describes, TSMs are not single-issue social movements. Rather, they are territorially anchored organizations such as urban associations, community groups, cooperatives, indigenous rural groups etc. TSMs' demand-making generally relates to the allocation of state economic resources.
18 Roberts, *Deepening Democracy*, 29–30.
19 Eduardo Silva and Federico Rossi (eds.), *Reshaping the Political Arena in Latin America: From Resisting Neoliberalism to the Second Incorporation* (Pittsburgh, PA: University of Pittsburgh Press, 2018).
20 Federico Rossi and Eduardo Silva, "Introduction: Reshaping the Political Arena," in Eduardo Silva and Federico Rossi (eds), *Reshaping the Political Arena in Latin America: From Resisting Neoliberalism to the Second Incorporation* (Pittsburgh, PA: University of Pittsburgh Press, 2018): 9.
21 Ibid.
22 Eduardo Silva, "Conclusion: Reflections on the Second Wave of Popular Incorporation for a Post-Neoliberal Era," in Eduardo Silva and Federico Rossi (eds), *Reshaping the Political Arena in Latin America: From Resisting Neoliberalism to the Second Incorporation* (Pittsburgh, PA: University of Pittsburgh Press, 2018).
23 Foweraker, *Polity*, 118–9.
24 I emphasize here that I do not advocate a boosting of executive power. A process which bends liberal norms entails enormous dangers, as numerous liberal scholars rightly stress. The conceptualizations advanced here, particularly "progressive centralization" should not therefore be understood as a normative target that aspiring democratizers should strive for. Rather, the conceptualization seeks to offer a more flexible, and accurate, tool for appraising empirical realities. Democratic deepening and extending should be understood as the objectives of democratization projects, bending liberal norms should not.
25 For a discussion of diminished subtypes and adjective+ concepts, see Gary Goertz, *Social Science Concepts: A User's Guide* (Princeton, NJ: Princeton University Press, 2006): 74–80.
26 Ruth Berins Collier and David Collier, *Shaping the Political Arena: Critical Junctures, the Labor Movement, and Regime Dynamics in Latin America* (Princeton, NJ: Princeton University Press, 1991).
27 Kenneth Roberts, *Changing Course: Party Systems in Latin America's Neoliberal Era* (New York: Cambridge University Press, 2015): 48.
28 For a discussion of historical causes see Arthur Stinchcombe, *Constructing Social Theories* (New York: Harcourt, Brace & World, 1968) and Santiago Anria, *When Movements Become Parties: The Bolivian MAS in Comparative Perspective* (Cambridge, New York: Cambridge University Press, 2019): 40–3.
29 Alexander George and Andrew Bennet, *Case-studies and Theory Development in the Social Sciences* (Cambridge, MA: MIT Press, 2005): 93.
30 Roberts, *Deepening Democracy*, 75.
31 Ibid.

32 Anria, *When Movements Become Parties.*
33 Juan Carlos Monedero, "Snipers in the Kitchen: State Theory and Latin America's Left Cycle," *New Left Review* 120, Nov/Dec (2019): 5.
34 Ibid.
35 Gerardo Munck, "Building Democracy... Which Democracy? Ideology and Models of Democracy in Post-Transition Latin America," *Government and Opposition* 50, no. 3 (2015): 378.
36 Barry Cannon and Peadar Kirby (eds.), *Civil Society and the State in Left-led Latin America* (London, New York: Zed Books, 2012): 202; John Brown, "Party-base Linkages and Contestatory Mobilization in Bolivia's El Alto: Subduing the Ciudad Rebelde," *Latin American Perspectives* 47, no. 4 (2020): 40–57.
37 Bob Jessop, *State Power: A Strategic-Relational Approach* (Cambridge: Polity, 2008).
38 Ibid., 1.
39 Diego Andreucci and Isabella Radhuber, "Limits to 'Counter-neoliberal' Reform: Mining Expansion and the Marginalization of Post-Extractivist Forces in Evo Morales's Bolivia," *Geoforum* 84, August (2017): 282.
40 Jessop, *State Power,* 6.
41 Bob Jessop, *The State: Past, Present, Future* (Cambridge: Polity, 2016): 96.
42 Michael Mann, *The Sources of Social Power, vol. 1: A History of Power from the Beginning to AD 1760* (New York: Cambridge University Press, 2012).
43 Eduardo Silva, *Challenging Neoliberalism in Latin America* (New York: Cambridge University Press, 2009): 33.
44 Kenneth Roberts and Steven Levitsky, "Conclusion: Democracy, Development, and the Left," in Steven Levitsky and Kenneth Roberts (eds), *The Resurgence of the Latin American Left* (Baltimore, MD: Johns Hopkins University Press, 2011): 407.
45 Kurt Weyland, Raúl Madrid, and Wendy Hunter (eds.), *Leftist Governments in Latin America: Successes and Shortcomings* (New York: Cambridge University Press, 2010).
46 Silva, *Challenging Neoliberalism,* 40.
47 Ibid.
48 Pepper Culpepper, "Structural Power and Political Science in the Post-crisis Era," *Business and Politics* 17, (2015): 396.
49 Evelyne Huber and John Stephens, *Democracy and the Left: Social Policy and Inequality in Latin America* (Chicago, IL: University of Chicago Press, 2012).
50 William Robinson, "Global Capitalism Theory and the Emergence of Transnational Elites," *Critical Sociology* 38, no. 3 (2012): 353–8.
51 Culpepper, "Structural Power."
52 Bob Jessop, *State Theory: Putting the Capitalist State in Its Place* (Cambridge: Polity, 1990): 248–72.
53 Mann, *The Sources of Social Power,* 26.
54 Silva, *Challenging Neoliberalism,* 38.
55 Jean Grugel and Matthew Bishop, *Democratization: A Critical Introduction* (London and New York: Palgrave Macmillan, 2014): 98.
56 Steven Levitsky and Lucan Way, "International Linkage and Democratization," *Journal of Democracy* 16, no. 3 (2005): 20–34; Lucan Way and Steven Levitsky, "Linkage, Leverage, and the Post-Communist Divide," *East European Politics and Societies* 21, no. 1 (2007): 48–66.
57 Levitsky and Way, "International Linkage," 21.
58 If analysing a European or North American context, the nature of elites, and what gives them power, would need to be adapted. See conclusion for discussion.
59 Foweraker, *Polity,* 100.
60 Sallie Hughes and Paula Prado, "Media Diversity and Social Inequality in Latin America," in Merike Blofield (ed), *The Great Gap: Inequality and the Politics of Redistribution in Latin America* (Pennsylvania: Pennsylvania State Press, 2011): 135.
61 Ibid.

62 Ben Ross Schneider, *Hierarchical Capitalism in Latin America: Business, Labor, and the Challenges of Equitable Development* (Cambridge: Cambridge University Press, 2013): 10.
63 Timothy Clarke and Liisa North, "The Limits of Democratization and Social Progress: Domination and Dependence in Latin America," in Liisa North and Timothy Clarke (eds), *Dominant Elites in Latin America: From Neo-liberalism to the 'Pink Tide'* (London: Palgrave Macmillan, 2018): 212.
64 Ibid.
65 Santiago Anria, "Democratizing Democracy? Civil Society and Party Organization in Bolivia," *Comparative Politics* 48, no. 4 (2016): 459–78.
66 Eduardo Silva, "Reorganizing Popular Sector Incorporation: Propositions from Bolivia, Ecuador, and Venezuela," *Politics & Society* 45, no. 1 (2017): 96.
67 Santiago Anria and Jennifer Cyr, "Inside Revolutionary Parties: Coalition-Building and Maintenance in Reformist Bolivia," *Comparative Political Studies* 50, no. 9 (2017): 1256, 1268.
68 Jenny Pearce, "Collective Action or Public Participation? Complementary or Contradictory Democratization Strategies in Latin America?" *Bulletin of Latin American Research* 23, no. 4 (2004): 483–504.
69 Jeffery Webber, "The Deadweight of Structure: A Response to René Rojas on Latin America's Pink Tide," *NACLA: Report on the Americas*, January 7th (2019).

2 Crisis of market democracy and making space for outsider Hugo Chávez

Venezuela in historical context

In this chapter, I examine the crisis of market democracy and the emergence of progressive anti-system outsider Hugo Chávez in Venezuela. The nature of the shallowing and narrowing of democracy, the development of an unstable democratic equilibrium, the form and extent of anti-neoliberal protests, party-system collapse, the coalescence of competing social blocs around divergent democratic models, and the nature of outsider-base relations are examined. The chapter concludes by raising questions regarding how such antecedent factors set the scene for, and fed back onto, post-election power struggles between the left-led government, an opposition bloc, and the popular base.

Making space for Hugo Chávez: Venezuela's crisis of market democracy

To understand why outsider Hugo Chávez was elected in Venezuela, to grasp what relationship Chávez had with the popular base, and to gauge the successes and failures of efforts to deepen and extend the quality of democracy, it is necessary to root such assessment in "the legacy of the illiberal Punto Fijo democracy" which began in 1958.[1] Moreover, in order to grasp the forms that emergent power struggles took following Chávez' election, it is necessary to identify which groups had dominated society and benefitted from the Punto Fijo era model, and whose status was challenged by the election of Chávez. The discussion of Venezuela's historical factors therefore examines the emergence of this Punto Fijo democracy; the rise and fall of the national populist era; the adoption of neoliberalism; popular protests against neoliberal political and economic exclusion, detailing the histories of societal mobilization; the emergence of contemporary Bolivarianism; and the election of outsider-candidate Hugo Chávez.

Punto Fijoism stage 1: inclusionary and exclusionary national populism

In 1930, with dictator Juan Vicente Gómez in power, Venezuela was the world's leading oil exporter with oil rents from foreign companies dominating

DOI: 10.4324/9781003262466-3

traditional agricultural exports. In this scenario, the landed oligarchy was converted into a "financial-rentier elite, with interests far beyond the country's borders."[2] The internal circulation of oil revenues fostered a local market of consumers, but without corresponding local producers. As such, imports became crucially important in the rentier state's model of development. A concentration of financial resources in urban centers fostered rapid urbanization which gave rise to an incipient construction industry. The

> transformation of agricultural lands into urban real estate became a central path to wealth and the basis for the formation of major *grupos económicos*, that is, diversified conglomerates centred on one or a few families linked by ties of marriage, business, and friendship.[3]

Gómez died in 1935 after 27 years in power, opening space for increased participation and representation. In 1945, the *Acción Democrática* (Democratic Action—AD) party joined a military conspiracy to remove Gómez' military successors, with AD playing a leading role in the governing junta known as the Trienio from 1945 to 1948. The election of AD candidate Rómulo Gallegos in December 1947 "provided AD with a political dominance that was strengthened by the party's association with the extension of suffrage, labor rights, and rural and social organization."[4] AD founded a national labor confederation, the *Confederación de Trabajadores Venezolanos* (Confederation of Venezuelan Workers—CTV) which incorporated the majority of Venezuela's organized workers and peasants. Changes to the hydrocarbons law during the Trienio were to prove pivotal in the country's oil policy and development. Under the 1910 Mining Code, a ground rent was levied and was paid as contract royalties. Under the law, the state was not the owner of subsoil resources and was simply paid rent for allowing private sector access to Venezuela's hydrocarbons. Under the AD government, however, this was revised and a new 50/50 profit-sharing agreement with oil companies was established. The boosted revenue for the AD government allowed it to "sow the oil wealth" by funding new welfare obligations established under the 1946 constitution.

The rentier nature of the Venezuelan state was institutionalized as national income was to be derived from collecting profits from transnational-led extraction of the state's hydrocarbon resources, with local industrialization marginalized. Indeed,

> Venezuela was tightly integrated into the US market for oil, while its entrepreneurs became salesmen and franchise-holders for US companies, importing cars, clothes and culture for an urban middle class prospering on public-sector employment and whitened by post-war immigration from Italy and Spain. Darker-skinned laboring classes swelled the informal economies of the urban periphery.[5]

The move away from dictatorship to democracy coupled with the establishment of a new nationalist oil policy "configured an association between citizenship and a distributionary state, with rent access mediated by the ruling party."[6]

AD's reform process, however, triggered a backlash from conservative sectors of the military, Catholic Church, and business community and in 1946 a new Christian Democratic party, *Comité de Organización Política Electoral Independiente*-COPEI, was formed to give conservative elites a partisan vehicle to represent their interests.[7] While COPEI emerged as an electoral vehicle for representation of conservative elite concerns, a military coup in 1948 toppled the Trienio with Pérez Jiménez taking power. However, by 1957 civilian, church, and military opposition to Jiménez' centralization of decision-making and refusal to hold free elections was growing. The Junta Patriótica, a multiparty interest group, called on the armed forces to defend the constitution and to remove Pérez Jiménez. As Coronil[8] stresses

> the turnaround of private sector leaders was a crucial factor in consolidating opposition to Pérez Jiménez. In 1948 … business leaders, alienated by AD's populist policies during the Trienio, strongly supported Pérez Jiménez. Yet by 1957 members of the business elite … had become critical of the state's unresponsiveness to their concerns and mismanagement of the economy.

and conspired with the principal political parties AD and COPEI, though not the Communist Party (PCV). While leading members of the local bourgeoisie had rejected the party system in 1948 and backed the military as a "party of their own," by 1957 when they realized that for Pérez Jiménez there was "no party other than himself, they began to accept a party system within which they could operate and, perhaps, which they could make their own."[9]

When Pérez Jiménez' most steadfast allies, colonels Casanova and Villate, informed him that he must leave the country immediately, he vacated the presidential palace. Leaders of the main party groupings—Rómulo Betancourt of AD, Rafael Caldera of COPEI, and leaders of other non-communist parties—agreed to a power-sharing pact in Caldera's home, the villa "Punto Fijo" in Caracas. Excluding the PCV was a signal to the United States and the private sector that the parties would offer a stable, moderate business environment. Indeed, the private sector was to have a strong voice in policymaking in the post-1958 governments. The Punto Fijo pact promised that the economic elite would be guaranteed of the right to private industry, the military was to be modernized and granted a seat at the executive branch, the Church would not be subject to government intervention, and workers were guaranteed of the right to organize.[10] AD and COPEI transformed into catch-all parties with COPEI reconciling its Christian Democratic ideology with its upper-middle-class constituency. AD meanwhile moved to the center-left, distancing the party's more radical members. The two parties converged around a moderate center and "forged a broad consensus for a state-led model of development that used ample oil revenues to moderate distributive conflicts."[11] Under this "pacted democracy,"[12] AD and COPEI secured a large electoral base through their dominant presence in the largest labor movements, and the parties consolidated their power by distributing leadership positions in unions, peasant organizations, the chamber of commerce, and the bar association amongst others. The two parties also negotiated and shared appointments to the judiciary, national electoral council, military, and state corporations.

The Punto Fijo pact provided for competition between AD and COPEI for access to oil rents, which were used to legitimize the regime via the provision of economic well-being and the promotion of societal development. The oil sector was nationalized in 1975 while an oil price boom between 1973 and 1977 saw GDP grow by 31 percent. Oil revenues allowed AD and COPEI governments to

> circumvent fiscal policy debates and reconcile seemingly incompatible class demands within a moderate, centrist policy path. Questions of re-distribution in a context of profound inequalities of land, resources and influence inherited from the colonial period were bypassed, with the narrow interests of 'white-gloved' patricians, hacendados and powerful business families (the Mendoza, Vollmer, Boulton, Phelps, Blohm and Delfino dynasties) accommodated.[13]

That is, AD and COPEI governments, using the vast oil wealth at its disposal, were able to simultaneously listen to the demands of private capital for accumulation and to the majority's demands for social and economic well-being.[14]

In a turbulent region with military regimes in power across the Southern Cone, many political scientists considered Venezuela to be a model of democratic stability. However, while democracy may have been stable, the pact increasingly divorced parties from representation of the popular sectors and there was little room for national social movements to emerge, as happened elsewhere in Latin America in the struggles against military or other authoritarian regimes.[15] While elections were held, freedoms and collective well-being were restricted as a result of massive inequality and exclusion, with little popular input in decision-making, a narrow choice of political candidates, clientelistic networks based around oil wealth, and often violent repression of dissent.[16] Closed-block list voting systems empowered the AD and COPEI leaderships to reward loyalists with places on the list and to punish critics—usually from the left—through omission.[17] The pacted-democracy was underpinned by the agreement to respect the political and economic relations that upheld the oil enclave and that were in turn sustained by it. Venezuela was to maintain its international role as a major oil producer "economically and politically tied to the geopolitical strategy of the United States in the hemisphere. This orchestration also assumed a commitment to contain the lower and working classes within a centralized system of limited reforms and benefits."[18]

The oil boom of the 1970s and the state's role in extracting rent from its natural resource deepened the corruptive practices of the state whereby oligopolistic networks of family-owned businesses received privileged access to credit, information, and preferential interest rates.[19] The political and economic elites mingled and there was a sense of solidarity amongst this dominant class which considered itself as the rightful custodian of the nation's oil. While there was a competition within this class for supremacy, the assumed common role as natural overseers of the nation's oil meant that internal class differences were to be resolved informally, that is, outside of the court and prison system. This intraclass partnership was underpinned by privileged access to public resources and oil monies. As Coronil[20] states, "the chronic blurring of boundaries separating the proper from the improper use of this privilege was both a condition for the existence of this class and an expression of its power."

While the Punto Fijo pact was undergirded by oil revenues and generous social spending, by the 1980s, falling oil prices and the Latin American debt crisis exposed the fragilities of the system. Despite the oil boom of the 1970s, Venezuela had borrowed heavily from international lenders to fund the massive spending on subsidies, industrial development, and social programs. The "oil bonanza encouraged state profligacy and inefficiency, leaving the country vulnerable to the global shocks that loomed on the horizon."[21] In 1982, a global recession alongside falling oil prices, in conjunction with an overvalued exchange rate triggered capital flight. As Cannon[22] notes, it was no longer possible to give to one sector without taking from another. The multiple fractures in the social body of Venezuela which had been concealed under a sea of oil money began to surface.

Punto Fijoism stage 2: the era of market democracy

Under COPEI President Luís Herrera Campíns, a fiscal and current account crisis and the subsequent currency devaluation in 1983 broke the basis of Punto Fijo social pact. In the absence of lubricating oil monies, the vast AD-COPEI patron–client network began to creak. While corruption was tolerated when there was enough oil money to trickle down to everyone, "when international oil prices collapsed, the inherent inequalities of the spoils system became intolerable. The money no longer filtered down to the middle classes and the popular sector. Only politicians and the rich, powerful, and well-born benefited."[23] For example, under Jaime Lusinchi's (AD) presidency from 1984 to 1989, an agency to manage preferential dollar exchanges for certain imports was established to make foreign debt repayments easier for the private sector. Lusinchi was simultaneously seeking to court local private sectors by maintaining a version of the protectionist and distributionist system he had inherited, while at the same time responding to international pressures from the IMF to adopt stabilization measures. However, business interests essentially looted the system, paying off politicians and shipping vast sums abroad. Despite debt servicing consuming almost 50 percent of Venezuela's foreign exchange, Lusinchi continued to spend to paper over the fault lines and keep some semblance of social accord.

During the 1988 presidential campaign, neither major candidate—Eduardo Fernández of COPEI or Carlos Andrés Pérez of AD—prepared the electorate for the "economic shock treatment that lay just around the corner."[24] Indeed, Pérez fostered the belief that his election would allow for a return to the affluence of his earlier term as president during the 1970s. Despite such promises, in February 1989, Pérez, who had been elected on a center-left, social-democratic platform, implemented a severe structural adjustment package known as the *gran viraje*—"the great turnaround"—under the guidance of the International Monetary Fund (IMF) in a classic example of "bait and switch" electoral politics. Pérez took office having to use over half the state's annual foreign exchange income to pay its creditors. Low oil prices, a lack of commercial loans, and low taxation pushed Pérez into adopting the IMF shock therapy approach to economic stabilization in the interest of international debt servicing and macroeconomic stability.

The structural adjustment package emphasized deep cuts in public spending, deregulation of prices including on food and transport, deregulation of interest rates, devaluation of the national currency and the introduction of a unitary foreign exchange rate, the introduction of a value-added tax, restructuring of the foreign debt, privatization of banks, airlines, telecommunications, ports, and other activities, while trade liberalization was called for. Decisions regarding the adoption of these neoliberal policies were taken by a closed group of free-market technocrats and businesspeople who were given top cabinet positions.[25] These technocratic decision-makers were schooled in the private business school Instituto de Estudios Superiores de Administración (Institute for Advanced Studies in Administration—IESA), and in analogy to Chile's Chicago Boys,[26] they were known as the IESA Boys.[27] Many of the technocrats who devised the "great turnaround" were associated with the Grupo Roraima which was formed in the early 1980s with the aim to advance a neoliberal solution to the crisis facing the national populist model.[28]

Though the drastic impacts of the neoliberal reforms on the quality of life for Venezuela's popular and middle-class sectors would worsen over the course of the 1990s, in 1989, the year in which shock therapy was applied, GDP contracted by more than 10 percent while poverty levels rose from 46 to 62 percent, with extreme poverty levels increasing from 14 to 30 percent. Following structural adjustment adoption, poverty was not confined to a minority of the population who had not benefitted from the sowing of oil monies. Poverty affected a majority of the population that was systematically excluded from the socio-economic model.[29] At the same time, businesses hoarded goods in the expectation that Pérez would lift price controls, triggering shortages and a consequent sense of "deception and impotence in the face of uncontrollable powers" amongst the populace.[30]

Eleven days after announcing the structural adjustment measures, on February 27, 1989, a 100-percent increase in bus fares sparked a spontaneous five-day rebellion known as the Caracazo which resulted in the deaths of between 246 and 1,500 people in riots and military responses, while thousands were arrested in popular neighborhoods, particularly those that had histories of left-wing guerrilla activity.[31] Protesters looted small shops whose owners had hoarded goods. The Caracazo was a howl of long-simmering rage as hungry and impoverished people rejected the government and the structural adjustment measures. It was also "a sign of the profound indignation and frustration most Venezuelans felt at the political exclusion from the policy-making process and their declining faith in the political system's capacity to solve public problems equitably."[32]

In the three years following the Caracazo, around 5,000 anti-neoliberal protests were recorded. However, the protests remained ad hoc, isolated events with weak organizational connections amongst protest leaders which would have allowed for more sustained, large-scale mobilization. The lack of a powerful coordinating movement was due to a combination of generally weak histories of popular sector organization; the informalized nature of labor which atomized popular sectors; a national union that had become embedded within one of the major political parties adopting neoliberal reforms; and state repression of left-wing popular sector organization.

Urbanization trends that had been rising throughout the 1980s accelerated rapidly following the adoption of structural adjustment reforms as rural migrants joined newly unemployed urban dwellers in seeking work in the informal economy. Such labor market conditions were not conducive to worker coordination or unionization. The CTV, meanwhile, despite calling several general strikes at crucial moments, never sustained leadership or coordination of anti-neoliberal mobilization.[33] The CTV was perceived to be part of the elite system as it had close historical ties to AD and because it had accepted neoliberal reforms under the belief it would be able to negotiate to soften their impacts.[34] Rather, uncoordinated strikes, marches and demonstrations in which each group focused on its own specific grievances, occurred almost daily.

It is important to emphasize here that popular voices critiquing AD and COPEI governments from the left were savagely repressed by the state, thereby limiting the potential for the development of coordinated and autonomous popular organizing. Luis Isturiz, a delegate for the *Partido Socialista Unido de Venezuela* (United Socialist Party of Venezuela—PSUV)[35] and member of the Comuna Símon Bolivar in El 23 de Enero, told me that before Chávez, "in the Fourth Republic, you couldn't meet up to discuss left-wing politics, they (state forces) took you prisoner, they disappeared you, they murdered you." A member of a commune in Petare told me that during the historical era before the election of Chávez

> the state persecuted and tortured the poor … We couldn't say anything against the government, that the president was a thief for example. We

> have family and neighbors who ended up disappeared because of their ideas ... And the media never interviewed us about the torture and disappearing of people.

A spokesperson for the Comuna Símon Bolivar in El 23 de Enero concurs, telling me that

> I used to live in fear because I was living in a family that supports the left. It was a very hard time. When we talk of the past, of the Caracazo, my daughter reminds me 'Well Mom, thank God we live in the Chávez era and those things don't happen anymore'. It is good to remember the past so that we can understand what we are living in the present, and what we want from the future.

More neoliberalism, more exclusion, popular-military movements, and the emergence of Hugo Chávez

The Caracazo was followed by two coup attempts in 1992 against Andrés Pérez, the first of which was led by Hugo Chávez. Chávez led the *Movimiento Bolivariano Revolucionario 200* (Bolivarian Revolutionary Movement-200-MBR-200), a clandestine group of officers who originally sought to reform the armed forces. The waves of protests following the Caracazo, though they failed to deliver a political alternative, did manage to block the realignment of the dominant political forces. It was in this unstable situation where power from the top was unable to govern, while power from the bottom was unable to offer a valid alternative,[36] that popular protesters galvanized behind "a military-led political opposition committed to profound institutional change and revenge against a rapacious ruling class."[37] The MBR-200 officers, who followed the ideals of Simón Bolívar and his continental project for democracy, felt the Venezuelan oligarchy had betrayed the country, that the CTV was a mere appendage of AD and COPEI,[38] and that the Punto Fijo pact had become corrupted and excluded the interests of the popular sectors. Given the marginalization of the left in Venezuela under the Punto Fijo system, the MBR-200 adopted an anti-party discourse, called for more participatory and direct forms of government, and emphasized that the mobilization and participation of citizens should be coupled with executive power and strong leadership that interprets the will of the people.[39] While the MBR officers were arrested after the failed coup, Chávez' one-minute address on national television in which he stated that the objectives of the coup had not been achieved, "*por ahora* (for now)," transformed him into a symbol of hope for many poor people who were struggling to survive and whose voices had long been excluded from the national debate.

In May 1993, the president was impeached on corruption charges and Rafael Caldera became the first elected president not to come from AD or COPEI. As the two parties who were the founding pillars of the political and economic order that was rapidly decomposing, AD and COPEI saw their vote shares in the presidential elections, as well as their numbers of seats in the chamber of deputies, decimated. Caldera had broken with COPEI and forged a makeshift coalition which included the small leftist party MAS. Caldera had stridently opposed the neoliberal model in his campaign, even going so far as to rationalize the 1992 coup as an expression of anger at Perez' reforms. Indeed, in an attempt to stabilize civil–military relations, in 1994 Caldera pardoned the rebellious junior officers of the coup, including Hugo Chávez.

Caldera faced a banking crisis as weak regulation and "blatant theft of government bailout funds by bankers (estimated at nearly US$7 billion) in the form of capital flight led to large-scale bank closures and government takeovers of many of the economy's largest commercial banks in 1994 and 1995."[40] The principal cause of the crisis was weak state capacity to regulate the financial sector, while campaign contributions from large financial groups to the Pérez presidential campaign also increased banks' leverage over the state.

Following the bailout, which cost the government the equivalent of 18 percent of GDP, with mounting outlays for subsidies and price controls, and in the context of low international oil prices, the fiscal deficit and inflation far exceeded government targets. In 1996, Caldera announced an agreement with the IMF on a $3.3 billion structural adjustment package in a dramatic reversal of pre-election promises. Furthermore, the tranche of reforms relating to currency rates and controls, gasoline prices, interest rates, sales taxes, and increased commitment to privatization had been devised by Teodoro Petkoff, the historic leader of the leftist MAS. As Ellner[41] summarizes, "these reversals of positions put in evidence the profound impact of neoliberalism on actors of different political leanings who were closely tied to the political system and accepted the established rules of the political game."

Meanwhile, the sudden deregulation of the economy triggered a shift in the business sector as the market rather than the state became the focus of attention. In a drive to dominate the market by whatever means necessary, business groups engaged in an "oligopolistic frenzy" and "oligopolistic wars" as they sought monopolization of raw material supplies, financing, and distribution channels.[42] Business groups also shifted their attention to constructing public opinion via the media, with economic elites investing aggressively in newspapers, magazines, and radio and television stations.[43] No major media organization was independent of a major conglomerate group by the 1990s.[44] Following neoliberal deregulation, centralized power was not displaced, but rather changed form as "the commanding heights … shifted from the state to these more diffuse and invisible private centers of public power."[45] Major conglomerates such as the Cisneros Group and the Polar Group deepened their investments in and domination of domestic productive structures.

The adoption of neoliberal policies and the move away from the political model associated with import substitution industrialization also dramatically weakened organized labor. AD and COPEI's labor bureaus had incorporated the organized working class into the nation's ruling bloc. In the 1990s, however, AD's labor bureau was stripped of "prerogatives including uncontested representation on party slates for public office."[46] Moreover, the labor bureau lost influence amongst workers due to its backing of neoliberal policies, especially the 1997 labor law reform.

While private business groups took advantage of the liberalizing reforms as the power of organized labor retreated, neoliberal reforms dramatically reduced the quality of life for popular sectors. Poverty increased from 36 percent in 1984 to 66 percent in 1995, while those living in extreme poverty increased from 11 to 36 percent.[47] By the end of the 1990s, minimum wages were 60 percent lower than those in the 1980s while public sector per-capita spending was 40 percent lower than levels in 1980. Between 1981 and 1997 unemployment almost doubled, with massive increases in numbers working in the informal sector, with the poorest of society bearing the brunt of a 37 percent decrease in average wages.[48] Informal sector employment rose from 41.3 percent of working Venezuelans in 1983 to 48.2 percent in 1998.[49] While in 1979 the richest 5 percent of the population earned 41.58 times more than the poorest 5 percent, by 1997 that ratio was 53.11 to one.[50] As the popular sectors bore the brunt of structural adjustments, the failure of the state to implement progressive tax reforms indicates how wealthier groups were able to resist shouldering the burden of reforms. Value-added tax rates increased but income and property taxes remained negligible, furthering income inequality and polarization of politics.[51]

The collapse of the Punto Fijo party system and the election of outsider-candidate Hugo Chávez

Worsening living conditions and the adoption of the packet of severe structural adjustments called for by the IMF in 1996 triggered a second wave of anti-neoliberal protests during Caldera's presidency, the characteristics of which were similar to earlier moments of contention. Public sector unions, teachers, students, transport workers, and neighborhood protests dominated this second wave, while oil workers occasionally joined in, as did militant unions controlled by the left-wing Causa Radical (Radical Cause-Causa R) party. The CTV even staged a second strike. However, like the previous wave, protests were decentralized, with no group framing mobilization around larger strategic objectives. By 1995, unionization rates had fallen to just 13.5 percent meaning that the unions were incapable of acting as a national glue to bind myriad anti-neoliberal protests together. Venezuela did not have a mass-based indigenous movement, and the CTV was too closely intertwined with AD to channel popular social resistance to market democracy.

Hugo Chávez emerged in this organizational void where traditional avenues of popular sector incorporation had come to be seen as part of the problem. However, while it is certainly true that protests were in general disorganized and uncoordinated, in some popular barrios, for example, El 23 de Enero in Caracas, popular organizations and collectives with strong histories of mobilization and organization existed. Such movements had their origins in the clandestine movement against the 1950s military regime, the post-transition era of guerrilla struggle in the 1960s, as well as in the cultural activism and urban committees of the 1980s.[52] As established corporatist institutions such as trade unions and political parties lost power, and as neoliberal reforms created deep unrest in popular areas, greater space emerged for unaffiliated barrio-based organizations, with their roots in longer-term social movements, to build their bases.[53] One such organization, the Asamblea de Barrios de Caracas, brought together representatives of around 200 barrios in the city to discuss the most pressing issues facing residents.[54] Though the organization only existed from 1991 to 1993, its members included MBR-200 militants and it contributed significantly to the formulation of plans for popular struggles in Caracas' barrios.[55]

However, while such organizations existed, by the late 1990s popular sector organizational power had been drained by almost two decades of neoliberal policies. As López-Maya and Lander[56] state, the anti-neoliberal popular movement "lacked an organic base, tradition, and networks" and was "disorganized, dispersed, and fragmented." Following the failed coup of 1992, the leaders of MBR-200 spent two years in jail, during which time they developed their plans and ideology, and once out of prison, they began forming a "civic-military" movement based on popular organizations like the Bolivarian Circles. The Bolivarian Circles were popular organizations formed in the 1990s to act as the organized expression of civilian support for the MBR. These small cells of up to 11 individuals swore to defend Bolivarianism and its principles.[57]

While Chávez drew inspiration from long-standing popular organization struggles, he acted as the glue that bound disparate communities together around the ideas of a more inclusionary democracy. For example, while popular actors had discussed building socialism before Chávez' election, a central actor in Venezuela's national commune movement told me that such discussions

> Were mainly theoretical ... they were not attached to anything concrete, anything real. It was an airy debate of what we could do. We used to read, to debate. We didn't have a solid foundation. Chávez' biggest contribution, regarding true democracy, was the revitalization, the redefinition, the deepening of the concepts, the radicalization of our thinking ... He helped us to see clearly how to create what we had read in books. He helped us discover how to put socialism into practice and make it part of our daily routine, of giving it flesh and bones.

As a member of a commune and resident of Zone 10 in the Petare barrio of Caracas told me, "Chávez awoke us, he ingrained strength in us so that even in bad times we would not lose our direction, that we would continue to struggle." This conscientization[58] of the popular sectors, the sentiment of being politicized and the belief that the state and the political system could in fact be used to improve the livelihoods of the poor, is a view that I heard throughout my fieldwork in the popular barrios of Caracas.

The waves of protest following the IMF-sponsored neoliberal adjustments encouraged MBR members to capitalize on the moment of electoral volatility by forming a political party. In 1997, the MBR changed its name to the *Movimiento V República* (Fifth Republic Movement—MVR)[59] as Chávez decided to directly seek the presidency. When Chávez announced his candidacy for the presidential elections of 1998, he was a relatively marginal figure with popularity in the single digits, but as Venezuela's economy declined and the party system continued to self-destruct, his candidacy surged. Chávez' candidacy represented a real threat to the existing status quo. He embodied the "decentralized demands for an alternative to neoliberalism by running on a platform that promised to overhaul Venezuela's democratic institutions and the political economy to encourage the political and economic inclusion of the popular sectors."[60] He "adopted a radical and polarizing anti-neoliberal discourse that offered to 'fry the heads' of the corrupt traditional elites and get Venezuela out of the crisis situation through deep social and political change."[61] The centerpiece of his campaign was a promise to convoke a constituent assembly and re-found the republic, promising an institutional rupture with the post-1958 political order dominated by AD and COPEI.[62]

In a last-ditch attempt to constrain Chávez, AD and COPEI abandoned their original presidential candidates, backing instead an anti-Chávez independent, Salas Römer. The move backfired, tainting Römer and crystallizing "the outsider/establishment cleavage that separated Chávez from the field,"[63] leading to the election of Chávez with 56 percent of the vote and a clear mandate for his plans to challenge the exclusionary market model of democracy that had come to dominate Venezuelan politics.

Summary of Venezuela's historical era: setting the scene for post-neoliberal struggles

The preceding discussion has highlighted how Venezuela's adoption of a market model of democracy in the 1980s and 1990s fostered such shallow and narrow citizenship quality for the popular sectors and sectors of the middle class that the party system, and indeed support for the democratic model itself, became unstable. The

> Two bait-and-switch processes of market reform had produced an overarching pattern of neoliberal convergence, one that encompassed Caldera and MAS as well as AD and COPEI – thus demonstrating the failure of partisan electoral competition to generate policy alternatives that accurately mapped onto the programmatic divide in Venezuelan society.[64]

Indeed, the decline in social-democratic discourse throughout the 1980s and 1990s witnessed the institutionalized, electoral Left "move to the right and become indistinguishable from it."[65] Decision-making became technocratic as the IMF and IESA-trained economists dictated policy limits with popular sectors and trade unions increasingly side-lined. As market policies were adopted, though some economic elite actors struggled, the impacts were most apparent for the popular sectors whose quality of life deteriorated drastically, while inequality levels spiraled. Working lives, and daily survival, became increasingly precarious as labor and welfare protection were non-existent for the informalized and excluded popular sectors. As the protectionist era of the Punto Fijo pact ended and became instead a market democracy based around an open economy, the nation split in two, with "an internationally connected upper class and its local associates (about many of whom it could be said that 'money is their country'" dominating, while an "impoverished majority" struggled to make ends meet.[66] It is hardly surprising that in such conditions, Venezuelan democracy faced a legitimacy crisis by the end of the 1990s.

With the market model of democracy becoming increasingly unstable, an abrupt fall in oil prices in 1998 led to an economic and fiscal disaster in Venezuela. This final trigger cause pushed the unstable democratic equilibrium beyond a tipping point. As "oil prices hit a historical low, provoking an acute sense of frustration among Venezuelans and reinforcing their repudiation of traditional elites, the parties, and moderate proposals,"[67] space for progressive-outsider Hugo Chávez widened. The divide in Venezuelan society became superimposed on an establishment/anti-establishment political cleavage, allowing Chávez to politicize inequalities and mobilize the popular constituencies that consistently opposed the neoliberal model.[68]

The market model of democracy simply rejected the notion that the state has a duty to protect vulnerable citizens from the worst excesses of the market. It fostered appalling levels of poverty and inequality. It was both the content of neoliberal reforms and the exclusionary nature of their adoption that (re)polarized Venezuelan society, tearing away the ISI-era oil-spending plaster that had assuaged societal tensions. Chávez did not create a polarized society as some commentators contend.[69] He was not a cause of a crisis of democracy. His emergence and election at the head of disjointed anti-neoliberal protests was a symptom of an underlying crisis fostered by elite domination of political institutions and their support for a market model of democracy that tended to their needs, and to the needs of global capital, at the expense of ordinary Venezuelans.

The antecedent era to Chávez' election set the stage for new struggles between competing social blocs around distinct visions of what Venezuelan democracy should entail. Chávez propounded a vision of a

> Bolivarian revolution that would replace the pale-skinned partidocracy with an inclusive polity, incorporating the *mestizo* majority. The invocation of Bolívar also indicated an international dimension of south-south solidarity, as a defence against the global predominance of Washington and the IMF.[70]

Using an array of ideological, economic, military, and political powers, traditional elite forces who had dominated the Punto Fijo era and who supported liberal democracy and market economics, as well as international actors such as the United States and the IFIs, would confront Chávez and insurgent popular sectors who sought to overturn decades of political and economic exclusion.

While the new left-led government would confront an opposition-bloc, the historic conditions of Chávez' emergence and the fragile popular organizational base would feed back onto the process. With weak and delegitimized labor organizations, and with barrio organizations having been battered by years of neoliberal assault, Chávez forged a partial vanguardist-type relationship with the popular sectors. That is, though he did not emerge organically from popular sector movements, neither did he emerge wholly independently of protest movements. His MBR/MVR organization and party, though forged in the military, was also shaped by interactions with autonomous barrio organizations. However, these barrio organizations were generally weak and fragmented, and Chávez acted as a coordinating hub that bound disparate pre-existing popular organizations, as well as non-organized popular sectors, together. As Collier and Handlin[71] emphasize, understanding this demobilized and fractured starting point of the popular base is crucial for thinking about how the Chavista project would unfold in the aftermath period.

In sum, with Chávez elected to power promising an immediate campaign against poverty and political exclusion, the stage was set for a new period of struggles between the government, elites who sought the protection of the status quo, international actors who sought to retain access to Venezuelan oil at preferential rates, and popular sectors who demanded a radical overhaul of the exclusionary market model of democracy. The process that was to emerge would be extraordinarily complex, with democratic quality simultaneously advancing and regressing over the duration of the process. I examine this post-election process in the following chapters.

Notes

1 Julia Buxton, "Foreword: Venezuela's Bolivarian Democracy," in David Smilde and Daniel Hellinger (eds), *Venezuela's Bolivarian Democracy: Participation, Politics, and Culture under Chávez* (Durham, NC: Duke University Press, 2011): xiii.
2 Juan Carlos Monedero, "Snipers in the Kitchen: State Theory and Latin America's Left Cycle," *New Left Review* 120, Nov/Dec (2019): 16.
3 Fernando Coronil, *The Magical State: Nature, Money, and Modernity in Venezuela* (Chicago, IL: Chicago University Press, 1997): 87.
4 Julia Buxton, "Continuity and Change in Venezuela's Bolivarian Revolution," *Third World Quarterly* 41, no. 8 (2020): 1373.
5 Monedero, "Snipers in the Kitchen," 16.
6 Buxton, "Continuity and Change," 1374.
7 Kenneth Roberts, *Changing Course: Party Systems in Latin America's Neoliberal Era* (New York: Cambridge University Press, 2015): 181.

8 Coronil, *The Magical State*, 208.
9 Coronil, *The Magical State*, 216.
10 Ana Mallen and María Pilar García-Guadilla, *Venezuela's Polarized Politics: The Paradox of Direct Democracy Under Chávez* (London: FirstForumPress, Lynne Rienner, 2017): 28–9.
11 Roberts, *Changing Course*, 181.
12 Terry Karl, "Dilemmas of Democratization in Latin America," *Comparative Politics* 23, no. 1 (1990): 1–21.
13 Buxton, "Continuity and Change," 1374.
14 David Smilde, "Introduction: Participation, Politics and Culture – Emerging Fragments of Venezuela's Bolivarian Democracy," in David Smilde and Daniel Hellinger (eds), *Venezuela's Bolivarian Democracy: Participation, Politics, and Culture under Chávez* (Durham, NC and London: Duke University Press, 2011): 3.
15 Daniel Hellinger, "Venezuela: Movements for Rent?" in Gary Prevost, Harry Vanden, and Carlos Oliva Campos (eds), *Social Movements and Leftist Governments in Latin America: Confrontation or Co-option?* (London: Zed Books, 2012): 140.
16 Maura Duffy, "(Re)conceptualizing Democracy: The Limitations of Benchmarks based on Neoliberal Democracy and the Need for Alternatives," *Third World Quarterly* 36, no. 8 (2015): 1476.
17 Buxton, "Continuity and Change," 1375.
18 Coronil, *The Magical State*, 228.
19 Jonathan Di John, "Economic Liberalization, Political Instability, and State Capacity in Venezuela," *International Political Science Review* 26, no. 1 (2005): 107–24.
20 Coronil, *The Magical State*, 358.
21 Roberts, *Changing Course*, 215.
22 Barry Cannon, *Hugo Chávez and the Bolivarian Revolution: Populism and Democracy in a Globalised Age* (Manchester and New York: Manchester University Press, 2009): 35.
23 Eduardo Silva, *Challenging Neoliberalism in Latin America* (New York: Cambridge University Press, 2009): 199–200.
24 Roberts, *Changing Course*, 217.
25 Silva, *Challenging Neoliberalism*, 199–200.
26 The Chicago Boys was the name given to a group of Chilean economists trained under Milton Friedman at the Department of Economics at the University of Chicago.
27 Sujatha Fernandes, *Who Can Stop the Drums?: Urban Social Movements in Chávez's Venezuela* (Durham, NC: Duke University Press, 2010): 22–3.
28 Eduardo Silva, "Business Elites, the State, and Economic Change in Chile," in Sylvia Maxfield and Ben Ross Schneider (eds), *Business and the State in Developing Countries* (Ithaca, NY: Cornell University Press, 1997): 182.
29 Silva, *Challenging Neoliberalism*, 203.
30 Coronil, *The Magical State*, 376.
31 See George Ciccariello-Maher, *We Created Chávez: A People's History of the Venezuelan Revolution* (Durham, NC: Duke University Press, 2013).
32 Silva, *Challenging Neoliberalism*, 205.
33 Silva, *Challenging Neoliberalism*, 195.
34 Steve Ellner, *El Sindicalismo en Venezuela en el Contexto Democratico (1958–1994)* (Caracas: Universidad de Oriente, 1995); Katrina Burgess, *Parties and Unions in the New Global Economy* (Pittsburgh, PA: University of Pittsburgh Press, 2004).
35 The PSUV is the party that evolved from the MVR. Its emergence is discussed in Chapter 3.
36 Andrés Antillano, "Algunas Notas Sobre Poder Popular y Socialismo en el Proceso Bolivariano," in Miriam Lang and Alejandra Santillana (eds.), *Democracia,*

Participación y Socialismo. Bolivia–Ecuador–Venezuela (Quito: Fundación Rosa Luxemburgo, 2010):117–123.

37 Hellinger, "Venezuela: Movements for Rent?" 143.

38 Smilde, "Introduction: Participation, Politics and Culture," 7; Steve Ellner, "Conflicting Currents Within the Pro-Chávez Labor Movement and the Dynamics of Decision Making," in Eduardo Silva and Federico Rossi (eds), *Reshaping the Political Arena in Latin America: From Resisting Neoliberalism to the Second Incorporation* (Pittsburgh, PA: University of Pittsburgh Press, 2018): 162.

39 Smilde, "Introduction: Participation, Politics and Culture," 7.

40 Di John, "Economic Liberalization," 113.

41 Ellner, "Conflicting Currents," 160.

42 Moisés Naím and Antonio Francés, "The Venezuelan Private Sector: From Courting the State to Courting the Market," in Louis Goodman, Jonathan Mendelson Forman, Moisés Naím and Joseph Tulchin (eds), *Lessons from the Venezuelan Experience* (Baltimore, MD: Johns Hopkins University, 1995): 189.

43 Di John, "Economic Liberalization," 114.

44 Naím and Francés, "The Venezuelan Private Sector."

45 Coronil, *The Magical State*, 376.

46 Ellner, "Conflicting Currents," 159.

47 Kenneth Roberts, "Social Polarization and Populist Resurgence in Venezuela," in Steve Ellner and Daniel Hellinger (eds.), *Venezuelan Politics in the Chávez Era* (Boulder, CO: Lynne Rienner, 2003): 59–60.

48 Smilde, "Introduction: Participation, Politics and Culture," 5.

49 Margarita López-Maya, *Del Viernes Negro al Referendo Revocatorio* (Caracas: Alfadil, 2005): 34.

50 López-Maya, *Del Viernes Negro*, 35.

51 Di John, "Economic Liberalization," 116.

52 Fernandes, *Who Can Stop the Drums*, 5–6; Alejandro Velasco, *Barrio Rising: Urban Popular Politics and the Making of Modern Venezuela* (Oakland: University of California Press, 2015).

53 Fernandes, *Who Can Stop the Drums*, 59–60.

54 Latinno.net, *Asamblea de Barrios de Caracas*: Retrieved https://www.latinno.net/es/case/19033/.

55 María Pillar García-Guadilla, "The Incorporation of Popular Sectors and Social Movements in Venezuelan Twenty-First-Century Socialism," in Eduardo Silva and Federico Rossi (eds), *Reshaping the Political Arena in Latin America: From Resisting Neoliberalism to the Second Incorporation* (Pittsburgh, PA: University of Pittsburgh Press, 2018): 64.

56 Margarita López-Maya and Edgardo Lander, "Participatory Democracy in Venezuela: Origins, Ideas, and Implementation," in David Smilde and Daniel Hellinger (eds.), *Venezuela's Bolivarian Democracy: Participation, Politics, and Culture under Chávez* (Durham, NC: Duke University Press, 2011): 75.

57 Kirk Hawkins and David Hansen, "Dependent Civil Society: The Circulos Bolivarianos in Venezuela," *Latin American Research Review* 41, no. 1 (2006): 102–32; Matthew Rhodes-Purdy, "Participatory Populism: Theory and Evidence from Bolivarian Venezuela," *Political Research Quarterly* 68, no. 3 (2015): 415–27.

58 The concept comes from Paulo Freire's book *Pedagogy of the Oppressed* (New York: Continuum, 1996).

59 The Punto Fijo pact era was known as the Fourth Republic.

60 Silva, *Challenging Neoliberalism*, 220.

61 Margarita Lopez-Maya, "Hugo Chávez and the Populist Left," in Steven Levitsky and Kenneth Roberts (eds), *The Resurgence of the Latin American Left* (Baltimore, MD: Johns Hopkins University Press, 2011): 219.

62 Roberts, *Changing Course*, 224.
63 Ibid.
64 Roberts, *Changing Course*, 223.
65 Smilde, "Introduction: Participation, Politics and Culture," 6.
66 Coronil, *The Magical State*, 383.
67 Lopez-Maya, "Hugo Chávez and the Populist Left," 219.
68 Roberts, *Changing Course*, 223.
69 For a critique of such analysis, see Cannon, *Hugo Chávez and the Bolivarian Revolution*, 41–6.
70 Monedero, "Snipers in the Kitchen," 17.
71 Samuel Handlin and Ruth B. Collier, "The Diversity of Left Party Linkages and Competitive Advantages," in Steven Levitsky and Kenneth Roberts (eds), *The Resurgence of the Latin American Left* (Baltimore, MD: Johns Hopkins University Press, 2011): 139–61.

3 Progressive and regressive centralization

The Hugo Chávez years, 1999–2013

In this chapter, I analyze the post-neoliberal democratization process in Venezuela under the presidencies of Hugo Chávez from 1999 to 2013, while in the following chapter, I examine the process during the presidencies of his successor, Nicolás Maduro. The chapters offer periodized accounts of the process, analyzing how the governing party and an opposition-bloc used an array of ideological, economic, military, and political sources of power to achieve their agenda while stymieing their adversary. Each "side" argued that their conceptualization of democracy was more democratic than their opponents. The governments of Chávez, and as will be discussed, to a lesser extent Maduro, sought to advance a post-neoliberal democracy that rejects the marketization of society prevalent under neoliberal-inspired models of democracy and called for greater substantive and participative rights for citizens. The opposition-bloc, though comprising several strands, was united by a rejection of Chávez, Maduro, and their "Bolivarian" ideology, and sought a return to a classic liberal market democracy. Throughout the chapters, I discuss the nature of democratic quality in liberal, deepened, and extended terms while I also refer to the historical era preceding Chávez' election, highlighting how certain antecedent features fed back onto the process.

The 1999 constitution and the general elections of 2000: setting the stage for battles ahead

Following his victory in the 1998 election, Chávez immediately called and won a referendum to convoke a constituent assembly. His coalition won 125 of 131 assembly delegates. The Constitutional draft was ratified in a referendum in 1999 with 71.8 percent of the vote. The Constitution Guidelines "present three foci around which politics should revolve, each one pertaining to a distinct and crucial dimension of the structural condition of exclusion, and all promoting popular organization and mobilization."[1] The first area focuses on "the correction of the unjust distribution of income and wealth"; the second focuses on "overcoming discrimination in access to fundamental human rights such as nutrition, health, housing, and education"; and the third focus is the "development of full citizenship, which is characterized by

DOI: 10.4324/9781003262466-4

members of society possessing attributes such as solidarity, responsibility, and participatory and democratic attitudes."[2]

The Constitution of the Bolivarian Republic of Venezuela (CRBV) sought to deepen democracy by guaranteeing citizens' rights to direct, semi-direct, and indirect participation, not only via the vote, but also via the "formulation, execution, and control of public administration."[3] As Hellinger[4] notes, the traditional liberal system of checks and balances based on the separation of powers was considered to be insufficient to prevent "the iron law of oligarchy." Instead, new participatory institutions were included in the Constitution to prevent a pacted democracy like the Punto Fijo democracy from occurring again. The guidelines of the Constitution identify both the state *and* society (citizens, families, and organized communities) as the key actors in social transformation. The state is seen as a "facilitator of empowerment for those who ought to make decisions and control public administration."[5]

Article 62 states that "the participation of the people in the formation, execution, and control of public matters is the means necessary to accomplish the protagonism (*protagonismo*) that will guarantee their complete development, both as individuals and as well as the collective." Articles 326, 70, and 184 call for "co-responsibility" where society is to play a "protagonist" role via participation in public affairs via "elections, petitioning, recall referendum, and public consultation" along with "the execution of welfare service projects at decentralized levels of government in which service delivery may be transferred to organized groups of society." According to the Constitution then, representative democracy is to be linked with participatory democracy to ensure that democratic participation is not simply via the ballot box but is accompanied by bottom-up oversight of, and participation in, decision-making processes of elected representatives.

The Constitution also called for an extending of democracy. The Exposition of Motives of the Constitution claims that the Republic has been "re-founded" so as to create "a more democratic society. Not only is it the state that should now be more democratic, but also society." The second article states that

> Venezuela is constituted as a Democratic and Social State of Law and Justice which in its legal order and actions holds as highest values life, liberty, justice, equality, solidarity, democracy, social responsibility and in general, the pre-eminence of human rights, ethics, and political pluralism.
> (CRBV 1999)

Indeed, social inequality is considered social exclusion, and the objective of the state's social policy must therefore be to build inclusion and deliver social rights.[6]

However, the ratification of the 1999 Constitution strengthened presidential powers, and by the end of 1999, "Chávez had weakened institutional checks and balances on executive authority and set the stage for new elections in 2,000 under the terms of his Bolivarian constitution."[7] In the 2,000 elections, none of the traditional parties ran a candidate, and Chávez won the election with 59.8 percent of the vote. The MVR captured 46.7 percent of the seats in the new National Assembly, while the MAS and allied leftist parties added another 15.1 percent, giving Chávez a strong legislative majority. With the de-legitimation of the Punto Fijo parties and the market model of democracy they cleaved around in the 1980s and 1990s, the 2000 elections gave Chávez and the MVR extensive political power over a fractious opposition as well as the ideological space to begin to implement the new CRBV.

While the political power of the government increased, its economic power remained weak. Chávez inherited an economy in recession, and oil prices were at a low of $8/barrel. As such, he followed relatively austere fiscal policies and declined to control prices and interest rates, though Chávez' oil minister, Alí Rodríguez, did seek to reassert Venezuela's position as a leader in OPEC, calling for an enforcement of production quotas to boost the price of oil.

The efforts to adhere to the new constitutional promises to deepen and extend democratic quality in comparison to that of the pre-existing Fourth Republic would witness the emergence of an array of tensions. As the government set out to advance a post-neoliberal model that deepened and extended democracy, while also strengthening executive powers to achieve such goals, an opposition-bloc comprised of elite families, business confederations, media organizations, political parties, the Catholic Church hierarchy, sectors of the military, traditional trade unions, the US government, and transnational neoliberal think tanks rejected the democratic potential of the post-neoliberal model and sought adherence to a liberal market democracy. Moreover, the efforts by Chávez to foster from above a more participatory power from below triggered a complex process that would at times witness a boosting of popular sector organizational and participatory capacity, while at other times such power from below was limited by the power from above.

Elite destabilization efforts, centralization, and promoting popular power: 2001–04

IEMP and transnational struggles

The period from December 2001 to August 2004 "saw an intense and protracted struggle between the Chávez government and opposition political and economic forces" comprised "mainly of those who have (or at least had) a solid place in formal society" such as members of the "traditionally conservative Catholic Church, industry, commerce, and construction."[8] While the political power of the government trumped that of the opposition parties, allowing Chávez to push forward with reforms, over the 2001–04 period, with support from the US government, the opposition-bloc of organizations and interests that had been protected during the Punto Fijo era democracy, and which lacked experience of being out of power, repeatedly challenged the legitimacy of the Bolivarian process and used an array of extra-institutional tactics to block the post-neoliberal democratization process.[9]

Following the 2000 election, the National Assembly passed an enabling law, allowing Chávez to rule by decree for one year. In November 2001, Chávez used this authority to issue 49 legislative decrees, including new laws that moved beyond political reform. The Law of Hydrocarbons reflected the oil nationalism of AD in the 1940s and the promises to "sow" hydrocarbon revenue for development. Royalty rates were increased from as low as 1 percent during the latter stages of the neoliberal era to 30 percent while the tax rate was kept at just below 50 percent. Moreover, the hydrocarbon law insisted on majority state ownership of any joint ventures. The law sought to reassert executive control over *Petróleos de Venezuela, S.A.* (PDVSA)—the state oil company, whose management over the previous decade had independently determined how to direct the company. Though it did not apply retroactively, the reformed hydrocarbon law transformed the relationship between the state and transnational extracting firms.[10] *Plan Zamora* meanwhile called for a new land tax and expropriation of underused and unused private holdings and farmlands while the Law of Banks obliged banks to finance priority economic activities at preferential interest rates.

The new laws were described by the elite business sector and their political and media allies as an attack on private property. Indeed, as Mallen and García-Guadilla[11] state, the decree laws

> Affected the interests of private media moguls whose wealth made them part of Venezuela's traditional elite. The increased government intervention in economic affairs and the perceived attack on the right to private property seemed to solidify the widely circulated claim that the Bolivarian Revolution was being modelled after the Cuban Revolution.

Despite Chávez' electoral victories, the traditional elite-bloc maintained sources of economic, ideological, and military power. Indeed, the initial strategy to respond to the "attacks on private property" was marked by the establishment of the Democratic Coordinator, "a heterogeneous grouping of political parties, NGOs, the business association FEDECAMARAS, the trade union confederation, and the CTV trade union, with Catholic Church and media support."[12]

In December 2001, utilizing their economic power and seeking to force the government to reverse the policies that challenged elite interests, the traditional unions with links to the Punto Fijo parties, especially the CTV with ties to AD, called a nationwide strike. On 2 April 2002, Chávez fired PDVSA executives live on TV, stating that they had received their positions via political connections, not merit. On April 9, FEDECAMARAS again called for a strike, with CTV leader Carlos Ortega calling on workers to join in. The opposition-bloc, via private media channels, repeatedly advertised an anti-Chávez demonstration rally with front pages reading "not one step backwards."[13] The opposition march began at the PDVSA headquarters, but protest organizers re-directed the march toward the presidential palace, Miraflores, located in the western sector of the city which is predominantly populated by popular sectors and Chávez supporters. Chavista leaders urged protest organizers to avoid Miraflores as there was a pro-government march taking place around the palace.

As the two blocs of marchers confronted each other, separated by the National Guard, unidentified snipers began shooting on protesters, killing both opposition and government supporters. The private television networks aired images of Chávez supporters shooting from the *Puente Llaguno* bridge and then cut to a shot of injured opposition protesters fleeing for cover. The private media network, *Venevisión*, owned by the Cisneros group, captured these images and rebroadcast them repeatedly, nationally and internationally, laying blame for the killings on pro-Chávez gunmen. Indeed, as Duno-Gottberg[14] states, over the 2000–03 period, the private media conglomerates had been attempting to split Venezuelans into two blocs—a respectable "civil society" of opposition supporters who were defending democracy and a dangerous horde of dark-skinned *Chavistas*. Despite the disinformation promoted by the politicized media, evidence later emerged that the journalist involved in filming the *Puente Llaguna* bridge had manipulated the scene; the opposition march never reached the bridge, and the men on the bridge who were shooting were in fact returning fire on opposition controlled municipal police who were firing on them.[15]

The scenes of Chávez supporters supposedly firing on unarmed opposition marchers below was used to call into question the government's legitimacy and the next morning the military high command claimed that Chávez had resigned. The country's traditional economic and political elites convened an interim government headed by FEDECAMARAS president Pedro Carmona. The Catholic Church hierarchy gave its support for the coup with cardinals and bishops meeting the coup plotters before the events unfolded, while also attending the swearing in of Carmona.[16] The interim government dissolved all constituent powers and the media reported that a transition in power had occurred.

Despite lacking political power or, indeed, precisely because they lacked political power, while retaining other sources of power, the opposition-bloc launched a coup d'état with the backing of private media stations. The headquarters of the coup was the home of Gustavo Cisneros, Venezuela's richest man and owner of *Venevisión* amongst other media outlets.[17] In the aftermath of the coup, via private media broadcasts, the coup-organizers revealed their tactics, with an admiral who participated saying "We had a deadly weapon: the media. And now that I have the opportunity, let me congratulate you."[18] *Venevisión* broadcast interviews with opposition leaders who openly explained how they had planned to mobilize civil society and then activate the armed forces to remove Chávez.

As Mallen and García-Guadilla[19] note

> capitalizing on its lion's share of ratings to influence the outcomes of the coup, commercial media failed to broadcast the reaction of Chávez' supporters. The public television station *Venezolana de Televisión* (VTV) and the government-run radio station *Radio Nacional Venezuela* were shut down.

However, word spread via text messaging, community radio stations, and the community television station CatiaTV that Chávez had not resigned and was in fact being held incommunicado. Popular sector supporters of Chávez, organized by the Bolivarian Circles, began marching, demanding the military return Chávez to power.[20] As police repressed and killed popular protesters, the four major private television stations—*Radio Caracas Televisión (RCTV), Televén, Venevisión* and *Globovisión*—acted in unison, airing cartoons and Hollywood movies. With thousands of popular sector protesters calling on the military to restore Chávez, the military split. A pro-Chávez faction in the form of the Palace Guard ousted the interim government while Chávez' cabinet contacted international media to emphasize that a coup had taken place. With the private media failing to report that the palace had been retaken by forces loyal to Chávez, ministers managed to restore VTV and broadcast that Chávez was being held captive. Popular protests surged, and with the palace surrounded, the military high command backed down from mass repression and Chávez was reinstated as president.[21]

The US government supported Chávez' overthrow openly—via White House statements advocating dubious claims regarding government repression of opposition protests purported by the opposition-controlled media—and more covertly via funding from USAID and the National Endowment for Democracy (NED) for opposition parties.[22] Indeed, as Buxton[23] notes, "opposition groups were able to sustain disruptive action despite a lack of broad-based support due to the United States, which channeled financial assistance to anti-government actors under the rubric of 'democracy promotion'."

In the period following the coup, elite-opposition forces in the form of the NED-funded Súmate—organized by María Corina Machado, a member of one of Venezuela's traditional elite families, pushed for a recall referendum. However, lacking sufficient political power to achieve their goal, the opposition reverted to alternative tactics to destabilize the Chávez government. The Supreme Court ruled that events of April 2002 did not constitute a coup d'etat and several of the absolved officers set up camp in the Plaza Francia in Altamira, declaring it a "liberated zone."[24] With the vocal support of the Catholic Church hierarchy, PDVSA management, PDVSA's merchant marine, and unions linked to the Punto Fijo parties, a national work stoppage was called for in December 2002. Apart from two daily newspapers, all other commercial media suspended publications on the first day of the strike. Later, in February 2003, the Venezuelan Press Block comprising the directors of 38 dailies called on citizens to support the strike and defend their liberties while private TV suspended daily programming to instead offer round the clock, deeply one-sided coverage of the strike alongside anti-government propaganda that sought to stoke fears amongst opposition supporters.[25]

The stoppage almost shut down the oil industry for three months. As Hellinger[26] emphasizes, the stoppage brought PDVSA management into direct confrontation with the state's sovereign ownership of the subsoil, with management lining up behind international interests in keeping Venezuela's oil cheaply available to foreign extractors and importers. The opposition tactics failed, however, as the government, called in loyal and retired workers and asked for help from abroad and fired about half of the 30,000 PDVSA employees. In the process, the government boosted their economic power, while substantially weakening that of the opposition-bloc by regaining control over the country's primary source of revenue, oil.

Other responses to efforts to fund democratic extending by boosting the state's control of the country's hydrocarbons saw business elites use their economic power "as they have done throughout history when they consider their interests threatened" to create a scarcity of important commodities.[27] The government responded to scarcities (which pushed up prices) by implementing price and exchange controls in February 2003. Businesses who participated in the strike were excluded from access to preferential dollar rates for imports. The private sector responded by reducing production and exporting more. To fill the gaps in the market (and to intimidate the private sector into maintaining production and distribution at normal levels) the government began expropriating companies. The government's efforts to counter the structural economic power of the traditional economic elite grouped in FEDECAMARAS set in motion the emergence of new business interests who would engage in a tactical alliance with the government. This faction of capital who retained access to state channels of funding would later be known as the *boliburguesía* (Bolivarian-Bourgeoisie).

In conjunction with a rebalancing of economic power between the government and the opposition-bloc, Chavista loyalists replaced leading members of the army who had participated in attempts to overthrow the government, thereby augmenting the military power of Chávez. There were also further efforts to replace pro-opposition judges in the judicial system

> and ensure the presence of justices committed to the government's agenda and quest for political domination: a court- packing scheme to reduce the presence of the opposition in the Court and increase the government's clout with the arrival of new justices loyal to Chávez and his renewed political establishment.[28]

The opposition-bloc's destabilizing use of their ideological power also triggered efforts by the government to rebalance the media landscape by promoting community and state media and by restricting the powers of the four principal private televisions stations—the "four horsemen of the Apocalypse," as Chávez described them. For example, CatiaTV, the community station that had countered the misinformation of the private media during the coup, quickly received a license in May 2002, one of many such efforts to challenge the ideological power of the opposition-bloc. The "media wars" between deeply politicized community and state media on the one hand and private media on the other would continue over the course of the post-neoliberal process.

State-sponsored spaces of participation

The reversed 2002 coup and the extra-institutional destabilization efforts by opposition to reforms constitute a fundamental turning point in the process.[29] While the events between 2001 and 2004 witnessed the emergence of struggles over ideological, economic, and military sources of power between the government and the opposition-bloc, the extra-institutional tactics of the opposition-bloc to impede the left-government, and the active role of popular sectors—partly mobilized by the Bolivarian Circles to bring Chávez back to office opened a new stage in the relationship between Chávez and the popular base.

The destabilization tactics highlighted Chávez' reliance on a base capable of engaging in defensive-mobilization at times of confrontation with oppositional forces and the government began to foster new spaces of popular sector participation. The president maintained that he would "devote his remaining time in office to enriching the lives of Venezuela's popular classes who had saved Chávez from his deposal, or worse."[30] As such, Chavismo entered a new stage of radicalization in response to both the opposition tactics and the support of popular sectors for the president and the process.

The aggressive destabilization tactics of the opposition-bloc in conjunction with the historical weakness of the popular sectors' organizational ties and capacity to engage in sustained, coordinated mobilization shaped the nature of relations that emerged between the Chávez government and the popular base. The government actively supported the construction of an organized popular power. That is, a popular power capable of engaging in bottom-up mobilization at times of acute confrontation with the opposition was fostered from above by the left-led government.

The governments' boosted control of oil revenues in conjunction with rising international oil prices dramatically expanded the economic power of the government to redistribute oil rents toward Venezuela's long-excluded popular sectors. In early 2003, the government introduced the *misiones*, a series of state-sponsored programs aimed at delivering the socioeconomic goals of the new Constitution to popular communities in the areas of health, education, and nutrition. The *misiones* are defined by the government as the "conjunction of constituted power and constituent power."[31] Their purpose was

> not only to bring the benefits of the welfare state to the poor, especially those in the informal sector, but to alter the governance of the economy

> from one emphasizing atomistic participation in the market to one relying on cooperatives, state coordination, and local know-how – in a word, what the government celebrates as 'endogenous development'.[32]

Over the duration of the post-neoliberal process, the *misiones* had a hugely positive impact on the quality of social citizenship for participants. Illiteracy was drastically reduced, while medical access and public education was extended to all the population.[33] There was a reduction in poverty, nutritional improvements for popular sectors, declining infant mortality rates, and a closing of the inequality gap.[34]

The *misiones* were not only designed to expand welfare and involve citizens in committees and popular organizations linked to the spending programs. They "were linked to a mobilization strategy in anticipation of a possible recall referendum,"[35] which the opposition did successfully convene in June 2004. Chávez altered his campaign strategy for the 2004 recall election by reducing his reliance on the MVR politicians and appealing to his supporters in the *misiones* and the Bolivarian Circles to form "electoral battle units."[36] The electoral battle units were tasked with mobilizing popular sectors to vote against the recall. Chávez easily won the referendum with massive popular backing.

This early formulation of party-base relations witnessed a combination of democratic extending via social spending, democratic deepening via new avenues of participation in local planning, alongside a protagonistic role in electoral mobilization in support of Chávez and the Bolivarian process. Given the nature and tactics adopted by the opposition to impede the democratization process, an ally-type relationship was forged between the government and popular sector members who engaged with the new state-sponsored spaces of participation. Extensive linkages were established and political ties forged via government payments to participatory spaces for sectors whose livelihoods and health had been ravaged during the market democracy era. Moreover, linkages took an intensive form whereby members of the new participatory spaces were integrated into the formal bureaucratic party structure, making them more dependable allies for the party and the Bolivarian process.

Progressive and regressive centralization: tensions in the process, 2004–13

Oil boom, changing international context, and a weakened opposition: opening space for a move toward 21st Century Socialism, 2004–07

Chávez' victory in the 2004 recall with 58.3 percent of the vote coupled with a strong increase in oil prices significantly boosted his political and economic power, putting the government in a position to deliver real benefits to their core bloc of supporters. A "demoralized opposition made little effort to contest local and gubernatorial elections later in 2004, allowing Chávez supporters to capture 21 out of 23 state governments and 90 percent of municipalities."[37] Furthermore, the following year, the main opposition parties boycotted national legislative elections entirely, allowing Chávez' MVR party, in conjunction with allied leftist parties to completely dominate the national assembly. In the 2006 presidential elections, the opposition coalesced behind Manuel Rosales of a new party, *Un Nuevo Tiempo* (UNT), but Chávez again won with a record 62.8 percent of the vote. The political dominance of the Chávez-led government over the opposition-bloc was secured, restricting opposition space for institutional avenues to block the reform process.

As oil prices rose in 2004, Western leverage over the Chávez government declined. The Bush administration was preoccupied with Iraq and the Middle East. Meanwhile, China and Russia, two countries who would not seek to restrict Chávez in an ideological sense, were seeking new trading partners in Latin America. Furthermore, the "Pink Tide"—that is, the election of left-leaning presidents across much of the region such as Lula da Silva in Brazil, Kirchner in Argentina, Morales in Bolivia, and Correa in Ecuador offered ideological and political support to the Venezuelan government.

While the ideological power of the opposition remained intact, with the military leadership aligned behind the government in the aftermath of the post-coup purge, and with complete domination of the political sources of power, executive oversight of booming oil rents, and a favorable international context, this conjuncture marked the beginning of a radicalization that transformed the Bolivarian process from a "Third Way," moderate government, to an anti-imperialist, openly socialist one that began to "experiment in all seriousness with direct democracy and non-capitalist relations, property, and production."[38]

No longer facing a national referendum on his rule, Chávez announced on his weekly television program *Aló Presidente* that the Bolivarian revolution should construct a "new socialism of the 21st century," distinct from the "real socialisms" of the 20th century where the "process of seeking and building is guided above all by values such as collectivity, equality, solidarity, freedom, and sovereignty."[39] Chávez stated that "popular power is the soul, nerve, flesh and bone, and essence of Bolivarian democracy, of a true democracy."[40] As de la Torre[41] delineates, unlike orthodox Marxist models, the proletariat is not the central subject of Venezuelan 21st-century socialism; rather, the subject is the *pueblo* understood as the huge mass made up of the unemployed, the poor, and the excluded. The goal of 21st-century socialism is the "construction of a revolutionary socialist democracy that will transcend representative liberal democracy"[42] with "real quotidian exercise of power by the great majority of common people."[43] Socialism of the 21st century therefore calls for a bottom-up revolutionary movement to transform social, economic, and political relations[44] in an attempt to advance the goals of the 1999 constitution by "reconfiguring institutions and thus individuals' activities according to the principles of equality and solidarity."[45]

State-sponsored spaces of participation: 2004–07

In terms of party-base relations, several new laws were introduced which sought to reformulate the role of popular participation. A key development was the passing of the 2006 Law of Communal Council. Communal councils (CCs) were initiated in part in response to existing practices of direct democracy among urban social movements.[46] Based on 200–400 households in urban areas, or 20 in rural areas, the communal councils were to become sites for deliberation, design, and delivery of public services, with over 120,000 communal councils established by the end of 2006. The CCs "are based on the idea that local-level citizen participation in the planning, implementation, and maintenance of community development projects establishes a platform on which a new 'protagonist' democracy can be built."[47] In a 2006 speech, Chávez called for the CCs to "be built as a subsystem of decision making and avoid becoming only adjuncts to the mayors, governors, or political parties." As such, the CCs represent attempts to "create a new set of state institutions that bypass the traditional state and distribute power in a democratic and participatory manner."[48]

The communal councils have received considerable attention from the academic community in recent years, receiving both praise and criticism.[49] For some, the CCs are not autonomous spaces for participation, but rather state-dominated institutions. Financial dependence on a rentier state and regulation by a charismatic president who centralizes decisions in the executive are said to neutralize grassroots actors' ability to articulate independent political claims and impact political decision-making.[50] While acknowledging the "rough edges" of CCs, other analysts have highlighted the potential benefits of increasing state funding to historically excluded sectors of society.[51] Another strand of scholarship suggests that the CCs "subject constituted power to constant constituent pressure, binding the two in a dialectical chain toward ever more radical and direct representation."[52] In such perceptions, the CCs offer the possibility of decentralizing power away from the state toward empowered publics.[53]

The debate over the impact of the CCs on the quality of democracy for participants reflects broader discussions regarding the Bolivarian process and the nature of state–society relations more generally. The CCs offered opportunities to both deepen and extend democratic quality. In terms of deepening the quality of political participation, the CCs provided spaces for direct participation for formerly disenfranchised sectors to have voice in shaping the conditions in which they live. The CCs encouraged neighbors to organize and participate actively in policymaking, helping to build/strengthen organizational ties within popular neighborhoods. The opening of spaces where popular sectors meet to discuss the needs of their geographical area, and the linking of these spaces to state institutions such as the Ministry of the Popular

Economy allowed for the involvement of local citizens in designing and implementing social policies that benefit their neighborhood/region. As such, the CCs also open avenues for extending democratic quality by boosting the quality of socio-economic citizenship for popular sectors in areas such as education, housing, and health.

While the CCs offer new institutional mechanisms that link popular organizations to the political arena and policymaking, which was essential to popular sector incorporation after decades of neoliberal disincorporation, the issue of whether or not the CCs allow for informal contestatory mobilization is less clear cut due to the lack of autonomy from the sponsoring party. It is absurd to suggest that impoverished popular sectors should not participate in the CCs so as to access funding as well as decide how this funding should be distributed. However, while the CCs contained the seeds required to move toward a radical-substantive democracy, the funding structure and the relationship with the ruling party also had built-in tensions which could become an issue if and when the ruling party diverged from popular demands, and there was a need for autonomous popular mobilization not against a common opposition, but against the party itself.

The emergence of a new umbrella party, the Partido Socialista Unido de Venezuela (United Socialist Party of Venezuela—PSUV), would also highlight the inherent possibilities and pitfalls of the Bolivarian democratization process for popular sector incorporation. Following the series of elite efforts to remove Chávez from power between 2002 and 2004 and following his landslide victory in the 2006 election, Chávez initiated the process of forming the PSUV, thereby bringing together the majority of political parties that supported him under one umbrella. The formation of the PSUV offered Chávez the opportunity to clarify the political–ideological objectives of his project of developing 21st-century socialism. Indeed, its creation "represented another of Chávez' efforts to organize the popular sectors and, in particular, to do so by constructing a political organization that would be more solid and cohesive—and thus more strategically useful—than the MVR."[54] The aim was to provide opportunity for grassroots input in policy formation, uniting leadership and base into one single body. It was hoped such a move could counteract bureaucratization and attendant issues of clientelism and corruption and ultimately foster an independent popular movement that was not dependent on the president or any one figure for its survival.[55]

The PSUV members were "drawn from the popular movement in the barrios and show resistance to slavish adherence to the *oficialista* line."[56] However, as Hellinger stated in 2012, the "PSUV has yet to show a willingness or ability to say 'no' to its charismatic leader."[57] As a key member of the commune movement and formerly of the left-wing student movement emphasized to me,

> There were plenty of leftist leaders before Chávez, who participated in the PSUV, who stood beside Chávez without seeing him as their leader.

> But the problem is that there was not enough space for critical debates inside the party. The party functioned like a military battalion, with Chávez directing it.[58]

A former ally of Chávez and long-time activist and commune organizer told me that

> the PSUV lacked bottom-up linkages. The PSUV was, and is, an organization that takes its own decisions. For example, when they want to run somebody for mayor, they just make their selection, they don't come to ask anybody from the local organizations what they think.[59]

Indeed, according to Webber,[60] the PSUV, despite initially generating enthusiasm and millions of new members, "never realized its potential due to its rigid verticalism, lack of internal debate, and the generalized absence of participatory democracy within the party." On one occasion,

> There were internal PSUV elections to determine candidates, and all 33 positions were won by people from the radical left bloc of the PSUV, not from the party leadership. When Chávez saw this, that the people from the base didn't want Diosdado Cabello or any of the party elite as their candidates, he just decided that 66 positions would be filled instead of 33, so he could handpick his candidates, while still claiming to support internal party democracy.[61]

As a result, the PSUV became a top-down structure which proved slow in responding to grassroots demands, while those social movements and popular organizers that did not align themselves with the PSUV were sidelined. Moreover, there is an issue in that very often members of local CCs were also members of the PSUV, thereby blurring the boundaries between party and base.

New regional organizations

Venezuela played a key role in developing new regionalist projects which promoted "new geographical and ideological boundaries while fostering new consensuses that are defined regionally, not globally."[62] The new projects were "supported by the mainly state-led practices, institutions and funding mechanisms in new social fields such as education, health, employment, energy, infrastructure and security" thereby "setting new regional boundaries beyond the historical hub of what defined US and market-led regionalism."[63]

In 2004, Venezuela led the process of establishing the Bolivarian Alliance for the peoples of our America (ALBA). ALBA rejects the logic of 1990s regionalism that was based on Latin American countries competing to lock-in deregulation and attract foreign investment; rather, ALBA seeks, in direct opposition to neoliberalism, to extend 21st-century socialism into a regional integration scheme.[64] ALBA proposed an "alternative model of development and accumulation underpinned by new principles of solidarity and complementarities."[65]

In 2007, Chávez formally cut ties to the IMF and World Bank having repaid all debts to the institutions. In 2008, Chávez supported the establishment of the Union of South American Nations-UNASUR which sought to develop an autonomous space for South American nations vis-à-vis Western leverage allowing for a "normative re-engineering and debating in relation to the purpose of regional integration beyond trade policy"[66] into the spheres of democratization, inclusion, social development, physical integration, defense, and identity.[67]

TeleSur, a pan-Latin American satellite television station sponsored by the governments of Venezuela, Argentina, Cuba, Ecuador, Nicaragua, Uruguay, and Bolivia, was established with the goal of providing a "counterweight to the 'imperialist' information provided by the regular television channels."[68] Furthermore, Venezuelan-led energy integration projects such as PetroCaribe developed bilateral trade agreements to provide subsidized oil to Bolivia, Peru, and Uruguay, as well as joint ventures for exploration with Argentina and Uruguay. Banco del Sur meanwhile was established to offer loans to member countries for the construction of infrastructure and social programs, reducing the influence of IFI institutions such as the IMF.

The new regional agenda opened debates over how best to serve participatory and redistributive democracy as well as how to boost regional autonomy, redefining the Latin American regional agenda. Reclaiming the region "became not only a way of resisting US power but a genuine reflection of what Latin American should mean in the face of the crisis of neoliberalism."[69] (Ibid.: 426). The new regional environment reduced US economic and ideological leverage over Chávez, and the region, as Venezuela actively replaced the United States in terms of under-writing debt and offering strategic injections of capital to regional allies. In this scenario, regional space and support for a post-neoliberal democratization process was boosted.

Continued IEMP power rebalancing: 2007–10

With dominance in the political sphere, the governing party sought to boost its ideological, economic, and military power while curbing that of the opposition-bloc during the 2007–10 period, opening space for a further radicalization of the process. Moreover, with no opposition political power in the National Assembly, progovernment rectors were installed in the electoral authority.

In the ideological sphere, the government sought to rein in sectors of the opposition-controlled media who had played an active role in seeking to destabilize the government in the 2001–04 period. Such practices led to charges by opposition-bloc members as well as scholars in the strictly liberal tradition that the Chávez-led process was damaging democratic quality. In 2004 the government passed the Law of Social Responsibility in Radio and Television which was intended to break the monopoly of the media conglomerates, foster independent media, and ensure that content promoted social justice and contributed to the formation of the citizenry, democracy, peace, human rights, culture, education, health, and the social and economic development of the nation (Article 1). The law allowed the government to air 70 minutes of its own programming on all channels and to penalize stations that air information that could incite violence. In 2010, the Law was extended to the Internet. The National Commission of Telecommunications, CONATEL, was established to oversee adherence to the new law. Though supposedly independent, CONATEL effectively fell under control of the Ministry of Infrastructure, and later the Ministry of Popular Power for Communication and Information.[70]

Unsurprisingly, the opposition labeled the new law as government censorship indicating the un-democratic character of the government—a tactic which they used from the outset of the process irrespective of the government's adherence to liberal norms. Corrales[71] decries the government's "use and abuse" of the new law to regulate media as "autocratic legalism" because it "arbitrarily" refuses to renew licenses of private media. Mallen and García-Guadilla[72] capture the reality of the scenario however, noting that while "it is difficult to impugn a government's right to regulate what is broadcast on television screens and radios within a country ... the 2004 Law ... had more to do with the political conflict." The politicized manipulation and presentation of events during the events of April 2002 "caused the government to take a narrow view of freedom of the press"

The 2007 refusal to renew the license of the "fierce anti-Chávez network RCTV,"[73] one of the four major television stations who participated in the media conspiracy to remove Chávez from office in April 2002, was a key moment in the battle over ideological space between the government and the opposition-bloc. RCTV was replaced by the government channel *Televisión Venezolana Social* (TVes). For the opposition-bloc and their supporters, the move represented a clear attack on the freedom of expression, while for the government and its support base it simply removed a manipulating force who abused the notion of freedom of information to incite destabilization and remove a democratically elected government from power. Smilde[74] suggests that the following the 2004 law, the establishment of CONATEL, and the refusal to renew RCTV's license, private media began to self-sensor and tone down their criticism of the government, thereby altering the balance of ideological power. While there was popular sector resistance to government interference in RCTV as it showed many widely watched programs, as one Chavista organizer told me

> At that moment in time, I supported the move. It was accepted because of the history of the media, of the tactics by the opposition in 2002,

> and throughout. They made it into a war. They used violence. And we accepted un-democratic actions by Chávez because we felt he was combatting an adversary.[75]

However, as the interviewee continues, the bending of liberal norms was a dangerous precedent, stating

> The RCTV thing, it was a mistake. Look at Venezuela today (2021 under Nicolás Maduro). In the heat of struggles you can lose sight of what you are fighting for. If you ask me today was it okay to interfere with the media, I have to say no because today the media doesn't criticize anything. It was too big a risk, even in confrontation with the opposition, because it allows authoritarianism to emerge.

In conjunction with efforts to curb the monopoly of opposition-controlled private media, the government-funded community radio and television stations. CatiaTV is perhaps the most famous example of a community television station which was politically supportive of the Bolivarian project and which received state funding for its survival.[76] The government also invested in revamping state media to help get the government's message out.

Liberal scholars rightly raise concerns regarding government intervention in the media landscape, and indeed as discussed later, media censorship by the government did worsen. To grasp government actions, however, it is useful to view the scenario through a wider lens that accounts for the power dynamics between an opposition-bloc intent on recuperating political power and a government intent on advancing a project which challenges elite interests. Moreover, while liberal critics may argue that government-funded community media cannot act as an independent critic of government behaviors, in a landscape dominated by private media which ignores the issues of poor Venezuelans—except when engaging in sensationalist evaluations of crime—state-funded community media does offer an alternative source of information that engages with the day-to-day experiences of *barrio* residents. The issue of state-funding of community media does, however, resonate with the wider issue of state-funding of participatory spaces and the balancing of activating participation on the one hand and the curbing of autonomous critical space on the other.

A further point on the rebalancing of ideological power requires clarification. While opposition critics and liberal analysts berate the government for its illiberal, anti-democratic actions, private media retained an absolute dominance in media viewership figures while the space for anti-government messaging and critique remained robust. As Hellinger and Spanakos[77] note, the two major newspapers "*El Universal* and *El Nacional*, continued to feature stories and editorials sharply critical of the government, and all sorts of blogs and social media provided ample flows of both reflective commentary and vitriolic rhetoric." Moreover, while the number of state channels increased from one in 2000 to six in 2010, notions that the Chávez government-controlled television was overstated as the channels enjoyed an audience share of just 5.4 percent whereas 94 of television content seen by Venezuelans was controlled by private media.[78]

Echoing the efforts to utilize the government's dominant political position to rebalance the distribution of ideological sources of power, there were also efforts to fracture the economic power of the opposition-bloc. Given the dominance of the governing party across all branches of the political sphere, alongside the collapse of the traditional parties which had acted as the conduits for economic elite control over the state, there was a shift in economic elite relations with the government. While the government had boosted state influence over the oil sector and the branches of the state, it was still reliant on the private sector to import key goods such as medicines and foods not produced in Venezuela. The private sector meanwhile relied on the state for access to controlled dollars for imports. In this scenario where the structural power of capital had been weakened but not eliminated, and where the political power of the left-led government trumped that of the opposition-bloc, both the government and sectors of the business community strategically selected to moderate their confrontational stance toward each other.

A key example is the "pact of no aggression" forged between Chávez and Gustavo Cisneros, head of a media conglomerate that includes *Venevisión*, the television network that participated in the media-led coup of 2002 and supported the oil strike of 2003. The network rebranded itself as "impartial" and that it would provide "neutral" news coverage in comparison to its previously politicized, overtly anti-government messaging.[79] Cisneros' change of tactic from aggressive efforts to foment destabilization and an overthrow of the government to a more moderate, though still critical position which advocated an electoral path to change was representative of a broader split in opposition-bloc tactics. For example, the RCTV television station run by the Phelps Group maintained their hard-line support for destabilization tactics—and lost their license in 2007.

Ellner[80] argues that the formation of ties with some private interests enabled Chávez to split the economic wing of the opposition-bloc, thereby limiting their structural power. For example, Chávez maintained cordial relations with the head of Banesco, one of the country's largest banks. In turn, Banesco benefitted from preferential treatment from the government. Chávez' aim was to give space to non-FEDECAMARAS businesspeople who would not seek to use their structural economic power to try and topple the government, while side-lining those sectors of the opposition-bloc who sought the removal of the government as quickly as possible and by any means necessary.

It would be a mistake to view these strategic selectivities, on the part of the government and the collaborating private interests, as indicating an alliance. They were born out of the prevailing balance of power. Indeed, the private sector would drop any pretense of support for the government at the first sign of a reformation of the political wing of the opposition-bloc later in the process. There is a further issue regarding the formation of ties with a less confrontational section of the private sector. While such strategic relations may have fractured opposition-bloc economic power, over time, and as discussed in detail in the following chapter, issues of corruption and a lack of government willingness to restrict policies that benefitted *boliburguesía* businesses but harmed popular sectors created tensions between the PSUV leadership and more radical sectors of the popular base.

The government also sought to boosts its economic independence from opposition-bloc businesses and transnational firms by engaging in a series of nationalizations and expropriations. In 2007, the government took a majority stake in four oil projects in the Orinoco belt worth an estimated US$30 billion. Two major oil transnationals, Exxon Mobil and ConocoPhillips, quit Venezuela in response and filed arbitration claims against the Venezuelan government. France's Total SA and Norway's StatoilHydro ASA received about $1 billion in compensation after reducing their holdings while Britain's BP and America's Chevron Corp remained as minority partners. In 2009, a major gas injection project was taken over by the government from Williams Cos at a cost of US$420 million. There were nationalizations of fertilizer companies, land owned by foreign companies, and oil rigs. In the banking sector, the government took over Banco Federal, stating that there were severe liquidity problems. The bank's owner, Nelson Mezerhane, was also a shareholder in the opposition television station *Globovisión*, owned by a member of one Venezuela's traditional elite families, Guillermo Zuloaga. Mezerhane accused the government of trying to apply pressure on the bank to force a shift in the vehemently anti-government programming of the station. Zuloaga fled Venezuela after authorities ordered his arrest for alleged profiteering by hoarding cars for sale, where he took up a roll in the libertarian Cato Institute.

In the military sphere, "the 2008 Organic Law of the Bolivarian Armed Forces changed the name of the military from the National Armed Forces to the Bolivarian National Armed Forces, invoking the defense of a specific political project rather than the nation."[81] Polga-Hecimovich argues that this law and subsequent reforms "reinforced Chávez' tendency to create a parallel military structure that would respond directly to him and his political-ideological project."[82] Given the military's history to step in in response to elite demands, in Venezuela and across the Latin American region, Chávez saw military allegiance to the Bolivarian process as essential for its long-term stability.

Popular power, party-base relations and the "communal state" 2007–10

In 2007, Chávez called for the "revolutionary explosion of communal power"[83] arguing that the CCs, as the instruments of constituent power, should face no restrictions. As such, he proposed a constitutional reform that would build a "Popular Power" which would act as a new layer to the government. The proposal called for a new hierarchy of communal power that would be brought under the power of the executive branch rather than local governments as previously formulated with funding for participatory initiatives to come directly from the central government rather than through municipalities as the 1999 constitution states.

The proposed reform however was narrowly rejected by the electorate.[84] Webber[85] points out that the defeat of the 2007 referendum, the first electoral defeat for Chavismo, was a "product of top-down decision making in the lead up to the referendum and skepticism about the bureaucratizing direction of the Bolivarian process" indicating popular dissatisfaction with increasing vanguardization and centralization of the process of change.

It is important here to highlight that the Bolivarian movement is comprised of a number of competing ideological and organizational tendencies. Radical Venezuelan intellectual Roland Denis suggests that the "bureaucratic-corporatist republic" in the form of the Bolivarian government seeks to lead the popular movements that give it legitimacy, while a second current, the "self-governing socialist body," possesses an "entirely different logic, based in self-government of land, social spaces, and spaces of production."[86] Indeed, these divisions can be seen within the PSUV which Hetland[87] classifies into right, left, and moderate wings. Hetland contends that "the popular sectors, particularly those organized into grassroots movements, tend to favor the party's left while the generals, the state bureaucracy, and the *boliburguesía* favor its right and moderate wings." The moderate and the right Chavista forces dominate the upper echelons of the PSUV.[88]

While the 2007 defeat temporarily set back Chávez' plans, in July 2008 Chávez announced 26 laws by executive decree. These laws contained significant elements of the failed 2007 reform and sought to bypass governors and mayors and give extensive new duties to the Communal Councils in issues regarding "national defence, agro-industrial policy, and the formation of the 'popular economy'."[89] The 2009 Law of Communal Councils, an organic law that sought to place the CCs on a par with any other form of public power, was adopted. Furthermore, new laws in 2010 including the *Ley Orgánica de las Comunas* (Organic Law of the Communes), the *Ley Orgánica del Sistema Económico Comunal* (Organic Law of the System of Communal Economy), and the *Ley Orgánica del Poder Popular* (Organic Law of Popular Power) were established. The aim was to increase popular power by allowing autonomous development and decision-making along with the production, distribution, exchange, and consumption of goods and services via the grouping together of multiple communal councils into *comunas* (communes).

The communes were envisaged as a new organizational form that brings dozens of CCs together in conjunction with productive units established on socialist norms in a given territory. A communal parliament comprised of members of each participating CC would decide what was to be produced and how it would be distributed. The attempts to broaden the CCs into a system of communes so as to simultaneously allow for greater deepening and extending of democracy brought "an increase in the conflicts between the state and its popular base."[90] The CCs and communes have the potential to be parallel structures to the state that allow for a radical deepening of democracy if they are capable of governing on their own. Clearly, however, the potential for deepening democracy via the construction of new institutions that foster bottom-up participation in planning and decision-making on a broad scale, and which receive funding from ministries controlled by the executive for projects designed from below, is coupled with the potential for a curbing of autonomy and scope for informal contestatory intermediation that challenges government decision-making.

A key factor influencing whether state-sponsored spaces of participation such as the CCs and communes can overcome the potential pitfalls of extensive and intensive linkages becoming impediments to autonomous participation is the levels of prior organizational experience of members. Cases where participants have histories of organizing and mobilizing that predate Chávez' election were more likely to maintain a critical support for the government while maintaining a confrontational stance toward public powers which they see as impinging on grassroots' autonomy. Conversely, those CCs and communes whose members have intensive linkages with the PSUV and whose members have shorter histories of autonomous organizing are less likely to challenge government decision-making.

However, it would be a fundamental misreading of realities to suggest, even in instances with weak organizational histories, that the efforts by Chávez to foster a more organized and connected popular sector capable of engaging in mass defensive mobilization at times of confrontation with the opposition lead to a docile and submissive base who simply cowed to Chávez' authority, and financing. Such crude interpretations of the use of executive powers and state financing to support popular sector participation miss the contested realities that exist on the ground, in the meetings of the CCs and the communes. The relationship between organized spaces of popular participation and the state is "built around the pursuit of contingent autonomy, neither fully independent from nor fully beholden to the state."[91] Conflict and negotiation between base and party is part of the daily construction of the post-neoliberal democracy. Chávez did not construct every popular movement, many of which preceded, and opened the space for, his election. At the same time, Chávez actively supported and interacted with the grassroots, and it was via top-down organizational efforts that new spaces of popular organizing were forged. It is this state of interdependencies between state and society, top and bottom, party and movement, that best describes the nature of democratic deepening in the Bolivarian process.

One example of grassroots organizing that makes use of state funding and support while understanding the dangers of losing autonomy is the National Network of Comuneros and Comuneras (NNCC) which was established in 2009 with the aim of promoting and linking communal councils (CCs) and communes in both urban and rural environments. While the CCs and communes were promoted by Chávez and the central state as a means of building popular power, the NNCC sought to use the state-sponsored framework to link diverse popular organizations "without the mediation of the state."[92] A spokesperson for the NNCC told me that the decision to maintain autonomy from the state was key because "we considered that the Minister for the Communes would change all the time. Given that the *comuna* is fundamental to our form of socialism, we could not depend on bureaucratic fluctuations, we had to maintain independence."[93] The Red Nacional grew to encompass diverse social, cultural and artistic groups, farmer, fisherman, and worker movements, as well as CCs and *comunas*. By 2017, the Red Nacional would go on to have a presence in 20 states, linking about 500 *comunas* and 100 social movements.

Groups like the Corriente Bolivar and Zamora (CRBZ) also have ideas for promoting socialism that are autonomous from the state. The CRBZ is comprised of the peasant organization, the Ezequiel Zamora National Campesino Front (FNCEZ), and the Simón Bolivar National Communal Front (FNCSB) which links together communal councils and *comunas*. The CRBZ represents one of the largest radical currents within Chavismo with a presence in 14 out of 23 states. As Azzellini[94] states, the establishment of the CRBZ was the result of "an autonomous focus of the FNCEZ that postulates the building of a revolutionary current with organizational autonomy within the Bolivarian movement." The CRBZ is a member of the PSUV but has "always had a critical position, a position of disagreement regarding certain practices we have questioned, a position that involves questioning corruption, bureaucratism and reformism."[95]

Organizations such as the CRBZ and the NNCC and their constituent *comunas* do receive some state funding for their projects, "but this has not prevented us from being critical of, or supporting, different projects to the government."[96] As such, although they collaborate with the government, "the focus … is the autonomous creation of a project for a socialist society."[97]

While there are examples of popular sectors whose associational and collective power has been boosted via state-led schemes and who have maintained autonomy from the state, the Chavismo model for deepening democracy has also fostered tensions between the government and the base. A central issue relates to the nexus between the state and society, the PSUV. A coordinator in the Comuna Rogelio Castillo Gamarra in Petare's José Filax Ribas *barrio* told me that while the base and the *comunas* work every day of the year to develop the local community, the party "only becomes active in the neighborhood six months or three months before an election. The party dictates what has to be done, when they come to the *barrio* they want to take control of what we do every day."[98] Moreover,

> While the push and support from Chávez was important to mobilize the people to participate in the CCs and the communes, to organize

> themselves, to study … there was always a tension with mayors, governors. Though they were PSUV officials, they often tried to co-opt and control the CCs and communes, to make sure they didn't act autonomously because they competed for funding with the local politicians. Sometimes the communes, asking directly to central government, got more funding than PSUV mayors.[99]

This created "a division between what people bring up in the CCs and the *comunas* and the decisions taken by the government."[100] As such, while "the *comunas* are an institution and we take our decisions independently while maintaining links with the government,"[101] there is "dissatisfaction regarding all those struggles that never achieve a conclusion due to bureaucratic blockages and corruption."[102]

Reconstituting opposition-bloc political power: the emergence of the MUD

With Chávez and the PSUV overcoming the opposition-bloc's extra-institutional destabilization efforts, while augmenting the IEMP powers of the governing party over the 2004–10 period, the opposition switched strategy and "embarked on a process of 'partidization' through the MUD (*Mesa de Unidad Democrática*, Democratic Unity Coalition), featuring a return to predominance of politics and political parties, a privileging of electoralism, and a unification of policy platforms and electoral strategies."[103] The MUD was established in 2008 and was composed of multiple parties across the political spectrum, but was dominated by Primero Justicia (PJ), Acción Democrática (AD), Voluntad Popular (VP), and Un Nuevo Tiempo (UNT), while the remnants of the Punto Fijo parties, AD and COPEI also joined. The removal of Chávez from power was the unifying goal across MUD parties.

While several of the new parties sought to distance themselves from the Punto Fijo era politics to appeal to the electorate, the leadership of the parties was comprised of individuals with links to the traditional political establishment and the country's elites. Leopoldo López formed the radical right-wing VP in 2009. López was active during the 2002 coup, signing the Carmona Decree which suspended the Constitution and dissolved the National Assembly and the Supreme Court. López flew to meet with functionaries of the Bush administration in the US multiple times, and he led the opposition march in April 2002. He is also a long-standing associate of Alvaro Uribe, ex-president of Colombia (2002–10) who was a hard-line opponent of Chávez. VP has ties to billionaire Lorenzo Mendoza, the CEO of Empresas Polar, Venezuela's largest food company, and long-time critic of Chavismo. Indeed, López[104] describes VP as a "Mendoza family franchise."

Another prominent voice of the radical right-wing opposition was María Corina Machado, who also had links to the traditional elites.[105] With the assistance of NED funding, she founded the Súmate organization which aimed to promote the 2004 re-call of Chávez. In 2005, Machado was photographed smiling and shaking hands with George Bush following her invitation to the White House to discuss the "perspective of civil society about democratic values and the spread of democracy in … Venezuela."[106] Machado comes from one of Venezuela's traditional economic elite families, the Machado-Zuloagas and her uncle owned *Globovisión*, one of the principal opposition television networks. Henrique Capriles, head of PJ, meanwhile, is a scion of one Venezuela's largest business families and ran his first electoral campaign for COPEI.[107]

The Venezuelan elite families are a representation of *Mantuanaje*, the name given to "the sectors that occupied the peak of the social pyramid since they arrived by European military invasion."[108] The families are linked to the notion "lineage," an "inherited nobility limited to the handful of elite Spanish-descended families from which opposition leaders like Machado, López, and Capriles are drawn."[109] During colonialism, these families fortified their commercial power by inter-marrying with others who shared the "mantuado lineage." These elite families are guided by an attitude of *sifrinaje*-snobbishness—and whose historic control over importations has facilitated a "natural" alliance with sectors of US power, especially with Republicans.[110]

The unified MUD discourse presents the participating parties as the defenders of democracy against an illiberal government that engages in arbitrary, authoritarian behaviors. While the MUD utilizes liberal democracy and the defense of institutional autonomy from executive oversight as their frame of reference, the bloc does not publicly discuss its positions on the social environment of politics. For example, attitudes regarding privatizations, state guarantees of social citizenship for vulnerable sectors, and liberalization of the economy are hidden behind a "defenders of democracy" discourse.[111]

In the 2010 legislative elections, the MUD's adoption of a unified candidate system led to the strongest electoral showing of the opposition since Chávez' first election, winning 47.2 percent of the vote compared to the PSUV's 48.3. In 2012, Henrique Capriles of PJ was selected by the MUD as their candidate for presidential elections. While PJ had received funding from the wealthiest Venezuelan families such as the Phelps, Zuloagas, and Mendozas, there was an effort to brand the party and its leader as representative of popular sector interests in order to win the election and remove the threat that Chávez represented to their historic dominance of the country's wealth and resources.[112] That is, while the MUD could rally the support of middle- and upper-class Venezuelans by presenting themselves as democratic opposition to an illiberal government, to garner popular sector support Capriles attempted to present his candidacy as a social democratic alternative to the neoliberalism of the 1980s and 1990s.

While PJ's efforts to present itself as a moderate party that would take popular sector interests into account helped the party establish itself in some popular zones, including in *Petare* in Caracas, as part of the MUD, Capriles and his party had to adopt a unified policy discourse. This was expressed most evidently in Guidelines for the Government of National Unity Program, 2013–19 (MUD 2012). Cannon's[113] analysis of the MUD's economic policies demonstrates the focus on private property as the principal means to economic progress, potentially reversing Chávez' nationalizations in areas such as telecommunications, banking, and food distribution. MUD policy proposals would also likely see greater private sector involvement in electricity and water services, altering how the services are delivered and priced. The Guidelines contain plans to reengage with multilateral lending agencies, restore "autonomy" to the central bank, and return expropriated business to their original owners. In terms of PDVSA, the state oil company, the opposition "accepts its present condition as a state-owned company but would remove it from immediate governmental control, open it to wider private sector involvement, and subject it to national and global competitive pressures."[114] PDVSA would thus reduce substantially its role in funding social and welfare provision. Cannon describes the MUD's economic policy as "gradual pragmatic productivism" which "would represent a major reversal of current government policy, despite some important continuities." Ultimately, despite some window dressing regarding social protections, the major leaders in the MUD sought a return to a market democracy—that is, support for liberal institutions underpinned by neoliberal economic rationale.[115]

However, the opposition-bloc's neoliberal inclinations are rarely openly discussed. Moreover, in the face of increasing popular discontent over crime, corruption, and government inefficiency, and with Chávez battling against cancer, the 2012 presidential elections witnessed an increasingly competitive electoral arena. However, following a massive electoral mobilization campaign, Chávez captured 55.1 percent of the vote to Capriles' 44.3 percent, while in governorship elections, the PSUV won 20 out of 23 states, though with the turnout at just 53 percent.

Transnational support for the opposition-bloc project

The opposition-bloc's efforts to build support for a return to a market democracy, and its rejection of the post-neoliberal model of democracy advocated for by the Chávez government, received transnational backing. The US' "democracy promoting agencies" such as USAID and the NED and its associated groups such as the International Republican Institute (IRI) funded and supported opposition parties and civil society organizations over the duration of the Chávez presidencies.[116] MUD parties such as AD and PJ attended IRI workshops about how best they could garner voter support, appeal to young voters, and speak with journalists. Transnational neoliberal think tank networks also provided funding and training to a range of Venezuelan civil society organizations opposed to Chávez' project, who in turn sought to advance their libertarian ideology through the media and political parties. The Atlas network was a key hub in this network.

According to former Atlas president, John Blundell, the aim of the network was to "litter the world with free-market think tanks" thereby adhering to

Atlas founder Anthony Fisher's strategy of having multiple institutes across countries, continents, and the world all advocating the same neoliberal-inspired policies. The strategy is built on the belief that while one institute advocating strict adherence to market principals is unlikely to sway public opinion, and consequently, public policy, a chorus of supposedly apolitical think tanks and civil society organizations promoting neoliberalism is more likely to be successful.[117] Atlas was funded by bankers, General Electric, Pfizer, Procter & Gamble, Shell, ExxonMobil, British American Tobacco, and Philip Morris amongst other Fortune 500 corporations. As Fischer[118] states, "both transnational capital and local economic groups or family firms ensure a comfortable financial basis for Atlas-affiliated think tanks in every region of the world." Moreover, "in spite of the frequent claims to independence from state funds, Atlas members have received funding from the US State Department and the National Endowment for Democracy (NED)."

According to the Atlas Network's Centre for Latin America website, the organization "collaborates with partners that understand how individual rights, limited government under the rule of law, and free markets tend to create prosperity and improve the prospects for peace." The Centre aims to improve "understanding of the benefits of trade and the dangers of protectionism, so that political leaders will be less inclined to indulge in demagoguery that could undermine beneficial trading relationships." It seeks to foster "enlightened political actors" who "will be 'pro-market' (since market competition produces innovation and lowers prices for consumers)." To advance its goals, the center provides its partners with training, grants, and networking opportunities.

The Atlas Network's Centre for Latin America has six partners in Venezuela, the flagship being Cedice Libertad. As early as 1998, Cedice received regular financial support from the NED affiliated Centre for International Private Enterprise with the overt objective of advocating a "change in government."[119] Though Atlas purports to not engage in partisan politics, its partner, Cedice, is closely affiliated with María Corina Machado who was one of the most vocal MUD opponents to the Bolivarian process. Cedice disseminates, educates, researches, and defends "the principles of free markets and individual freedom to build a society of free and responsible individuals." The other five Venezuelan partners of the Atlas Network promote the same free-market ideology through the media and seek to educate a new generation of political leaders steeped in libertarian ideology.

The Atlas Network is part of a broader Latin American network that includes the International Foundation for Liberty (FIL) and Liberal Network of Latin America (RELIAL). The FIL is headed by Mario Vargas Llosa, and its principal objective is "the defence and promotion of the principals of liberty" and the adoption of strategies to "fight in the field of ideas against those who threaten such values." With support from intellectuals and think tanks in the United States, Europe and across Latin America, the FIL seeks to shape public opinion by highlighting the benefits of private property, limited government, and free markets. On the FIL board of directors is Rocio Guijarro, the general manager of Cedice in Venezuela, who completed the Advanced Management Program at the Instituto de Estudios Superiores de Administración (IESA), the same business school that trained the technocrats who designed Venezuela's neoliberal "great turnaround" under Carlos Andrés Pérez in the late 1980s and 1990s.

The RELIAL network is comprised of Latin American political parties and think tanks who support free-market economics and is part of the Liberal International global network that includes like-minded organizations in Europe and North America. RELIAL's mission is to contribute to the growth of liberal think tanks and parties in the region and to raise the profile of economic liberalism in political discourse. Venezuela's Cedice is a partner organization.

This brief discussion of transnational support for opposition-bloc parties and affiliated think tanks highlights the battle for ideological primacy not only in Venezuela, but in any scenario where a government is elected on a mandate to deepen and, particularly, extend democracy to the socio-economic sphere. While the electoral efforts of the opposition to regain political power failed up until 2013, the constant anti-government, pro-market propaganda coming from myriad sources sought to delegitimize the government precisely for responding to its mandate to take a more proactive role in protecting vulnerable citizens from the excesses of the market.

Framing the Chávez-led government as a fundamental threat to liberty, democracy, and ultimately economic well-being ensured that MUD parties and candidates could count on the support of middle-class Venezuelans, while also eroding confidence amongst some popular sectors. The Venezuelan think tanks and organizations, with funding and ideological backing from regional and international allied groups, were also capable of reaching out to student movements, ensuring that they would mobilize against the "anti-liberal, authoritarian" government. Indeed, the Washington-based Cato Institute, a member of the Atlas Network, awarded the US€500,000 Milton Friedman Prize for Advancing Liberty in 2008 to Yon Goicoechea for his role in mobilizing student protests against the refusal to renew RCTVs license.[120]

Moreover, the international think tank network, alongside US state agencies, shaped perceptions of the Bolivarian project at an international level as anti-democratic. With multiple reports coming from multiple sources in multiple countries, all proclaiming that democracy was under threat in Venezuela, this became the defining depiction of the Bolivarian process in international media.[121] The infiltration of the student movement and the shaping of international media perceptions of the process, along with continued support for opposition-bloc civil society organizations from the international neoliberal think tank network would become crucial factors in mobilizing, and framing understandings of, deadly anti-government destabilization efforts following Chávez' death in 2013.

IEMP struggles, transnational interference, and progressive to regressive centralization under Chávez

Summarizing the 1999–2013 period, there were complex and paradoxical impacts on the quality of democracy. There is little question that Chávez' and the PSUV's use of political power bent liberal norms. However, strict adherence to liberal norms is not the only component of a high-quality democracy. It is necessary to ask why illiberal actions were taken and what political power was used to do. In the case of Chávez and the PSUV, there was a dual use of political power. On the one hand, it was used to confront an opposition-bloc who dominated ideological and economic spheres of power and who were willing to use both institutional and extra-institutional tactics to block the post-neoliberal process. Moreover, the political power of the PSUV and Chávez was used to push forward with reforms that sought to simultaneously deepen and extend the quality of democratic citizenship for popular sectors in political and socio-economic terms. On the other hand, there were abuses of political power by the ruling party which were not used to curb the power of a recalcitrant elite so as to advance a popularly mandated democratization process but rather were used to bypass the results of a referendum, to use decree powers to illegitimately curb the power of an elected incoming national assembly, and to curb space for oversight of the ruling party's actions from critical voices coming from below.

The 2004–13 period of the Bolivarian process witnessed the beginning of a move from progressive centralization toward regressive centralization. While strict adherence to liberal norms may have limited the scope of the project to challenge opposition-bloc resistance to a deepening and extending of democratic quality for long-excluded popular sectors, there is an enormous danger where progressive centralization slides toward regressive centralization. That is, while a strong executive may help to overcome elite opposition to reforms that are in fact democratizing, where executive power is not limited by a separation of the branches of state power, and where it is not tethered to a critical popular base capable of mass mobilization against undemocratic (though not necessarily illiberal) executive actions, there is a danger that regressive centralization will slide toward authoritarian centralization. With the death of Chávez in 2013, the re-emergence of extra-institutional opposition-bloc tactics, worsening transnational conditions, and an economic crisis, the stage was set for such a process.

Notes

1 Margarita López-Maya and Edgardo Lander, "Participatory Democracy in Venezuela: Origins, Ideas, and Implementation," in David Smilde and Daniel Hellinger (eds), *Venezuela's Bolivarian Democracy: Participation, Politics, and Culture under Chávez* (Durham, NC: Duke University Press, 2011): 64.

2 Ibid.

3 CRBV 1999; López Maya and Lander, "Participatory Democracy in Venezuela," 59.
4 Daniel Hellinger, "Defying the Iron Law of Oligarchy I: How Does 'El Pueblo' Conceive Democracy," in David Smilde and Daniel Hellinger (eds), *Venezuela's Bolivarian Democracy: Participation, Politics, and Culture under Chávez*, (Durham, NC and London: Duke University Press, 2011): 28.
5 López Maya and Lander, "Participatory Democracy in Venezuela," 64.
6 Ibid., 63.
7 Kenneth Roberts, *Changing Course: Party Systems in Latin America's Neoliberal Era* (New York: Cambridge University Press, 2015): 259.
8 David Smilde, "Introduction: Participation, Politics and Culture – Emerging Fragments of Venezuela's Bolivarian Democracy," in David Smilde and Daniel Hellinger (eds), *Venezuela's Bolivarian Democracy: Participation, Politics, and Culture under Chávez* (Durham, NC and London: Duke University Press, 2011): 9–10.
9 Julia Buxton, "Continuity and Change in Venezuela's Bolivarian Revolution," *Third World Quarterly* 41, no. 8 (2020): 1380.
10 See Daniel Hellinger, "Oil and the Chávez Legacy," *Latin American Perspectives* 44, no. 1 (2017): 54–77; Antulio Rosales, "Auge y Colapso del Socialismo Bolivariano: Estado, Rentismo, y Revolución Bolivariana," in Pablo Andrade (ed), *Nuevos Enfoques para el Estudio de los Estados Latinoamericanos* (Quito: Universidad Andina Simón Bolívar/ Corporación Editora Nacional, 2020): 223–50.
11 Ana Mallen and María Pilar García-Guadilla, *Venezuela's Polarized Politics: The Paradox of Direct Democracy Under Chávez* (London: FirstForumPress, Lynne Rienner, 2017): 77.
12 Barry Cannon, "As Clear as MUD: Characteristics, Objectives, and Strategies of the Opposition in Bolivarian Venezuela," *Latin American Politics and Society* 56, no. 4 (2014): 54.
13 Mallen and García-Guadilla, *Venezuela's Polarized Politics*, Chapters 3 and 4.
14 Luis Duno-Gottberg, "Mob Outrages: Reflections on the Media Construction of the Masses in Venezuela," *Journal of Latin American Cultural Studies* 13, no. 1 (2004): 115–35.
15 Pascal Lupien, "The Media in Venezuela and Bolivia: Attacking the 'Bad Left' from Below," *Latin American Perspectives* 40, no. 3 (2016): 232; Mallen and García-Guadilla, *Venezuela's Polarized Politics*, 57.
16 David Smilde and Coraly Pagan, "Christianity and Politics in Venezuela's Bolivarian Democracy: Catholics, Evangelicals, and Political Polarization," in David Smilde and Daniel Hellinger (eds), *Venezuela's Bolivarian Democracy: Participation, Politics, and Culture under Chávez* (Durham, NC: Duke University Press, 2011): 326.
17 Alan MacLeod, "Was Hugo Chávez to Blame? Media Depictions of Polarization in Venezuela, 1998–2013," *Bulletin of Latin American Research* 39, no. 3 (2020): 362–79.
18 As quoted in Maurice Lemoine, "Venezuela's Press Power: How Hate Media Incited the Coup against the President," *Le Monde Diplomatique*, August (2002).
19 Mallen and García-Guadilla, *Venezuela's Polarized Politics*, 58.
20 See Chapter 2 on Venezuela's historical era for more on the Bolivarian Circles.
21 Mallen and García-Guadilla, *Venezuela's Polarized Politics*, 58–9.
22 Cannon, *Hugo Chávez and the Bolivarian Revolution*, 91; Trudy Coker, "Dimensions of Democracy in Contemporary Venezuela," *Social Justice* 40, no. 4 (2014): 88–105.
23 Buxton, "Continuity and Change," 1380.
24 For a detailed background on Venezuela's judiciary, the previous links between the courts and Punto Fijo parties, and the efforts by both the government and

the opposition to utilize courts to advance their agendas/restrict their opponents, see Raul Sanchez Urribarri, "Courts between Democracy and Hybrid Authoritarianism: Evidence from the Venezuelan Supreme Court," *Law and Social Inquiry* 36, no. 4 (2011): 854–84.

25 See Mallen and García-Guadilla, *Venezuela's Polarized Politics*, Chapter 4 for excellent discussion of Venezuela's "media wars."

26 Hellinger, "Oil and the Chávez Legacy."

27 Steve Ellner, "Social and Political Diversity and the Democratic Road to Change in Venezuela," *Latin American Perspectives*, 40, no. 3 (2013): 67.

28 Sanchez Urribarri, "Courts between Democracy and Hybrid Authoritarianism," 871.

29 George Ciccariello-Maher, "Constituent Moments, Constitutional Processes: Social Movements and the New Latin American Left," *Latin American Perspectives*, 40, no. 3 (2013): 141.

30 Tim Gill, "Whither Venezuelan Bolivarianism?," *NACLA Report on the Americas* 48, no. 4 (2016): 367.

31 Ministerio del Poder Popular para la Comunicación y Información, "Socialismo del Siglo XXI: La Fuerza de los Pequeños," (Caracas: MINCI, 2007).

32 Kirk Hawkins, Guillermo Rosas, and Michael E. Johnson, "The Misiones of the Chávez government," in David Smilde and Daniel Hellinger (eds), *Venezuela's Bolivarian Democracy: Participation, Politics, and Culture under Chávez* (Durham, NC: Duke University Press, 2011): 190.

33 Atilio Boron, "El Balance de la Revolución Bolivariana: Logros, Fortalezas, Debilidades y Errores," in Daniel Chávez, Hernan Ouviña, and Mabe Thwaites Rey (eds), *Venezuela: Lecturas Urgentes Desde el Sur* (Buenos Aires: CLACSO, 2017): 34.

34 Edgardo Lander, "El Balance de la Revolución Bolivariana: Logros, Fortalezas, Debilidades y Errores," in Daniel Chávez, Hernan Ouviña, and Mabe Thwaites Rey (eds), *Venezuela: Lecturas Urgentes Desde el Sur* (Buenos Aires: CLACSO, 2017): 36.

35 Hellinger, "Defying the Iron Law of Oligarchy I," 33.

36 Hellinger, "Venezuela: Movements for Rent?" 146; Daniel Hellinger, "The Second Wave of Incorporation and Political Parties in the Venezuelan Petrostate," in Eduardo Silva and Federico Rossi (eds), *Reshaping the Political Arena in Latin America: From Resisting Neoliberalism to the Second Incorporation* (Pittsburgh, PA: University of Pittsburgh Press, 2018).

37 Roberts, *Changing Course*, 262.

38 Ciccariello-Maher, "Constituent Moments," 141.

39 Dario Azzellini, "The Communal State: Communal Councils, Communes, and Workplace Democracy, *NACLA Report on the Americas* 46, no. 2 (2013): 26.

40 Arturo Sosa, "Reflexiones Sobre el Poder Comunal," in Margarita López Maya (ed), *Ideas para debatir el socialismo del siglo XXI* (Caracas: Editorial Alfa, 2007): 52.

41 Carlos de la Torre, "In the Name of the People: Democratization, Popular Organizations, and Populism in Venezuela, Bolivia, and Ecuador," *European Review of Latin American and Caribbean Studies* 95 (2013): 31.

42 Ibid.

43 Vladimir Acosta, "El Socialismo del Siglo XXI y la Revolución Bolivariana. Una Reflexión Inicial," in Margarita López Maya (ed), *Ideas para debatir el socialismo del siglo XXI* (Caracas: Editorial Alfa, 2007): 22.

44 Marta Harnecker, "Apuntes para un Socialismo Distinto, Popular y Democrático," in Miriam Lang and Alejandra Santillana (eds.), *Democracia, Participación y Socialismo. Bolivia–Ecuador–Venezuela* (Quito: Fundación Rosa Luxemburgo, 2010): 125.

45 Roger Burbach and Camila Piñeiro, "Venezuela"s Participatory Socialism," *Socialism and Democracy* 21, no. 3 (2007): 184.
46 Sujatha Fernandes, *Who Can Stop the Drums?: Urban Social Movements in Chávez's Venezuela* (Durham, NC: Duke University Press, 2010).
47 Matt Wilde, "Contested Spaces: The Communal Councils and Participatory Democracy in Chávez's Venezuela, *Latin American Perspectives* 44, no. 1 (2017): 141.
48 Sara Motta, "Populism"s Achilles' Heel: Popular Democracy beyond the Liberal State and the Market Economy in Venezuela," *Latin American Perspectives* 38, no. 1 (2011): 37.
49 For good discussion, see Iselin Åsedotter Strønen, *Grassroots Politics and Oil Culture in Venezuela: The Revolutionary Petro-State* (Cham: Springer Nature, 2017).
50 Greg Wilpert, *Changing Venezuela by Taking Power: The History and Policies of the Chávez Government* (London: Verso, 2007); Rafael Uzcátegui, *Venezuela, la Revolución Como Espectáculo: Una Crítica Anarquista al Gobierno Bolivariano* (Caracas and Madrid: Libertario, 2010).
51 Steve Ellner, "A New Model with Rough Edges: Venezuela's Community Councils," *NACLA Report on the Americas* 42, no. 3 (2009), 11–4.
52 Ciccariello-Maher, "Constituent Moments."
53 Dario Azzellini, "Constituent Power in Motion: Ten Years of Transformation in Venezuela," *Socialism and Democracy* 24, no. 2 (2010): 8–31.
54 Gabriel Hetland, "From System Collapse to Chavista Hegemony: The Party Question in Bolivarian Venezuela, *Latin American Perspectives* 44, no. 1 (2017): 17–36.
55 Cannon, *Hugo Chávez and the Bolivarian Revolution*, 60.
56 Hellinger, "Venezuela: Movements for Rent?" 146.
57 Ibid.
58 Interview online, January 2021.
59 Electronic interview with commune activist and organizer in Lara state, March 23, 2021.
60 Jeffrey Webber, "Latin America: From Reform to Resistance," (G. Souvlis interviewer), *Salvage* (2016): Retrieved http://salvage.zone/online-exclusive/latin-america-from-reform-to-resistance-an-interview-with-jeffery-webber-part-1/.
61 Online interview with commune organizer, February 2021.
62 Pia Riggirozzi and Diana Tussie, "The Rise of Post-Hegemonic Regionalism in Latin America," in Pia Riggirozzi and Diana Tussie (eds), *The Rise of Post-Hegemonic Regionalism* (Dordrecht, Netherlands: Springer, 2012): 6.
63 Ibid.
64 Pia Riggirozzi, "Region, Regionness and Regionalism in Latin America: Towards a New Synthesis," *New Political Economy* 17, no. 4 (2011): 434; Asa Cusack, *Venezuela, ALBA, and the Limits of Postneoliberal Regionalism in Latin America and the Caribbean* (New York: Springer Nature, 2018).
65 Riggirozzi, "Region, Regionness," 434.
66 Pia Riggirozzi and Diana Tussie, "Regional Governance in South America: Supporting States, Dealing with Markets and Reworking Hegemonies," in Pia Riggirozzi and Christopher Wylde (eds), *Handbook of South American Governance* (Abingdon and New York: Routledge, 2017): 170.
67 Riggirozzi, "Region, Regionness," 432.
68 Margarita Lopez-Maya, "Hugo Chávez and the Populist Left," in Steven Levitsky and Kenneth Roberts (eds), *The Resurgence of the Latin American Left* (Baltimore, MD: Johns Hopkins University Press, 2011): 225.
69 Riggirozzi, "Region, Regionness," 432.
70 Mallen and García-Guadilla, *Venezuela's Polarized Politics*, 94.

71 Javier Corrales, "The Authoritarian Resurgence: Autocratic Legalism in Venezuela," *Journal of Democracy* 26, no. 2 (2015): 42.
72 Mallen and García-Guadilla, *Venezuela's Polarized Politics*, 87.
73 David Smilde, "From Partial to Full Conflict Theory: A Neo-Weberian Portrait of the Battle for Venezuela," in Tulia Falleti and Emilio Parrado (eds.), *Latin America Since the Left Turn* (Philadelphia: University of Pennsylvania Press, 2018): 151.
74 Ibid.
75 Online interview, activist and popular organizer in the communes movement, February 2021.
76 For an excellent discussion of how community media related to the Bolivarian state see Naomi Schiller, *Channeling the State: Community Media and Popular Politics in Venezuela* (Durham, NC: Duke University Press, 2018).
77 Daniel Hellinger and Anthony Spanakos, "The Legacy of Hugo Chávez," *Latin American Perspectives* 44, no. 1 (2017): 12.
78 Lupien, "The Media in Venezuela and Bolivia," 227.
79 Ociel Alí López, *¡ Dale Más Gasolina!: Chavismo, Sifrinismo y Burocracia* (Caracas: Casa Nacional de las Letras Andrés Bello, 2015): 134.
80 Steve Ellner, Class Strategies in Chavista Venezuela: Pragmatic and Populist Policies in a Broader Context," in Steve Ellner (ed.), *Latin America's Pink Tide: Breakthroughs and Shortcomings* (Lanham, MD, Boulder, CO, New York and London: Rowman & Littlefield, 2020).
81 John Polga-Hecimovich, "Bureaucratic Politicization, Partisan Attachments, and the Limits of Public Agency Legitimacy: The Venezuelan Armed Forces under Chavismo," *Latin American Research Review* 54, no. 2 (2019): 482.
82 Ibid.
83 López Maya, "Hugo Chávez and the Populist Left," 227.
84 Following the 2007 referendum defeat which included a clause allowing for the re-election of sitting presidents, a 2009 referendum was passed by 54-46 percent, abolishing the two-term limit for sitting presidents. According to Chávez, the results would allow him to remain in power long enough to push forward and establish the basis for the move to 21st century socialism.
85 Webber, "Latin America: From Reform to Resistance."
86 Susan Spronk, Jeffrey Webber, George Ciccariello-Maher, Roland Denis, Steve Ellner, Sujatha Fernandes, Michael Lebowitz, Sara Motta, and Thomas Purcell, "The Bolivarian Process in Venezuela: A Left Forum," *Historical Materialism* 19, no. 1 (2011): 247–8.
87 Hetland, "From System Collapse."
88 Ibid., 28, 31.
89 Luis Vicente León and David Smilde, "Understanding Populism and Political Participation: The Case of Venezuela," *Woodrow Wilson International Center for Scholars* 3, April (2009): 5.
90 Azzellini, "The Communal State," 29.
91 Alejandro Velasco, "'We are Still Rebels': The Challenge of Popular History in Bolivarian Venezuela," in David Smilde and Daniel Hellinger (eds), *Venezuela's Bolivarian Democracy: Participation, Politics, and Culture under Chávez* (Durham, NC and London: Duke University Press, 2011): 181.
92 Interview with NNCC coordinator, Caracas, 2016; on.
93 Interview with spokesperson for NNCC, Caracas, 2016.
94 Dario Azzellini, *Communes and Workers" Control in Venezuela: Building 21st Century Socialism from Below* (Leiden: Brill, 2016): 71.
95 Kevin Rangel, "CRBZ: Venezuela's Left must Unite Behind Maduro to Defeat Imperialism," *Venezuela Analysis*, March 8 (2018): Retrieved https://venezuelanalysis.com/analysis/13711.

96 Interview with NNCC spokesperson, Caracas, 2016.
97 Azzellini, *Communes and Workers'' Control*, 72.
98 Interview, Caracas, 2016.
99 Online interview with former left-wing student leader and commune organizer, February 2021.
100 Interview with NNCC coordinator, Caracas, 2016.
101 Interview with member of the Comuna Rogelio Castillo Gamarra, Caracas, 2016.
102 Interview with NNCC coordinator, Caracas, 2016.
103 Cannon, "As Clear as MUD," 49.
104 López, "*¡ Dale Más Gasolina!*"
105 Jennifer Cyr, "Que Veinte Años no es Nada: Hugo Chávez, Las Elecciones de 2012 y el Continuismo Político Venezolano, *Revista de Ciencia Política (Santiago)* 33, no. 1 (2013): 377.
106 Machado cited in Jonah Gindin, "Democracy vs Bush-o-cracy in Venezuela, "*Venezuela Analysis* June 1 (2005): Retrieved https://venezuelanalysis.com/analysis/1160.
107 Cyr, "Que Veinte Años no es Nada," 377; Hellinger, "The Second Wave of Incorporation," 266.
108 López, *¡ Dale Más Gasolina!*, 104.
109 George Ciccariello-Maher, *Building the Commune: Radical Democracy in Venezuela* (London and New York: Verso Books, 2016): 56.
110 López, *¡ Dale Más Gasolina!*, 104–5.
111 See Ybiskay González, "Democracy as Political Strategy of the Venezuelan Right," *Revista CIDOB* 126 (2020): 163–84.
112 López, *¡ Dale Más Gasolina!*, 128–9.
113 Cannon, "As Clear as MUD".
114 Ibid., 59.
115 Julia Buxton, "Situation Normal in Venezuela: All Fouled Up," *NACLA Report on the Americas* 49, no. 1 (2017): 6; Cannon, "As Clear as MUD."
116 For details, see Tim Gill, "Newly Revealed Documents Show how the AFL-CIO Aided US Interference in Venezuela," *Jacobin* May 8 (2020): Retrieved https://jacobinmag.com/2020/08/venezuela-hugo-chavez-afl-cio-united-states; Tim Gill and Joseph Brown, "Two Decades of Imperial Failure: Theorizing U.S. Regime Change Efforts in Venezuela from Bush II to Trump," *Class, Race and Corporate Power* 8, no. 2 (2020).
117 See Karin Fischer, "The Atlas Network: Littering the World with Free-Market Think Tanks," *Global Dialogue* 8, no. 2 (2018):10–11.
118 Ibid.
119 Lee Fang, "Sphere of Influence: How American Libertarians are Remaking Latin American Politics," *The Intercept* August 9 (2017): Retrieved https://theintercept.com/2017/08/09/atlas-network-alejandro-chafuen-libertarian-think-tank-latin-america-brazil/.
120 Jeffrey Webber, *The Last Day of Oppression, and the First Day of the Same* (London: Pluto, 2017): 39.
121 MacLeod, "Was Hugo Chávez to Blame."

4 From regressive to authoritarian centralization

Nicolás Maduro, 2013–21

Following Chávez' death, a range of new power struggles in the development of a post-neoliberal democracy emerged. Nicolás Maduro, Chávez' hand-picked successor, narrowly defeated MUD-candidate Henrique Capriles with 50.6 percent of the vote to 49.1 in the April 2013 election. Nearly victorious, "the opposition swarmed at the sight of fresh blood."[1] Indeed, from the moment of Maduro's election, "the political and economic pressures imposed on Venezuela have been relentless."[2] With economic conditions deteriorating and an international environment becoming less favorable for the government, and having barely scraped electoral victory despite Chávez having easily won elections just a month previously, Maduro set about solidifying his position by tightening his alliance with the military hierarchy. The 2013–21 period would thus witness an intense struggle between the opposition-bloc with the backing of international allies and the ruling PSUV party, with deleterious consequences on the quality of democracy for popular sectors. While the Chávez era had witnessed progressive centralization creep toward regressive centralization, the Maduro era would see a whole-scale slide toward authoritarian centralization.

The beginning of the economic downturn and opposition tactical shifts: 2013–14

The year 2013 witnessed the beginning of an economic slide for Venezuela. By April, the month-on-month inflation had reached 6 percent. While the economy struggled, the country began to witness scarcities of basic products. Oil prices fell by 50 percent from June to December 2014. With oil revenues accounting for approximately 95 percent of export earnings and 60 percent of budget revenues, the economic power of the government was hobbled.

Maduro inherited a budget deficit of around 20 percent of GDP while social spending had been underpinned by external debt, principally from Chinese institutions. Facing a fiscal deficit, toward the end of 2012, Chávez had introduced a rationing of foreign currencies to the private sector. Maduro continued this rationing of US dollars while printing local currency. Expanding the supply of the Venezuelan Bolivar in conjunction with fixing

DOI: 10.4324/9781003262466-5

foreign exchange rates increased the demand for available dollars. However, given declining levels of dollars from oil sales, the government further restricted dollar supplies, fostering a black market for the dollars sold by the government. The gap between the official and black-market dollar rates created enormous incentives for corruption, while also leading to scarcities of goods as dollars that were purportedly to be used to pay for imports were instead sold at enormous profit on the black market.

Scarcities of foodstuffs, hygiene products, medicines, and household goods were worsened by speculation, hoarding, and selling government-regulated goods across the Colombian border. The government described such behaviors by the private sector as amounting to an "economic war." As discussed in detail later, there is little doubt that there were efforts by private sector interests to create shortages and thus foment anti-government sentiment. However, the principal factor was the government's own policies.

By March 2014, the Venezuelan Central Bank stated that the shortfall of staple goods in the country averaged 29.4 percent. Medicines and medical supplies were affected. It was increasingly difficult to find some items such as cooking oil, powdered milk, toilet paper, and pre-cooked maize (needed to make arepas), with the shortfall reaching over 85 percent.[3] Though the situation eased somewhat over the course of 2014, the issues of inflation, shortages, and corruption were to be defining features over the eight years of Maduro's presidencies.

While the opposition-bloc had turned toward an electoral strategy to regain state power from 2010–13, Capriles' narrow electoral defeat was followed by a refusal by MUD parties to recognize the results, even though the international community, with the notable single exception of the United States, did so almost immediately. Following the narrow defeat in the presidential elections, Capriles called for municipal elections scheduled for later in the year to be a referendum on Maduro's leadership. However, the PSUV won 49.24 percent compared to the opposition's 42.72. Meanwhile, the PSUV and its allies won 76 percent of the mayoral elections and 14 of the 24 gubernatorial elections. The inability of the opposition-bloc to present a political project capable of winning power via the ballot box deepened a rift between the major MUD parties over which was the best route to achieve their aim of recouping control over all branches of the state—moderation, negotiation, and continuation of an electoral strategy, or an extra-institutional push to destabilize the government and bring about regime change.

Given the weak economic position of Maduro's government, he called on the opposition to meet him and work on a plan for national reconciliation. Capriles responded and was photographed shaking Maduro's hand at the presidential palace. However, for the ultra-right sector of the MUD, represented by Leopoldo López and VP as well as Maria Corina Machado and Vente Venezuela, such calls to dialogue were unacceptable as they were convinced that an electoral strategy would take too long. Rather, given the economic issues facing the country, they sought to

> take advantage of the government's weakness and the people's discontent at the shortages, inflation and crime to provoke violent confrontations (which had to include deaths), attempting to create a state of ungovernability in order to denounce the government as dictatorial and repressive.[4]

They instigated a campaign via social, private domestic, and international media to instigate "*La Salida*" ("The Exit") calling for massive protests to "ignite the streets with struggle" and make the country ungovernable for Maduro.[5] As Lander cogently summarizes, according to the strategy, the

> protests had to be as violent and politically costly to the government as possible. This seems to be the main reason why, right from the start, these actions had a minority but well-organized violent component: barricades, Molotov cocktails, snipers, attacks on public buildings, burning of public transport vehicles.

Barricades in the wealthy eastern side of Caracas were set up and manned by student organizations from the private universities.

In two months of street barricades and marches—both peaceful and armed, there were violent clashes with the police and army. Forty three people died and many were wounded while hundreds were arrested, including Leopoldo López. Those killed included opposition activists, security force members, and citizens uninvolved with the clashes. Seeking to ideologically isolate the Maduro government, "global corporate media – often using photos from other countries – then constructed the image these opposition groups sought, describing the protesters as defenseless victims of a repressive government."[6] The student groups, López, and Machado had been in receipt of US funding and political support for years from the US "democracy promotion" agencies, and the events of February 2014 "are likely to have been planned with the aim of creating a Ukraine-style 'orange revolution' scenario."[7]

Responsibility for the deaths has been heavily debated, though it would appear that while heavy-handed state repression was certainly a factor, the "dominant narrative of government repression" in the mainstream, and social media provides only part of the reality.[8] Meanwhile, the jailing of leading opposition politicians Antonio Ledezma and Leopoldo López on charges of fomenting a coup against the government sparked "an international outcry and condemnations from organizations accusing Maduro of political repression."[9] Domestic private media reporting of the events was somewhat more muted due to the rebalancing of ideological sources of power that had occurred over the duration of Venezuela's post-neoliberal process. Moreover, following an obscure change of ownership in the once fervently oppositional *Globovisión* in 2013, the channel did not report on the February protests. However, while Maduro managed to survive the protests, his international image was badly damaged via the international and social media campaigns. Meanwhile, the United States, seeing Maduro's vulnerability, introduced a range of sanctions thereby discouraging Western banks and investors from doing business in Venezuela at a time when the country was in desperate need of foreign currency.

While Maduro emerged from the 2014 protests in a weakened position, the 2014 violence fractured the political unity of the opposition-bloc grouped in the MUD. With AD and PJ stating that an alternative to Maduro should come about peacefully and via electoral means, while VP and Machado's support base rejected dialogue with the government, the MUD entered into crisis and its general secretary, Ramón Guillermo Aveledo, resigned. While Capriles and other MUD parties such as AD refused to openly support the violent efforts to force Maduro from power, this should not be interpreted as representing a newfound willingness to respect the electoral victories of the PSUV or the gains of the Bolivarian process. It was simply a tactical decision based on the given distribution of power. As such, while the more radical and moderate branches of the opposition political bloc differed in terms of the tactics they saw as most efficient to remove Maduro, the end goal was the same—end the Bolivarian process and restore the elite families to the top of the pyramid where they had reigned until Chavismo disrupted the social order.

The differences between the moderate and radical wings of the MUD also relate to the speed and intensity in which they would "de-Bolivarianize" democracy, with PJ and AD advocating a more moderate return to market democracy than VP who supported a rapid marketization of society.[10] Despite these differences, neither wing of the MUD was capable of offering a political project that resonated with the majority of popular sectors as, in the eyes of voters, both ultimately represented a return to Punto Fijo era exclusionary democracy. Hence, despite the dire economic situation in the country, and despite stating that they would respect the 1999 Constitution—in stark contrast to 2002 electoral success remained elusive for the MUD up to 2014. Moreover, "La Salida" protests were interpreted as a delegitimate tactic by a wealthy elite who refused to respect the legitimacy of the Bolivarian process. However, 2015 was to prove a key turning point as a rapid deterioration in living standards and the emergence of corruption scandals by state personnel triggered electoral protest against Maduro and the PSUV by formerly allied popular sectors.

National assembly elections, 2015

In the December 2015 legislative elections, the PSUV was trounced in the urban barrios whose residents were "sending a powerful signal—either by abstaining or voting for the opposition—of their displeasure with the government."[11] The PSUV were punished for the endless lines found around the country as people queued for scarce goods, for inflation levels that had reached 100 percent, and for rising poverty levels.[12] The opposition gained a two-thirds supermajority in the National Assembly giving them substantial legislative power for the first time since Chávez' 1999 election. Given the deepening economic crisis facing the country, the MUD parties put aside their internal differences to push for electoral success in the 2015 elections, with the social democratic AD and Un Nuevo Tiempo gaining support in rural and popular urban areas traditionally supportive of the PSUV.

With the opposition-bloc winning control over a branch of government for the first time since 1999, while Maduro retained control over the judiciary, military hierarchy, and the state oil company PDVSA, a new stage in government-opposition struggles began that witnessed the country move from a scenario of regressive centralization toward authoritarian centralization.

In December 2015, the Venezuelan Supreme Court (TSJ) reduced the opposition's number of elected deputies by three due to alleged irregularities in their elections. The move aimed to block the MUD from having a two-thirds super-majority which would have allowed them to make fundamental changes to laws established over the course of the Bolivarian project. This "prompted the National Assembly to unilaterally reincorporate the suspended deputies in July leading the TSJ to 'declare congress illegitimate', effectively neutering that body and any legislation it may pass."[13]

MUD parties activated a recall process of Maduro with the National Electoral Council (CNE) on 9 March 2016. The government controlled CNE, however, found 600,000 of the 1,957,779 signatures collected invalid, which meant that this stage of the process was not completed until 24 August. The next step for the opposition was to collect the signatures of 20 percent of registered voters, a process that required completion by the end of October, with signatures approved by the end of November if the referendum itself was to be held by the end of the year. This timing was important as a referendum victory before year's end would have meant the removal of Maduro and new elections, which the opposition would probably win. If not, Maduro's vice president would replace him, making the whole process much less appealing, if not meaningless, from the MUD's point of view.

In October, the CNE found 53,658 irregular signatures, effectively suspending the entire process indefinitely. Additionally, the CNE had earlier announced the postponement of the regional and municipal elections due that December until an undetermined date in early 2017. With these moves, plus a legal prohibition on a number of MUD politicians including the governor of Miranda state and presidential candidate, Henrique Capriles, the National Assembly declared Venezuela in a coup d'état situation and requested international help. This was not long in coming, when the Secretary General of the Organization of American States (OAS), Luis Almagro, called for the Inter-American Democratic Charter to be invoked against Venezuela—as he had previously attempted but failed to do in May—a process that could lead to Venezuela's suspension from that organization.

The actions of the TSJ further delegitimized Maduro in the international arena, making previously untrue claims that the Bolivarian process was anti-democratic appear much closer to reality. The events that transpired from

2015 onward and the government's refusal to respect electoral outcomes would also seriously delegitimize the government in the eyes of many formerly allied popular sector groups, opening the stage for party-base tensions.

Deepening economic crisis, increasing corruption and militarization, 2016–17

The year 2016 witnessed a deepening of the economic and social crisis. Oil prices dipped to $34/barrel, GDP declined by 25 percent between 2013 and 2016, and inflation was estimated at 720 percent, with food inflation reaching 1,400 percent.[14] Foreign debt repayments averaged about US$10 billion per year, while capital flight was estimated to be US$23 billion between 2003 and 2013. Both latter phenomena drew scarce dollars away from paying for food imports, which fell 40 percent in the first half of 2016 alone.[15] With little domestic production, scarcities of vital goods, medicines, and food soared. Poverty levels rose from 48.4 percent in 2014 to 87 percent in August 2017.[16] While falling oil prices, US sanctions, and elite hoarding tactics certainly worsened the crisis, the single greatest cause was government mismanagement of its currency.

While currency manipulation was first undertaken as an emergency response to the oil industry strike of 2002, by 2016 it had become a byzantine three-tiered currency control system: the lower official rate of 10:1 (bolivares to dollars) applied to "essential imports"; a second official rate for non-essential imports known as DiCom, rose via a "managed float" from 200 to 697: 1 in 2017; and finally, a fluctuating black-market rate stood at 4,229: 1. Imports financed by overvalued government regulated dollars meant that every time the government sold ten dollars to private companies, it was in fact giving away nine dollars for free.[17] This lucrative transfer of oil rent to the private sector was the most onerous burden on the Venezuelan nation imaginable. The enormous gulf in rates created serious incentives for corruption whereby businesses and state/military officials with access to dollars at the lower official rate could then resell them at black market rates, making enormous profits.

Indeed, it was not simply the traditional opposition-bloc elites who engaged in such practices, with widespread accusations that government and military elites charged with managing the supply of US dollars for purchasing price-controlled goods, as well as the supply of food and medicines, were heavily involved in corruption.[18] The outcome was a shortage of dollars for food imports, lengthy queues for the little food that was available, and a greatly inflated black market for those same goods. As Velasco[19] notes, the oil boom "simultaneously masked and fed corruption as dollars were plentiful. But when dollars became scarce as oil prices plummeted, the breach no longer held."

In June, a specially commissioned UNASUR team of experts, many of them identifying with the left, presented a comprehensive set of proposals to the government to help manage the crisis. Among the recommendations involving monetary policy were an immediate end to the tiered currency system and the free floating of the BF on the markets, a lifting of price controls and of all energy subsidies (not just gasoline), with direct government subsidies to consumers to soften the blow, and the indexing of all salaries to the monthly inflation rate until inflation stabilizes. Additional recommendations included the selling of all non-strategic assets, a tax on financial transactions, wealth taxes, and assistance for the informal employment sector which developed under the present crisis (such as the reselling of price-controlled goods). The government declined to adopt any of the UNASUR experts' recommendations, making it one of "the most astonishingly static governments Latin America has seen for many years."[20]

There are a number of reasons for this inactivity. First, many in the government saw the UNASUR proposed reforms as a *paquetazo* resembling IMF neoliberal reforms of the past.[21] This problem was particularly acute as Maduro could not be seen to deviate from Chávez' anti-neoliberal positions, for fear of alienating his base. For Sutherland,[22] however, the economic policies of the government did not make the government anticapitalist, as it claimed. Rather, the transfer of public wealth generated through oil rents to private hands via mismanaged currency policies was more generous than Venezuela's capitalists could ever have dreamed of. Moreover, as Hetland[23] suggests, too many people were employed by the state and, in particular, the military, who benefited from the system, mostly through corruption. Given Maduro's lack of economic power and the rising levels of popular discontent, he could not risk alienating the military for fear of their heeding opposition calls for a coup.

The tame efforts by the government to tackle the currency situation were accompanied by changes to important cabinet positions, with an increasing military presence in powerful roles. In August, Maduro appointed General Nestor Reverol as Minister for Interior Justice, days after a US Federal District court issued an indictment against Reverol over allegations of accepting bribes from drug-traffickers between 2008 and 2010. Maduro aimed to build a core team whose exit costs were too high to allow them to desert the government, as they would likely face charges in the United States if the MUD were to achieve executive power. López Maya argues that

> illicit businesses contribute in an important way to explain the military support for Maduro, which is essential if he is to remain in power. Therefore, he continuously opens more business opportunities for this elite, grants them privileges, and ensures salary increases for the military amidst the country's catastrophic economic crisis.[24]

Domestic turbulence coincided with a stark political realignment elsewhere. Two of the most geopolitically important countries in Latin America, Argentina and Brazil, turned sharply to the ideological right in 2016, with the elections of Mauricio Macri in the former and the installation of Michel Temer as President in the latter. In September, the founding members of Mercosur (Argentina, Brazil, Paraguay, and Uruguay) agreed that Venezuela would not assume the pro tempore presidency of the bloc, and by early December, Venezuela had been suspended from the organization. Meanwhile, the Secretary General of the OAS, Luis Almagro, continued to seek the application of the Democratic Charter against Venezuela, declaring in August that democracy in Venezuela had "ended." With the election of Donald Trump in November, and Republican domination of both Houses of Congress, there was a hardening of US policy toward Venezuela.

Institutional rupture, violent protest, the national constituent assembly, and transnational destabilization, 2017

With the CNE postponement of regional and municipal elections due to take place in December 2016, Chávez' proclamation that Venezuela's process of building socialism differed from the Soviet Union due to its adherence to electoral democracy was violated. In March 2017, the government controlled Supreme Court stripped the opposition controlled National Assembly of its authority to legislate, temporarily taking that power for itself. While Maduro backtracked on this position and the Supreme Court rescinded the decision a few days later, and while the National Assembly had taken unconstitutional measures, such as to "snap their fingers and grant amnesty to all so-called political prisoners, some of whom had engaged in very violent actions,"[25] the initial move was heavily critiqued, even by Chavista sympathizers such as attorney general Louisa Ortega Díaz who decried it as a "rupture with the constitutional order."

By closing off constitutional avenues for the opposition, the government played into the hands of the more radical sectors of the MUD. The result was a wave of almost constant street protests for three months. While it would be erroneous to suggest that all of these protests incited violence, in many of the mobilizations, there were attacks on public buildings, lynching and burning alive by right-wing activists of brown and black men "just for looking like Chavistas"[26] and the use of *guarimbas*—violent protests that involved the barricading of streets with burning tires and the hanging of galvanized wire across intersections to decapitate motorcyclists. International media coverage, especially in the United States, ignored much of this violence[27] highlighting instead incidences of violence carried out by state forces and government supporters.

In the midst of protests Maduro "doubled down on the loyalty of the security forces and the risk of alienating even his Chavista supporters by calling for a constituent assembly to rewrite the 1999 constitution,"[28] a move Maduro claimed was necessary to overcome the political impasse and violence in the country and to advance the country's revolution. Without holding a consultative referendum in advance—unlike in 1999 when Chávez relied on popular support to convene a constituent assembly—on June 30 a vote was held to elect the 545-member National Constituent Assembly (ANC). The electoral process faced accusations of bias to guarantee that, despite the majority of the population not supporting either the constituent process or the Maduro government, Madurismo wins a majority. The election of the 545 delegates was split between 181 "sectoral" and 364 "territorial" representatives, with sectoral members chosen by members of communal councils, labor, peasant organizations, students, pensioners, and other groups who must first be selected by the government controlled CNE. The opposition decried the move as an attempt to avoid facing presidential elections in 2018 and declined to participate.

Once convened, the ANC quickly moved to remove attorney general Ortega Días from office, accusing her of "serious failures in the exercise of her role" and replaced her with Tarek William Saab, a close ally of Maduro. Ortega Díaz stated that her removal was due to her investigations into corruption and abuses of human-rights cases against high-ranking government officials and members of the ANC.

At the international level, Florida Senator Marco Rubio openly threatened the Dominican Republic, El Salvador, and Haiti with punishment if they failed to cooperate with Washington's plans to delegitimize the government of Venezuela. The Trump administration and Secretary of State Rex Tillerson openly called for regime change, which emboldened the radical sectors of the opposition who did not seek a negotiated or peaceful solution to the political impasse and whose aim was "not only to get rid of Maduro, but to destroy Chavismo itself."[29] Furthermore, US sanctions against Venezuela, and the threat of further sanctions, led to investors withdrawing money and the black-market dollar exchange rate falling 45 percent in just four days (in the first weeks of August 2017). Meanwhile, the Lima Group was established in August by 12 countries with the purported aim being to "restore democracy" through peaceful means. The group was comprised primarily of conservative-led regional governments and was supported by the United States, the Venezuelan opposition, and the overtly partisan Organization of the Americas.

In October 2017 gubernatorial elections, despite popular discontent, opposition-bloc pressure and transnational efforts to destabilize Maduro, the PSUV trounced the MUD, winning 18 of the 23 states. Utilizing its ideological sources of power, the MUD rapidly contested the "shock" results through its social and international media connections, claiming fraud and that it had been robbed. However, while the government certainly engaged in efforts to hinder the MUD, such as via the CNE's refusal to substitute candidates after the opposition's primaries as well as its decision to move the electoral centers of 700,000 voters 72 hours before the election, it was declines in voter turnout in opposition strongholds from the 2015 electoral victory that was by far the biggest driver of change in vote share.[30]

The "shock" results and lack of opposition turnout may be partially explained by the divisions in MUD strategy, with Maria Corina Machado, Leopoldo López, and Antonio Ledezma calling for abstention of the elections and continued (violent) mobilization, while other parties of the coalition such as Un Nuevo Tiempo and Avanzada Progresista telling supporters it would be better to confront the government via the ballot box.[31]

While divided tactics on how to remove Maduro certainly impacted the election results, the MUD's issues are of a more fundamental nature. Kronick and Rodríguez[32] suggest that the principal cause for low opposition-voter turnout appears to have been the lack of policy proposals that respond to actual voter concerns, with efforts simply aimed at regime change. The opposition did not represent a solution to the increasing authoritarian centralization of the Maduro regime that promised to avoid a return to the late-stage Punto Fijo market democracy. Despite an enormous amount of head-scratching and opinion pieces by liberal analysts seeking to try and explain how Maduro manipulates conditions to prevent the opposition from winning, the reality is that MUD contains so many actors and interests linked to traditional elite families and to newer business elites that it is not considered a legitimate option for swathes of the population. To make significant and repeated electoral gains required demonstrating a policy matrix that would respond to popular sector needs. To do so, however, would go against the very ideological make-up of the opposition whose ideological project is underpinned by support for a market democracy.

Following the MUD's incapacity to offer a coherent program other than a generic anti-government position, the October election results "practically destroyed" the opposition-bloc, with the rifts that had always existed coming to the fore in the aftermath of the defeat.[33] With "the opposition more divided than ever, the government … wasted no time in capitalizing on the moment to announce plans for municipal elections" in December.[34] In disarray, the MUD called for an electoral boycott, which the main constituent parties adhered to. The PSUV and allies won 308 of the 335 municipalities. With their electoral tactics leaving the opposition-bloc's political power in disarray, they were more dependent than ever on support from their international allies.

In response to the October elections, the US Department of Treasury added ten more Venezuelan officials to its sanctions list, stating that the elections "were marked by numerous irregularities that strongly suggest fraud helped the ruling party unexpectedly win a majority of governorships."[35] Furthermore, the sanctions were placed on individuals supposedly involved in "undermining electoral processes, media censorship, or corruption in government-administered food programs in Venezuela." These sanctions were a response both to election results which boosted the political power of the government and to Maduro's efforts to boost his economic power via a proposed meeting with creditors to discuss a restructuring of Venezuelan debt. The Trump administration warned that "US bondholders that attended this meeting could put them in violation of US economic sanctions against Venezuela" which could lead to penalties of 30 years in prison and up to $10 million dollars in fines for businesses.[36]

Considering that over 95 percent of Venezuela's export revenue comes from oil sales, cutting off the government's access to dollars would leave the economy without the hard currency needed to pay for imports of food and medicine. The Trump strategy appeared "to be to prevent an economic recovery and to worsen the shortages (which include essential medicines and food) so that Venezuelans will get back in the streets and overthrow the government."[37] As Weisbrot summarizes, "this is what regime change efforts are all about: delegitimation — if the election results don't concur, they must be declared fraudulent — and economic strangulation." Supporting US efforts at regime change, Argentina's pro-neoliberal president Mauricio Macri stated that the Trump administration "should dramatically tighten its *sanctions on Venezuela* by *imposing a full embargo* on its *oil* exports to the US."[38] US secretary of state Rex Tillerson visited conservatively led Mexico, Peru, Colombia, and Jamaica seeking to drum up support for an escalation of sanctions to include restrictions on the oil industry. Tillerson went so far as to suggest that Maduro could be toppled by his own military, while stating that "we are looking at options and we are looking at how to mitigate the impacts on US business interests."[39]

Illegitimate elections, sanctions, and a tale of two presidents: 2018–20

With the MUD coalition still in disarray, in January 2018, the ANC called on the electoral board to convene presidential elections in April. The Lima Group and the United States rejected the calls, stating that the ANC was illegitimate, that there would be insufficient time to ensure the elections met international standards for transparency and oversight, and that there was a lack of time for opposition parties to prepare. The MUD boycotted the elections, deferred until May 20, though Henri Falcón, a former ally of Chávez who was part of the MUD, decided to participate. Falcón was ejected from the MUD for doing so. Despite leading in polls, Falcón was told by US officials that he would face fines if he participated. As Weisbrot[40] notes, hardliner Marco Rubio dictated US foreign policy regarding Venezuela and negotiated or electoral strategies were rejected in favor of the maximum pressure approach of seeking to use sanctions to foster public uprisings leading to a military intervention and the removal of Maduro from office. Unsurprisingly, with the major opposition parties refusing to participate, Maduro won the May elections, though his 68 percent vote share was higher than most polls had predicted. However, 54 percent of registered voters abstained.

While it was government ineptitude and mismanagement that fostered the economic crisis, the US strategy to worsen the crisis via sanctions crippled the economic power of Maduro's government, with appalling impacts on the livelihoods of Venezuelans. Maduro's government was banned from profiting from any sales of oil to the United States, cutting access to foreign exchange. The sanctions also targeted any private firm or bank that engaged with the government, triggering a corporate exodus of firms with operations in Venezuela while blocking firms from buying the country's oil.[41] With no foreign exchange revenues, shortages of goods, foods, and medicines worsened. Moreover, US companies were banned from exporting the additives required to refine Venezuela's heavy crude into gasoline, leading to severe shortages at the petrol pumps.

A report by economists Jeffrey Sachs and Mark Weisbrot highlights that the major impacts of US sanctions were borne by the civilian population. By exacerbating Venezuela's existing economic crisis, the sanctions disproportionately harmed the poorest citizens via reduced caloric intake, rising disease and mortality rates, and displacement as millions fled the country's worsening depression and hyperinflation.[42] Indeed, a damning report by a UN Special Rapporteur outlined that the sanctions by the United States and European Union not only contravened international law, but were having a devastating impact on a range of basic human rights such as access to food, medicine, and education.[43]

The sanctions "worked" in that they did eventually lead to massive popular protests in the barrios against Maduro, "the first time I saw such mass protests against the Revolution coming from the barrios. They were enormous, in Los Magallanes de Catia, La Vega, Petare. They were angry with the crisis, dollarization, shortages, lack of public services."[44] Jiménez notes that these were spontaneous protests, not organized by any particular party. It "was like 1989 (the Caracazo), with local barrio leaders coordinating the protests."

While the "maximum pressure" approach by the United States aimed to trigger popular unrest and a consequent military uprising, sanctions were also targeted on military officials supportive of Maduro with the hope they would lead to defections. The outcome, however, witnessed a deepening of ties between Maduro and military officials whose control over vast tranches of the Venezuelan economy and illicit currency exchange programs ensured their support for the maintenance of the Maduro regime, while regular citizens suffered.

While the opposition-bloc rejected electoral competition in 2018, calling instead for an international blockade to force Maduro from power, in 2019 there were efforts to utilize political sources of power in conjunction with international destabilization efforts. In early 2019, president of the National Assembly Juan Guaidó from the radical VP party declared himself "interim president," a move immediately recognized by US officials and regional conservative-led governments. Guaidó argued that the May 2018 election was not legitimate and therefore, the second in line—the president of the National Assembly—should be declared interim president. Around 50 countries, including 19 European Union members soon recognized him as the legitimate head of state.

Atenea Jiménez suggests that when the opposition-bloc saw the popular protests in the barrios against Maduro, the radical wing pushed Guaidó forward to take advantage of the moment of popular unrest. However, "as soon as Guaidó emerged, the popular protests subsided. Guaidó demobilized the protests because popular sectors did not want to assist Guaidó in any way."[45]

The United States announced a freeze on all Venezuelan government assets in the United States, including Citgo, a subsidiary of state oil company PDVSA and the eight-largest refinery based in the United States. Guaidó named a new board for Citgo and would then use funds generated from the firm to finance efforts to topple Maduro, which he could access because the US handed control over Venezuela's national bank accounts in the United States to him.[46]

Guaidó's team of "ambassadors" and advisers comprised numerous individuals linked to organizations funded by the NED and the International Republican Institute, as well as Maria Corina Machado's Vente Venezuela party.[47] Guaidó's *Plan País* set out his plans to rejuvenate the economy. As Cannon[48] delineates, "Juan Guaidó's 'Venezuela to Come' is a Venezuela we have seen before—one for the elites, at the expense of lower socioeconomic sectors and the working class." The document outlines how "empowering Venezuelans to overcome structural poverty" should be tied to the reestablishment of free-market principles, "which will supposedly enable society to organize itself to solve its problems." *Plan País'* goals of stabilizing the economy, reactivating the oil economy, attending to the humanitarian crisis, and ensuring access to public services are to be funded by "massive" financing from four key sources: "multilateral finance organizations and countries interested in the restoration of democracy and development in Venezuela;" a "profound" debt restructuring; macro-economic and regulatory restructuring to attract international investment; and, recuperation of illegally sourced wealth.

A leaked Inter-American Development Bank document detailed how a US$48 billion infusion of capital would be used to boost the Venezuelan economy, once Maduro was removed from office. The plans outlined a four-year plan to open the economy to foreign investment through privatization, structural reforms, and public-private partnerships.[49] The funding would allow an incoming president, be that Guaidó or another opposition-bloc politician, to claim an immediate victory by benefitting from international assistance that was denied to the Maduro government, while simultaneously stripping Venezuela of its public assets.

The strategy of the radical wing of the MUD was clear: make the "economy scream" with the backing from international allies, leading to such despair that ordinary Venezuelans back regime change by any means necessary; and then, once in power, offer immediate short-term responses to a crippling humanitarian scenario while quietly rolling back on Bolivarian efforts to move away from a marketized model of citizenship. Trump supported pro-neoliberal Guaidó as it aligned with his regime's desire to topple the leftist governments in Cuba, Nicaragua, and Venezuela—the "troika of tyranny" as Trump's national security adviser John Bolton described the countries. While the aggressive stance sought to drum up the electoral support of Latin Americans living in Florida, the objectives of US foreign policy under Trump toward Latin America remained the same as under previous presidents—to remove parties and president who rejected a neoliberal model of regional integration dominated by the United States. Bolton was not shy in proclaiming this mission, noting that

> the recent elections of like-minded leaders in key countries, including Ivan Duque in Colombia, and last weekend Jair Bolsonaro in Brazil, are positive signs for the future of the region, and demonstrate a growing regional commitment to free-market principles, and open, transparent, and accountable governance.

Indeed, Bolton told Fox News "we're in conversation with major American companies now … It will make a big difference to the United States economically if we could have American oil companies really invest in and produce the oil capabilities in Venezuela."[50]

In conjunction with efforts by the domestic opposition-bloc and their international allies to cut the economic power of the Maduro government, the Guaidó and Leopoldo López wing of the opposition also sought to fracture Maduro's military support by promoting a coup in April 2019. The two men and a small group of soldiers gathered near the La Carlota airbase in Caracas, calling on the military hierarchy to rise up against Maduro. However, the so-called "Operation Freedom" failed to fracture the military's backing for Maduro, and the efforts to foment a coup were quickly put down by loyal troops.

In late 2019, 18 opposition-bloc National Assembly members split from their parties, facing accusations they had received bribes from pro-government forces. This dissident group, together with the pro-government vote, took control of the National Assembly in January 2020 when lawmakers elected a new congressional leadership as happens every year (in 2019, Guaidó was chosen). Guaidó sought re-election, but lost to a legislator from the PJ party, Luis Parra, one of the dissident assembly members. The Assembly named a new leadership comprised of dissident legislators previously aligned with the opposition. However, the National Guard had blocked the entrance to the Legislative Palace, impeding the entrance of opposition members who government authorities had disqualified from holding public office. With Guaidó and the banned legislators struggling to gain entry, the lawmakers inside hastily elected the new leadership.[51] Guaidó convened an alternative meeting at the headquarters of newspaper El Universal and claimed that he had received enough votes to remain as head of the Assembly, crucial given that his status as "interim president" depended on his holding the role. Both processes were highly dubious and broke from Venezuela's legal norms and resulted in the farcical scenario where there were two presidents and two National Assemblies.[52]

In February 2020, Guaidó went on an international tour to galvanize his role as "legitimate" leader of Venezuela. He received bipartisan applause when he appeared at the US State of the Union event. However, as Iber[53] and Ellner[54] both argue, the fact that Guaidó's major backers were international rather than domestic gave weight to the belief amongst ordinary Venezuelans that any government he may head in a post-Maduro scenario would be "made in the USA." Moreover, as discussed below, Guaidó's international support allowed Maduro to maintain the support of some of the Chavista base by portraying himself as a barrier against a return of imperialist domination of domestic issues.

The failure by the radical bloc of the opposition and their international allies to remove Maduro, despite efforts to hobble his political, economic, and military sources of power led to a bizarre incident in May. An ex-US Green Beret, Jordan Goudreau was captured off the coast of Venezuela. He had apparently been hired by a "strategy committee" headed by JJ Rendón, a political strategist tapped by Guaidó to identify how Maduro could be removed from power. Rendón stated that Guaidó told the "strategy committee" that all options were on, or under, the table regarding tactics to remove Maduro. An agreement signed by Guaidó and Silvercorp USA—an organization headed by Goudreau—emerged indicating that Maduro was to be captured. Following Goudreau's capture, Guaidó initially claimed the event was a false positive. Then, he admitted the event was real, but that he had no part in in it. However, following Rendón's disclosure that he had paid US$50,000 to Goudreau for costs, Guaidó's team released a statement announcing that he accepted the resignation of Rendón as advisor and called on the international community to support his interim presidency.[55]

Despite Guaidó's efforts to brush aside the event, it furthered the divisions within the opposition-bloc. PJ published a statement rejecting the May events, outlining that armed uprisings would "end up frustrating our people and destroying the confidence of those fighting for political change."[56] The uprising also provided Maduro with a perfect story to justify his increasingly authoritarian centralization of power. In June, the Supreme Court (TSJ) appointed new rectors to the National Electoral Council (CNE) that according to opposition parties, the United States, and the European Union did not allow for independent oversight of elections. The TSJ then intervened in the leading opposition parties AD, PJ, and VP, replacing the party leaders. For AD, the new head was Bernabé Gutiérrez, a long-time party member and brother of one of the newly appointed CNE members. The existing AD leadership expelled him immediately. In PJ, José Britto was installed as a leader. Britto was one of the "dissident" National Assembly members from the January debacle. PJ had however expelled Britto since December due to allegations of political corruption.[57] In the case of VP, José Gregorio Noriega, Guillermo Luces, and Lucila Ángela Pacheco were appointed by the TSJ. Norriega had been expelled from VP after being implicated in bribing legislators to vote against Guaidó in the January National Assembly election; Luces was expelled after voting for Luis Parra in the January elections; and

Pacheco was a former legislator from the PSUV.[58] Maduro justified his actions by accusing the opposition parties of robbing Venezuela's wealth and plotting a foreign invasion.

In August, members of the National Assembly coalition headed by Guaidó issued a statement rejecting participation in upcoming legislative elections slated for December, citing the TSJ interference in the leaderships of PJ, AD, and VP as well as CNE irregularities regarding participation in the elections. The EU called on Maduro to postpone elections to allow for oversight into improving the transparency of electoral conditions, though Maduro rejected such calls stating that according to the Constitution elections had to be held within the year before a new National Assembly term begins. The legislative elections were held in December with the PSUV winning 91 percent of the seats. Turnout appeared to be an abysmal 30 percent. Unsurprisingly, the new National Assembly installed in January 2021 was rejected by the Lima Group, the OAS, and the United States, with Guaidó receiving international backing.

How has Maduro stayed in power? International backing, military support, and allied private sector interests

Maduro retained international backing from China and Russia that was vital to his remaining in office. Apart from offering sources of credit, in the face of economic collapse and US sanctions, China and Russia continued to import Venezuelan oil as payments on outstanding debts. Both countries traded scarce foodstuffs and medicines for oil in 2018 and 2019 while China sent humanitarian aid following the outbreak of the Covid-19 pandemic. Russia also acted as an intermediary for Venezuelan oil exports, helping to skirt US sanctions.

While China and Russia offered economic support, the military remained the key to Maduro's survival. The influence of the military in multiple spheres of economic activity and the access to dollars that Maduro granted branches of the armed forces, as well as their roles as PSUV candidates elected to govern seven of the country's 23 states, ensured that the military's top brass refused to respond to Guaidó's calls for an uprising.

While international support and the military were key facets helping Maduro retain power, relatively cordial relations with some private capitalists also explain his longevity. While the *bolíbourgeosie* has been discussed previously, the collapsing economic conditions and US sanctions saw a further thawing of relations between Maduro and some former adversaries in the private sector. Just as during Chávez' time in power, Maduro's capacity to divide the political wing of the opposition and maintain control over all branches of the state, at the same time that international pressures compounded an economic crisis, meant that both sides needed each other, and a compromise was reached.

For example, despite a previously tense relationship, Lorenzo Mendoza, the head of Venezuela's largest private company Empresas Polar, stopped publicly criticizing the Maduro government in return for more favorable economic policies.[59] As mentioned previously, Mendoza had links to the most radically critical opposition party, VP. The government began to ease price controls on goods that Mendoza had called for. The measures allowed a small sector of capital to survive, providing some breathing space for Maduro as he confronted US sanctions. Some previously nationalized firms were returned to private operators while expropriated lands were leased to private interests, indicating a reversal of the policies of Chávez. Strong pro-labor laws that prevented workers from being fired without government approval were disregarded, and unions were dismantled. Strict currency controls were eased allowing importers easier access to dollars while also allowing transactions to be carried out in dollars. However, access to these new imports was restricted to those sectors of the population with access to dollars, only about one in ten Venezuelans. Non-price-controlled foodstuffs produced by Venezuelan companies like Polar were unaffordable to the vast majority.

Perhaps, the clearest evidence of the Maduro government's backtracking on the post-neoliberal economic policies of the Chávez era was the "Anti-Blockade Law." According to Vice President Delcy Rodríguez and Foreign Affairs Minister Jorge Arreaza, the new law aimed to offer a "basket of projects" to foreign investors including in oil, gas, and mining, thereby, in the words of VP Rodríguez, allowing Venezuela "to take a step forward, to go on an economic offensive" against the US-led sanctions.[60] The "Anti-Blockade Law" was approved by the ANC and authorized Maduro to suspend the Constitutional and legal impediments to reforming oil laws, including the 1975 nationalization law requiring majority state ownership, management, and administration of extractive enterprises.[61] Moreover, the ANC authorized Maduro to negotiate contract terms with foreign investors without any public oversight.

The content of the "Anti-Blockade Law" was passed to allow Maduro adopt proposals by PDVSA's Executive Office for Planning to a presidential commission tasked with "restructuring" the company so as to boost production. The proposals represented a significant reversal of oil policies from the Chávez era, and in fact closely echoed the stances of opposition politicians Henrique Capriles,[62] Leopoldo López,[63] and Juan Guaidó.[64] As Hellinger[65] emphasizes, the proposals by PDVSA

> closely mirror the neoliberal *apertura petrolera* (oil opening) of the 1990s, which sought to raise productions by reducing royalties and taxes heavily, relaxing national ownership and control over joint ventures between PDV and foreign companies, and transferring dispute resolution from national courts to international forums.

The ANC process granting Maduro executive powers under the Anti-Blockade Law, while side-lining opposition parties who do not recognize or participate in the body, also excluded any debate or space for critical voices from within the broader Chavista movement. Some ANC members were not provided a copy of the text of the new law before voting began while others were blocked from entering the palace to vote.[66]

The ANC's decision-making process regarding the adoption of the "Anti-Blockade Law" was the most evident case of a top-down domination of state-sponsored spaces of participation that were supposedly designed to boost the capacity of organized popular sectors to engage with a left-party and a left-led government, thereby ensuring bottom-up oversight of a process of radical-substantive democratization. Some ANC members openly criticized the content of the proposals to restructure the oil economy, the granting of powers to a president to negotiate with foreign companies without any capacity for public oversight, and the centralized and exclusionary manner in which such executive powers were granted in the ANC.[67] A number of critical leftist political, worker, and popular sector organizations also outlined their rejection of the Law and how it was adopted, stating that the law represented a return to neoliberalism under the tutelage of an exclusionary and totalitarian government.[68]

Rather than engaging with popular critiques regarding the obscure powers granted to the president, Maduro utilized the US sanctions to delegitimize leftist critics, stating that

> There are a lot of things that cannot be discussed about PDVSA. This is like a war. Can you say where your army is going to advance? The people on the left that have criticized PDVSA. … Haven't they noticed the imperialist bombardment against the industry?[69]

This notion of "unity, unity, unity" against opposition destabilization tactics was a recurring feature, not only under Maduro but under Chávez too. However, while unity may be essential to push forward a radical and substantive democratization process, over the course of Maduro's presidencies, it rang increasingly hollow as "unity" came to signify loyalty without internal debate or discussion. I turn now to a discussion of the evolution of party-base relations under Maduro.

Evolving party-base relations under Maduro: 2013–21

While corruption, militarization of the reform process, and the increasingly difficult realities of day-to-day survival fostered tensions between sectors of the popular base and the PSUV, mass-mobilized critique remained somewhat limited. First, given the evolution of party-base relations and the lack of a shared history of autonomous organizing and mobilizing, popular critique of the process was more moderate than one may have expected. It is important here to re-emphasize that the Chavista base should not be understood as one monolithic bloc. It is comprised of various groups with distinct histories and relations to the state. However, for popular sectors who had limited experiences of organizing and mobilizing outside of and against the state before Chávez' election, critiquing Maduro—who was Chavez' hand-picked successor—was understood as counter-revolutionary.

While Chavismo had always relied on a powerful executive, popular sectors had maintained support for the Maduro government because there was a sense that the power was being centralized in "their" government. A common sentiment heard in the José Felix Rivas *barrio* in Petare was that "the government is ours, we chose it, and we voted for it. They are like a part of us."[70] Furthermore, popular actors who had never participated in the political process before the 1998 election of Chávez not only began voting, but were incorporated as citizens, both in a political and in a social sense as they engaged in state-sponsored participative and deliberative spaces such as the CCs, *misiones*, and *comunas*. When one considers that the Chavista governments fundamentally transformed the quality of citizenship of the popular sectors who for decades had been excluded from society, it should not be wholly surprising that overt anti-government critiques were somewhat muted.

While Chavismo boosted popular incorporation, the tying of participatory spaces to resources from the central government also had a deleterious impact on the ability of the popular base to challenge the government. The most obvious example of this during Maduro's presidencies emerged during the economic crisis. The severe food shortages following the economic collapse hit popular sectors hardest, and as such, they were deeply dependent on the government providing subsidized food bags via the *Comités Locales de Abastecimiento y Producción* (Local Committees for Supply and Production—CLAPs) program. The CLAPs originated in April 2016 as partnerships between grassroots organizations and the government to provide food distribution that could overcome the issues of the black market for scarce foodstuffs by getting items directly into people's homes at government-regulated prices. However, the program was heavily criticized by presidential candidate Henri Falcon as being a "cynical form of political patronage … rife with corruption."[71] McCoy[72] states that the CLAPs were part of a system of "social control and intimidation" whereby "political party check-in booths near voting centers" required "hungry voters to register with the party's card and show that they voted in order to get a bag of subsidized food."

While the historical formation of state-sponsored spaces of participation partly explains the lack of contestatory mobilization by popular sectors against government corruption and oversight of a deteriorating economy, a second factor is fundamental to understanding party-base relations. In a polarized scenario with an aggressive opposition ready to pounce on any divisions within the rank and file of Chavismo, popular actors were in a tough position. There was a common sentiment in the *barrios* that the opposition parties were "part of a continuation of the war against the *pueblo*"[73] and that if they were to replace Maduro there would be a return to the exclusion experienced under market democracy. Furthermore, open critiques of the government were limited as there was a belief amongst many interviewees in Petare and El 23 that any popular critique of the government would be "misrepresented by media sources beholden to traditional elites and forces of imperialism." This does not mean there was no popular critique, but rather that public demonstrations of party-base rifts were kept in check. As one *comuna* leader in Petare told me,

> the problems regarding how the *comunas* interact with the state are discussed amongst Chavistas, but at a public level, the *comunas* go hand in hand with the party … We stand by our political party in the face of the MUD.[74]

However, elite destabilization efforts led the government to over-emphasize loyalty, foment intolerance, and allow political fealty to serve as a cover for corruption. As Ellner notes, "a favorite slogan of both Chávez and Maduro, 'Unity, unity and more unity' is often used to exhort followers to close ranks and set aside internal criticism to focus on facing down a ruthless enemy."[75] The lack of space for popular critique of the project allowed "a bureaucracy of the right to be replaced by a bureaucracy of the left,"[76] whereby PSUV inefficiencies and corrupt practices go unpunished, fomenting *desgaste* (exhaustion) with the process amongst many popular sectors. As a *comuna* member from Petare highlights,

> the people leading the government entities and the party have turned everything into a bureaucracy; you now need to have a *palanca* (a contact or influence) just to speak with them. These people are backed by the party, but not by the people like it was supposed to be. And what happens? I am stuck if I don't have a contact to receive my complaint.[77]

Like in

> the Soviet Union and other countries seeking to develop socialism, initiatives have been bureaucratized. People don't want to participate in such a scenario; they don't see any change, it seems to just be more of the same, and in the end, the popular movements just remain entrenched in their own spaces.[78]

The

> government bureaucratized the process, it isolated the revolutionary base and its revolutionary potential. It wasn't just blocked by the opposition, but by the same party that was supposed to be pushing the project. The struggle to get a commune registered for example. To do this you have to register with the state. But the mayors and municipal politicians who are part of the PSUV opposed the idea of autonomous communes.[79]

Chávez

> Called on us to participate. He had the best intentions. He pushed for a revolution, but he was impeded by his own leadership circle. He called for parallel popular power to the state, but he never ended the traditional state. The people who staffed the state institutions were not revolutionaries. They might have put on a red shirt (the color of the PSUV), but the commune, the communal councils, these were the antithesis of the traditional state so of course they opposed us ... Local and regional politicians boycotted our communal run businesses, they would not renew the registration of communes they could not infiltrate and control.[80]

The emergence of the government-sponsored National Constituent Assembly (ANC) following the PSUV's loss in the 2015 parliamentary elections represents a critical juncture in party-base relations. On the one hand, the ANC fostered a spike in popular mobilization as some grassroots Chavista organizations, particularly those that came into existence after the election of Chávez, actively mobilized the base to participate in the election process.

However, while the ANC may have acted as a mobilizational tool for some, for many Chavista sympathizers the ANC damaged the move toward radical democracy while the election process of candidates "made it clear that Maduro would sooner steal than lose an election if his political survival was at stake."[81] Indeed, for critical popular sector voices and organizations, the refusal to accept the 2015 electoral loss and the establishment of the ANC marked the beginning of a transition from an era that combined elements of progressive and regressive centralization to a period of authoritarian centralization.

While the ANC process clearly hindered opposition participation, leftist candidates who sought to run on an alternate ticket to that of the PSUV were also side-lined. In El 23 de Enero for example, exclusion of local Chavistas from the ANC led to protests, highlighting a widening gap between the government and the PSUV on the one hand, and the popular base on the other. On the 30 of June 2017, the announcement of the ANC election results which showed that the slate of representatives from El 23 was going to be comprised entirely of PSUV candidates led to protest with local *colectivos*—armed civil groups in popular *barrios* who have been key supporters of the Bolivarian process—crying fraud.[82] Valentín Santana, leader of La Piedrita—one of the longest-serving *colectivos*—had been postulated for the ANC by a coalition of local groups, independent of the PSUV. His proposals had included loyalty to Chávez, more independent power for the communes, a war against the bureaucracy, and maximum penalties for corrupt traitors. The exclusion of Santana and other local independent candidates and the subsequent protests highlighted the sense that more radical leftist currents were being excluded in the government-controlled ANC.

A "Chavismo-no-Madurista" movement made up of "critical Chavistas" was, albeit tentatively, becoming more vocal. The *Marea Socialista* (Socialist Wave) group, for example, represented a critical-left voice distinct from the PSUV. They denounced the lack of universal citizen participation in the formation of the ANC. In August 2017, deputies Eustoquio Contreras, Germán Ferrer, and Ivone Tellez separated from the PSUV to form an alternative Left bloc in the National Assembly. UPP 89, a new political party comprised of Leftist groups emerged in opposition to the PSUV, claiming to represent and adhere to the ideals Chávez. Furthermore, the Communist Party and the Patria Para Todos (Fatherland for All—PPT) party sought to construct a space for a leftist critique within Chavismo.

The elections for mayors in December 2017 saw the PSUV win 308 out of 335 municipalities. However, the centralized, top-down nature of candidate selection further stoked the growing rifts between the radical popular base of Chavismo and the PSUV leadership. In several states in the run-up to the elections, allies of the PSUV in the Gran Polo Patriótico—the coalition of Chavista parties—sought to select their own candidates rather than allowing the PSUV to determine the entire ticket. The case of Angel Prado, a commune leader in the El Maizal commune in the state of Lara, is emblematic of base-party tensions.

A press release signed by dozens of Venezuelan intellectuals and social movement activists described how the National Electoral Council (CNE) sought to block Prado's candidacy.[83] However, Prado overcame the CNE efforts to prevent his name from appearing on the electoral ticket and ran as a candidate for PPT. Furthermore, despite Prado gaining 57.45 percent of the vote compared to the PSUV candidate Jean Ortiz' 34.07, the CNE awarded Prado's votes to Ortiz due to alleged irregularities. The press release highlighted the growing tension between some sectors of the base and the government, stating that

> This conflict between the constituent power of the communal people … and the bureaucracy clearly expresses a revolutionary disjuncture. If the state (the CNE and the ANC presidency) and a part of the ruling elite continue to deepen the decisions they have been making, they will be moving away from democratic legality and their commitment to socialism.

While the government dominated the municipal elections, the growing critical Chavista bloc did have some electoral success, with 500,000 votes cast across the country for the PPT and Communist parties, creating a "leftist reference point within Chavismo."[84]

However, despite some organizations—especially those with strong organizational histories—having the capacity to challenge the PSUV leadership, they were side-lined by the PSUV, fracturing the potential for mass informal contestatory mobilization to erupt. Even when popular organizations maintained a critical support for the government in the face of elite and international pressures, "the government largely accepted the support while challenging the critique, labeling those who questioned the process in the time of difficulty as anti-revolutionaries or *derechistas* (Right-wingers)."[85] A key popular sector organizer at the national level told me that

> We brought together 50–60 communes and 300 social organizations. We debated about the direction of the process for three days. We had government ministers, deputies in attendance. But our suggestions about responding to the economic crisis were ignored. In fact, when we critiqued the government, we were called traitors. They (PSUV officials) made people afraid to come out and complain. The government used the pockets of communal council members to keep them quiet ... They would threaten to cut off their funds. It was a form of social control. Anybody labelled a traitor had the doors of the state closed to them.[86]

The consequence of such PSUV responses to critique on those popular sector members who had not organized politically before Chavismo was that they remained silent, even as the process slid further from the original goals of the post-neoliberal project.

In the run-up to 2018 presidential elections, just as within the opposition-bloc, there was debate within the critical Chavista organizations over whether to participate or not. *Marea Socialista* stated that

> The regime has engaged in electoral window-dressing beginning with the fraudulent Constituent Assembly. The elections for governors and mayors, and now with the 'presidential', they are attempting to maintain a democratic appearance where in fact there is only a state-led politics of repression, intimidation, and terror toward a population exhausted from the economic crisis and the social disaster.[87]

However, despite the widening rift between critical Chavistas and the PSUV leadership, the Communist Party and the PPT backed Maduro's candidacy for the elections. The PCV gave their support as they recognized that "the growing immoral, illegal, and criminal interventionist aggression from US imperialism and its allies in Europe against the Bolivarian process puts at the risk the national liberation" project set in motion by Chávez.[88] Similarly, the PPT stated that despite issues of "sectarianism, bureaucracy and corruption" in the government, it was necessary to defend Maduro against "imperialism" and the "unconventional warfare" being waged against the country. The radical CRBZ group also backed Maduro, stating that "beyond any internal contradictions there may be in regards to methods and practices, we understand that the current moment demands that we close ranks because there is a greater contradiction to resolve: the confrontation with imperialism."[89]

Marea Socialista captured the realities of the 2018 moment, highlighting the authoritarian centralization of power by Maduro and the PSUV leadership, at the same time that he made use of US sanctions to justify such actions. The group stated that the indiscriminate detention of opposition politicians accused of conspiracy; detention of citizens for protesting worsening economic conditions; violent repression and killings of Chavista activists who protested against the government; and the extra-judicial killings carried out by the state security forces in popular barrios in the name of security indicated that the PSUV bureaucracy headed by Maduro and Diosdado Cabello was systematically seeking to eliminate every aspect of democracy and to instill fear in those who challenged the leadership's strategies.[90] While the progressive centralization of Chávez supported the mobilization and participation of popular movements to resist imperial politics, the authoritarian centralization by Maduro allowed for indiscriminate repression of the population while simultaneously seeking the support of sectors of capital by delivering them the nation's resources in order to manage to deliver something to a desperately impoverished popular sector, thereby preventing mass popular uprisings.

The efforts to sideline and repress more radical demands from below and to instead work with branches of the private sector to keep the economy—and Maduro's government afloat were doubly destructive. Apart from their obviously undemocratic nature, repressing critical voices also fractured the very unity required to confront oppositional destabilization tactics. During Maduro's presidencies

> the *comuna* project has been overlooked … In the face of economic warfare he chose to make an alliance with the bourgeoisie. But we feel this was an error; if we are talking about economic warfare, about class struggle, then you should be behind the people in order to confront the enemy of the popular sectors.[91]

By sidelining critical popular sectors while confronting the radical wing of the opposition-bloc and international destabilization efforts, "the Madurista bureaucracy with its pro-neoliberal, authoritarian and anti-popular politics … have demoralized the very social base necessary to face such aggression."[92]

Following the presidential elections in 2018, the PSUV held a party congress with Maduro and party vice president Diosdado Cabello calling for unity amongst Chavistas against the opposition. Maduro needed a united party with all factions supporting him as it became increasingly evident that economic reforms that could trigger popular discontent were required. As such, continuing the trend under his leadership, internal critics who questioned the verticalist nature of the PSUV were pushed aside. A key voice in the commune movement told me that critical union leaders were being detained for months without trial while state armed forces were killing antagonistic voices under the veil of a clampdown on local gang activity.[93]

Maduro announced plans to gradually increase gas prices over two years. Rising gas prices had been the spark for the 1989 *Caracazo*, and Maduro's willingness to even discuss such measures highlights the complete fracturing of his economic power, as well as his belief that contestatory mobilization could be controlled. As a commune organizer in Lara state told me,

> today we have a government that has made a neoliberal pact with the opposition, with the owners of capital ... We are returning to the latifundio and to labor flexibilization like we had in the 4th Republic. They don't allow union organization. We are losing all of the rights of the workers that we worked for with Chávez. They have criminalized the left ... We have unionists in prison for defending our labor rights.[94]

As discussed above, the Maduro-controlled ANC and the "Anti-Blockade Law" opened the way for a return to neoliberal style management of Venezuela's resources. In many regards, Venezuela's post-neoliberal process came full circle under Maduro. While the traditional elite may have lost control over access to the favorable rents that were paid by foreign extractive capitalists, a new PSUV bureaucracy with the backing of a military elite had replaced them. Meanwhile, spaces for a deepened quality of democratic participation had ossified while the quality of social citizenship declined to levels worse than during the crises of the 1980s and 1990s. While popular sector voices and interests were excluded under the programmatically aligning AD-COPEI Punto Fijo party system, now they were excluded by a simultaneously polarizing-converging PSUV-MUD party system in which both sides sought to obliterate the other in order to determine who would recoup the spoils of a rentier oil economy managed according to neoliberal rational.

I return to discuss the Venezuelan case and the conjunctural historical and emergent factors which shaped the emergence, development, and outcomes of the post-neoliberal process in Chapter 8. The long-term legacies of the process are then outlined. Following a comparative analysis of the Venezuelan and Bolivian processes, the broader lessons from the cases for democratic theory and for progressive outsider-led efforts to escape the confines of market democracy are discussed. In the following chapters, I turn to an examination of the Bolivian case.

Notes

1 George Ciccariello-Maher, *Building the Commune: Radical Democracy in Venezuela* (London and New York: Verso Books, 2016): 77.

2 John Bellamy Foster, "Chávez and the Communal State: On the Transition to Socialism in Venezuela," *Monthly Review* 66, no. 11 (2015): 12.

3 Figures cited in Edgardo Lander, "Venezuela: Terminal Crisis of the Rentier Petro-State? *TNI*, October 2 (2014), Retrieved https://www.tni.org/en/publication/venezuela-terminal-crisis-of-the-rentier-petro-state.

4 Ibid., 8.

5 Ciccariello-Maher, *Building the Commune*, 12; Foster, "Chávez and the Communal State," 12.
6 Lander, "Venezuela: Terminal Crisis," 9.
7 Ibid.
8 Ciccariello-Maher, *Building the Commune*, 53.
9 From System Collapse to "Chavista Hegemony: The Party Question in Bolivarian Venezuela," *Latin American Perspectives* 44, no. 1 (2017): 18.
10 Barry Cannon, "As Clear as MUD: Characteristics, Objectives, and Strategies of the Opposition in Bolivarian Venezuela," *Latin American Politics and Society* 56, no. 4 (2014): 49–70.
11 Alejandro Velasco, "Christmas in Caracas? Worse than the Grinch," *The Nation*, December 16 (2016): Retrieved https://www.thenation.com/article/christmas-in-caracas-worse-than-the-grinch/.
12 Hetland, "From System Collapse," 17.
13 Barry Cannon and John Brown, "Venezuela 2016: El Año de Vivir Peligrosamente," *Revista de Ciencia Política Santiago* 37, no. 2 (2017): 616.
14 Miguel Angel Santos, "Venezuela: Running on Empty," *LASA Forum* XLVIII, no. 1 (2017): 58–61.
15 Gabriel Hetland, "Why Is Venezuela in Crisis?" *The Nation* August 17 (2016): Retrieved https://www.thenation.com/article/why-is-venezuela-in-crisis/.
16 Provea, *Situación de los Derechos Humanos en Venezuela* (Caracas: Provea, 2017): Retrieved https://www.venezuelablog.org/prologue-proveas-2017-annual-report-state-human-rights-venezuela/.
17 Manuel Sutherland, "A Critique to the Political Economy of 'XXI Century Socialism': Private Sector Takeover of Oil Revenue, Import Policy and Capital Outflow," *Estudios Latinoamericanos* 38 (2016): 39–63.
18 Mike Gonzalez, "Being Honest about Venezuela," *Jacobin* August 7 (2017): Retrieved https://www.jacobinmag.com/2017/07/venezuela-maduro-helicopter-attack-psuv-extractivism-oil.
19 Alejandro Velasco, "Explaining the Venezuelan Crisis," *TRT World* October 25 (2016): Retrieved http://www.trtworld.com/opinion/why-is-the-venezuelan-economy-so-prone-to-collapse-213821.
20 Julia Buxton, "Venezuela after Chávez," *New Left Review* 99 (2016): 15.
21 Mark Weisbrot, "Venezuela's Economic Crisis: Does It Mean that the Left Has Failed?" *Truth-out.org* October 23 (2016): Retrieved http://www.truth out.org/news/item/38094-venezuela-s-economic-crisis-does-it-mean-that-the-left-has failed.
22 Sutherland, "A Critique to the Political Economy of 'XXI Century Socialism.'"
23 Hetland, "Why Is Venezuela in Crisis?"
24 Margarita López Maya, "Populism, 21st-Century Socialism and Corruption in Venezuela," *Thesis Eleven* 149, no. 1 (2018): 77.
25 Gabriel Hetland, "The State of the Left in Latin America: A Disillusioned Revolution in Venezuela," *NACLA* July 21 (2017): Retrieved https://nacla.org/news/2017/10/04/state-left-latin-america-disillusioned-revolution-venezuela.
26 Interview with activist in the communes movement, Caracas, 2016.
27 Daniel Hellinger, "Constituent Assembly Is Obstacle, Not Solution to the Crisis," *Venezuela Dialogue* June 29 (2017): Retrieved https://venezueladialogue.com/constituent-assembly-is-obstacle-not-solution-to-the-crisis/.
28 Ibid.
29 Gonzalez, "Being Honest about Venezuela."
30 Dorothy Kronick and Francisco Rodríguez, "15 O. Fraud or Fatigue?," *Venezuela Blog* October 26 (2017): Retrieved https://venezuelablog.org/15o-fraud-fatigue/.
31 Gonzalez, "Democracy as Political Strategy."
32 Kronick and Rodríguez, "15 O. Fraud or Fatigue."

33 Tomás Straka, "La Tragedia de la Oposición Venezolana," *Nueva Sociedad* November (2017): Retrieved http://nuso.org/articulo/la-tragedia-de-la-oposicion-venezolana/.
34 Geoff Ramsey, "Venezuela's Opposition Coalition in Crisis: A Primer," *Venezuela Blog* October 27 (2017): Retrieved https://venezuelablog.org/venezuelas-opposition-coalition-crisis-primer/.
35 US Department of the Treasury, "Treasury Sanctions Ten Venezuelan Government Officials," November 9 (2017): Retrieved https://www.treasury.gov/press-center/press-releases/Pages/sm0214.aspx.
36 Mark Weisbrot, "Trump Doubles Down on Sanctions and Regime Change for Venezuela," *Alter Net* November 13 (2017): Retrieved https://www.alternet.org/world/trump-doubles-down-sanctions-and-regime-change-venezuela.
37 Ibid.
38 Financial Times, "US Urged to Impose Full Embargo on Venezuelan Oil," *Financial Times* November 8 (2017): Retrieved https://www.ft.com/content/286ad07a-c415-11e7-b2bb-322b2cb39656.
39 Luc Cohen, "Tillerson Raises the Specter of US Sanctions on Venezuelan Oil," *Reuters* February 4 (2018): Retrieved https://www.reuters.com/article/us-argentina-usa-tillerson/tillerson-raises-specter-of-u-s-sanctions-on-venezuelan-oil-idUSKBN1FO0P3.
40 Mark Weisbrot, "Trump Administration tries to Torpedo Venezuelan Elections as it Intensifies 'Regime Change' Efforts," *CEPR* March 3 (2018): Retrieved https://cepr.net/trump-administration-tries-to-torpedo-venezuelan-elections-as-it-intensifies-regime-change-efforts/.
41 Gill and Brown, "Two Decades of Imperial Failure;" Steve Ellner, "After Elections, Intransigence in Venezuela," *NACLA* May 25 (2018): Retrieved https://nacla.org/news/2018/05/29/after-elections-intransigence-venezuela.
42 Jeffrey Sachs and Mark Weisbrot, "Economic Sanctions as Collective Punishment: The Case of Venezuela," *CEPR* April 25 (2019): Retrieved https://cepr.net/report/economic-sanctions-as-collective-punishment-the-case-of-venezuela/.
43 UN Human Rights Council, "Preliminary Findings of the Visit to the Bolivarian Republic of Venezuela by the Special Rapporteur on the Negative Impact of Unilateral Coercive Measures on the Enjoyment of Human Rights," February 12 (2021): Retrieved https://reliefweb.int/report/venezuela-bolivarian-republic/preliminary-findings-visit-bolivarian-republic-venezuela.
44 Online Interview, Atenea Jiménez of the National Network of Communeros, 2021.
45 Ibid.
46 Luc Cohen and Brian Ellsworth, "New U.S. Sanctions on Venezuela Protect Citgo from Seizure – Guaido," *Reuters* August 6 (2019): Retrieved https://www.reuters.com/article/venezuela-politics-usa-citgo-idUSL2N2520PJ. Marissa Luck, "Two Venezuelan Governments, Two Boards Battle for Control Over Citgo Petroleum," *Houston Chronicle*, July 18 (2019): Retrieved https://www.houstonchronicle.com/business/energy/article/Two-Venezuelan-governments-two-boards-battle-for-14106364.php.
47 John McEvoy, "Juan Guaidó's Regime Change Lobby," *Venezuela Analysis* June 30 (2019): Retrieved https://venezuelanalysis.com/analysis/14604.
48 Barry Cannon, "Juan Guaidó's Policy Proposals: 'The Venezuela to Come' or the Venezuela that has already been?" *NACLA* March 12 (2019): Retrieved https://nacla.org/news/2019/03/12/juan-guaid%C3%B3%E2%80%99s-policy-proposals-%E2%80%9C-venezuela-come%E2%80%9D-or-venezuela-has-already-been. Barry Cannon, "Socialism Equals Death, Market Equals Life: Anti-socialist and Pro-Market Policy Discourse among the Contemporary Venezuelan Opposition," *Les Cahiers de Framespa* (online) 36 (2021).

49 Rafael Moro Martins and Ryan Grim, "Secret IDB Proposal would give $48 Billion Infusion to Boost Venezuela's Economy – But only after Regime Change," *The Intercept* April 18 (2019): Retrieved https://theintercept.com/2019/04/18/venezuela-idb-maduro-guaido/.

50 Cited in W. J. Hennigan, "Inside John Bolton's Month-Long P.R. Campaign against Venezuela's Government," *TIME* January 30 (2019): Retrieved https://time.com/5516920/inside-john-boltons-month-long-p-r-campaign-against-venezuelas-government/.

51 Ociel Alí López, "Venezuela's Opposition at a Crossroads," *NACLA* February 22 (2020): Retrieved https://nacla.org/news/2020/03/03/venezuela%E2%80%99s-opposition-crossroads-disponible-en-espa%C3%B1ol.

52 For excellent discussion see Francisco Rodríguez, "¿Cuál es la Verdadera Relación de Fuerzas en la Asamblea Nacional de Venezuela?" January 11 (2020): Retrieved https://franciscorodriguez.net/2020/01/11/cual-es-la-verdadera-relacion-de-fuerzas-en-la-asamblea-nacional-de-venezuela/.

53 Patrick Iber, "The Ongoing Crisis in Venezuela: A Forum," *Dissent* February 7 (2020): Retrieved https://www.dissentmagazine.org/online_articles/ongoing-crisis-venezuela-maduro-guaido.

54 Steve Ellner, "Regime Change made in the U.S.A," *NACLA* February 8 (2019): Retrieved https://nacla.org/news/2019/02/10/regime-change-%E2%80%9Cmade-usa%E2%80%9D.

55 For details of the above discussion see links to an array of sources cited in Rafael Uzcátegui, "Venezuela: The Card Game Under the Table," *Venezuela Blog* May 13 (2020): Retrieved https://www.venezuelablog.org/venezuela-card-game-table/.

56 Primera Justicia, "La Dirección Nacional de Primero Justicia, Teniendo en Cuenta la Grave Crisis que Vive el País," May 8 (2020): Retrieved https://twitter.com/Pr1meroJusticia/status/1258799584035430401/photo/1.

57 David Smilde and Dimitris Pantoulas, "Maduro Uses Supreme Court to Remake Opposition," *Venezuela Blog* June 17 (2020): Retrieved https://www.venezuelablog.org/venezuela-weekly-maduro-uses-supreme-court-remake-opposition/.

58 Human Rights Watch, "Venezuela: Rulings Threaten Free and Fair Elections," *HRW* July 7 (2020): Retrieved https://www.hrw.org/news/2020/07/07/venezuela-rulings-threaten-free-and-fair-elections.

59 The discussion of Mendoza is drawn from the article by Anatoly Kurmanaev, "Venezuela's Socialists Embrace Business, Making Partner of a 'Parasite'," *The New York Times* February 23 (2020): Retrieved https://www.nytimes.com/2020/02/23/world/americas/venezuela-economy-polar.html.

60 TeleSur, "Venezuela's New Anti-Blockade Law to Protect Foreign Investment," *TeleSur* October 14 (2020): Retrieved https://www.telesurenglish.net/news/Venezuelas-New-Anti-Blockade-Law-To-Protect-Foreign-Investment-20201014-0001.html.

61 Daniel Hellinger, "Maduro's Brown New Deal for Venezuela," *NACLA* February 5 (2021): Retrieved https://nacla.org/venezuela-pvd-oil-maduro.

62 Reuters, "What Does Henrique Capriles Want for Venezuela," January 27 (2012): Retrieved https://www.reuters.com/article/uk-venezuela-capriles-policies/factbox-what-does-henrique-capriles-want-for-venezuela-idUKTRE80Q1IQ20120127.

63 Leopoldo López and Gustavo Baquero, "Venezuela Energética: Propuesta para el bienestar y el Progreso de los Venezolanos," (2017): Retrieved https://www.leopoldolopez.com/wp-content/uploads/2018/04/ResumenejecutivoVE.pdf.

64 Cannon, "Juan Guaidó's Policy Proposals."

65 Hellinger, "Maduro's Brown New Deal for Venezuela."
66 Maru Morales, "Algunos Constituyentes Desconocían Texto de 'Ley Antibloqueo' y a Otros les Impidieron Entrar al Palacio," *Crónica Uno* October 9 (2020): Retrieved https://cronica.uno/algunos-constituyentes-desconocian-texto-de-ley-antibloqueo-y-a-otros-les-impidieron-entrar-al-palacio/.
67 Maru Morales, "Constituyentes Earle Herrera y María Alejandra Díaz Cuestionan Secretismo de 'Ley Antibloqueo'," *Crónica Uno* October 8 (2020): Retrieved https://cronica.uno/earle-herrera-maria-alejandra-diaz-cuestionan-secretismo-ley-antibloqueo/.
68 Aporrea, "Diversas Organizaciones Convocan a Firmar en Rechazo a la Ley Antibloqueo y Exigiendo un Referendo Popular," *Aporrea* October 12 (2020): Retrieved https://www.aporrea.org/actualidad/n359531.html.
69 Maduro cited in "Presidente Maduro Prorroga la 'Comisión Presidencial Alí Rodriguez Araque' en Pdvsa," *Aporrea* October 8 (2020): Retrieved https://www.aporrea.org/energia/n358105.html.
70 Interview with communal council participant in José Filix Rivas, Petare.
71 Cited in Andreina Aponte and Ana Isabel Martinez, "For Poor Venezuelans, a Box of Food May Sway the Vote for Maduro," *Reuters* March 12 (2018): Retrieved https://www.reuters.com/article/us-venezuela-politics-food/for-poor-venezuelans-a-box-of-food-may-sway-vote-for-maduro-idUSKCN1GO173.
72 Jennifer McCoy, "Could a Challenger Unseat Maduro in Venezuela?" *Latin American Advisor* March 16 (2018): Retrieved http://venezuelablog.org/wp-content/uploads/2018/03/LAA180316.pdf.
73 Interview with communal council member, Petare, August 2016.
74 Interview, Petare, July 2016.
75 Steve Ellner, "Venezuela's Fragile Revolution: From Chávez to Maduro," *Monthly Review* 69, no. 5 (2017): 10.
76 Interview with commune and UBCh member in Petare, June 2016.
77 Interview, Petare, July 2016.
78 Interview with activist in the commune movement, Caracas, July 2016.
79 Electronic interview with national commune organizer, March 2021.
80 Ibid.
81 Alejandro Velasco, "The Pyrrhic Victories of Venezuela's President," *Current History* 117, no. 796 (2018): 73–6.
82 Alejandro Velasco, "Chavismo en Crisis, Chavismo en Disputa," *Nueva Sociedad* 271 (2017): 4–12.
83 Statement cited in Rachael Boothroyd Rojas, "We Demand Recognition for the Chavista and Communard Peoples' Right to Participation," *Venezuela Analysis* December 13 (2017): Retrieved https://venezuelanalysis.com/analysis/13549.
84 Eduardo Samán cited in "La Victoria Más Importante es que se Logró Crear una Referencia Dentro del Chavismo de Izquierda y Tenemos que Consolidarlo," *Aporrea* December 16 (2017): Retrieved https://www.aporrea.org/ddhh/n318588.html.
85 Interview with organizer in the Comuna Rogelio Castillo Gamarra, Petare, August 2016.
86 Electronic interview, March 23, 2021.
87 Marea Socialista, "'Presidenciales' e Internacionalización de la Crisis: Adónde va Venezuela?" *Aporrea* February 13 (2018): Retrieved https://www.aporrea.org/actualidad/n320956.html.
88 Cited in Rachael Boothroyd Rojas, "Leftist Parties Back Maduro as Opposition's Henri Falcon Confirms Presidential Candidacy," *Venezuela Analysis* February 27 (2018): Retrieved https://venezuelanalysis.com/news/13685.

89 Kevin Rangel, "CRBZ: Venezuela's Left Must Unite behind Maduro to Defeat Imperialism," *Venezuela Analysis* March 8 (2018): Retrieved https://venezuelanalysis.com/analysis/13711.
90 Marea Socialista, "Presidenciales."
91 Interview with long-time political activist and commune organizer, Caracas, July 2016.
92 Marea Socialista, "Presidenciales."
93 Online interview, 2019.
94 Online interview, March 2021.

5 Crisis of market democracy and making space for outsider Evo Morales

Bolivia in historical context

In this chapter, I examine the crisis of market democracy and the emergence of outsider Evo Morales in Bolivia. The nature of the shallowing and narrowing of democracy, the development of an unstable democratic equilibrium, the form and extent of anti-neoliberal protests, party-system collapse, the coalescence of competing social blocs around divergent democratic models, and the nature of outsider-base relations are examined. The chapter concludes by raising questions regarding how such antecedent factors set the scene for, and fed back onto, post-election power struggles between the left-led government, an opposition bloc, and the popular base.

The protest waves that erupted in response to market democracy and the subsequent election of Evo Morales must be understood against the backdrop of Bolivia's 1952 revolution and the national-populist era that followed. Many of the key actors and institutions that would influence later democratization moments emerged out of and in response to this period. As such, the discussion of Bolivia's historical factors examines the emergence of the nationalist-populist state in the 1960s and 1970s; the adoption of neoliberalism; the waves of popular protest against marketizing reforms and the exclusionary nature of their adoption; the emergence of Evo Morales and the MAS movement-party; and the election of outsider-candidate Morales to the presidency.

Revolution, coups and counter-coups: limited national populism and military regimes

Pre-1952, Bolivia was marked by the promotion of liberal capitalism based around tin and silver exports and witnessed a tiny white-mestizo elite control the state as indigenous land was occupied and converted into enormous landholdings. Following a revolution in 1952, a nationalist-populist accumulation model emerged with the state playing a much more active role in the productive process. The democratic regime was dominated by the *Movimiento Nacionalista Revolucionario* (National Revolutionary Movement—MNR) party led by Víctor Paz Estenssoro and Hernán Siles Suazo. At the heart of the 1952 struggles was the miners' union which would become the militant core of the principal trade union confederation, the *Central Obrera*

DOI: 10.4324/9781003262466-6

Boliviana (Bolivian Workers Central—COB). Facing the militant miners under the COB, the MNR government nationalized the mines and a state mining company, COMIBOL was established to manage tin extraction.[1] Agrarian reform as well as extensive state employment boosted the legitimacy of the new government, while a state oil and gas company YPFB was also established. Import substitution industrialization policies were adopted with subsidies, price regulations, as well as credit agencies for the major agrarian and mining sectors. Moreover, the quality of popular sector social citizenship was boosted via subsidized basic foodstuffs, energy, utilities, transport, and credit for farmers. A corporatist system emerged with COB-affiliated urban and peasant unions, industry associations, and government officials given key positions in ministries and credit agencies that regulated their corresponding sectors.

The MNR, however, was never a socialist party, and as the COB mobilized against moderate MNR policies, including calling for general strikes, the corporatist system that maintained the ISI period collapsed in 1964. The government headed by Paz Estenssoro was ousted in a coup and replaced with a populist military regime led by former vice president René Barrientos and army chief Alfredo Ovando Candía. In 1971, with the leftist General Juan Jose Torres in power, the domestic and regional right, as well as an anti-communist Nixon administration, supported a right-wing coup led by Hugo Banzer. Until 1974, Banzer ruled via the Nationalist Popular Front that included the increasingly right-leaning MNR as well as the fascist *Falange Socialista Boliviana* (Bolivian Socialist Falange—FSB). Banzer ousted the civilian parties in 1974 and four years of a brutal military regime followed that saw the COB outlawed and leftist leaders tortured and disappeared. It is important to note that under the dictatorship, millions of dollars of cheap credit subsidized the agro-capitalists in the eastern province of Santa Cruz who would later expand into finance, industry, and the services sector.[2]

During the Banzer regime, and drawing from the left-wing of the MNR, the *Movimiento de Izquierda Revolucionario* (Leftists Revolutionary Movement—MIR) party formed in the early 1970s. The MIR would play a central role in Bolivian politics in the 1980s and 1990s. Moreover, under pressure for a return to democracy from US president Jimmy Carter, Banzer called elections in 1978 and forged the *Alianza Democrática Nacional* party (National Democratic Alliance—ADN) which would also go on to play a central role in Bolivian politics.

Following fraudulent elections that saw Banzer's chosen candidate, Juan Pereda, elected ahead of the left-leaning former president Hernán Siles, a dizzying series of military coups and counter-coups were the background to a new stage of democratization struggles in which labor and peasant mobilization were crucial in restoring civilian leaders to office. During the transition to democracy, the COB played a central role in helping the peasant movement to form a politically independent, unified campesino organization, the *Confederación Sindical Unica de Trabajadores Campesinos Bolivianos* (Unitary Syndical Confederation of Peasant Workers of Bolivia—CSUTCB) who represented highland peasants. Massive strikes and roadblocks led by the COB and CSUTCB brought the country to a halt and military rule was ended with Siles taking office at the head of a coalition of leftist parties, the *Unidad Democrática Popular* (Democratic Popular Union). The coalition would implode, however, as a combination of the Latin American debt crisis and an economy in tatters after years of military mismanagement meant that Siles sought to adopt an orthodox economic stabilization program. With the COB and CSUTCB mobilizing against the reforms, and with inflation reaching astronomical levels, Siles called for elections in 1985, the year that would mark a radical shift towards a marketized citizenship regime.

The turn to market democracy

A fragmented multiparty system emerged following the long period of military-dominated rule where the MNR, ADN, and the MIR engaged in "promiscuous power-sharing"[3] for nearly 20 years in what was known as a "pacted-democracy."[4] A "neoliberal oligarchic" regime began in 1985 with the introduction of an orthodox neoliberal structural adjustment program called the New Economic Policy.[5] As Webber[6] describes,

> this cycle was defined by the rise of domestic financial capital subordinated to transnational companies and international financial capital, the dramatic liberalization of trade, the penetration of foreign capital of the Bolivian economy, and the wholesale privatization of the country's natural resources, strategic state-owned enterprises, and public services.

The New Economic Policy was designed by the IMF and implemented under decree 21060 by Paz Estenssoro (1985–89) of the formerly revolutionary MNR party. Currency devaluation, free-floating exchange rates, and interest rate liberalization were adopted while price and wage controls were eliminated. Public sector spending declined and state lending and subsidies to the mining and traditional agricultural sector were restricted. Value-added taxes were adopted, and tariffs were slashed to encourage international trade. A central aim of the reforms was to destroy the COB, in particular the militant miners' unions. The majority of state-owned mines were shut, with the mining workforce cut from 30,000 to 7,000. Thirty-one thousand public sector jobs were lost, and 35,000 manufacturing jobs were lost to international competition and economic contraction. Moreover, labor reforms led to a flex-labor force that gave employers freedom to hire and fire at will.[7]

The "imposition of the New Economic Policy by 'shock treatment' caused profound economic and political exclusion of the popular sectors, deeply threatening their livelihood and leaving them without defences within established political institutions."[8] While popular sectors were excluded from policymaking, and bore the socio-economic burdens of the reforms, the Bolivian financial and mining elite played instrumental roles alongside IFI advisors and US-trained state technocrats in the implementation of the neoliberal model.[9] Gonzalo Sánchez de Lozada, a millionaire and large stockholder in COMSUR—one of Bolivia's largest mining companies—was designated as head of the economic change team by Paz Estenssoro.

De Lozada became president (1993–97) and adopted further neoliberal reforms that eroded the quality of political and socio-economic citizenship for popular sectors. A privatization drive under the 1994 Capitalization Law saw the majority of shares of publicly owned companies in energy, telecommunications and transport transferred to multinational corporations.[10] Under the capitalization plan, there was a drive to establish Bolivia as a gas hub for energy integration within the global market. De Lozada worked with the World Bank to write a new hydrocarbons law with the aim to offer ideal investment conditions (low tax, high profits) to attract private multinational oil and gas companies to extract Bolivian resources. The World Bank did not want to trigger popular unrest and so avoided a wholesale privatization of state-owned YPFB. However, the state firm was to be sidelined and the most lucrative new sites of exploration were to be offered to foreign companies. YPFB was to be "capitalized" with private money, effectively transforming it from a public to a private company whose social and redistributive capacities would be strangled as the firm focused on competing with foreign businesses for access to Bolivian exploration blocks. As Gustafson[11] emphasizes,

> the World Bank plan would allow the Bolivian government some revenue. Indeed, the government was not viable, nor could it pay its mountainous debt, if the bank did not account for this. Yet the law sought to appease investors by offering them generous conditions such as lower taxation (50 percent) and royalty rates (12.5 percent). The idea was to keep the government and YPFB on minimal fiscal life support, and to prioritize the return to foreign investors and creditors.

The plan was enshrined in the 1996 hydrocarbons law "written by and for fossil capital."[12] The privatization plan for Bolivia's natural resources would, however, trigger mass popular movements in the early 2000s.

The deepening turn toward a market democracy under de Lozada witnessed the simultaneous narrowing and shallowing of democratic quality for popular sectors as the interests of capital were organized into policymaking while the interests of popular sectors were organized out. One of the biggest impacts of the privatization drive was the radical flexibilization—meaning precaritization—of work. Labor market shifts included massive job losses; subcontracting of work to non-unionized labor, including child labor; the creation of obstacles to unionization via the atomization of workers as factories were replaced by smaller workshops; and informalization of work as the number of informal workers without social security, health benefits, or decent wages grew from 60 percent of the workforce in 1985 to 68 percent in 1995.[13]

A shift in agricultural policy witnessed transnational corporations and large domestic agricultural enterprises based in the *media luna*[14] departments

Santa Cruz, Beni, Pando, and Tarija lead a drive to insertion in the global economy. Cotton, sugarcane, peanuts, soy, timber, and fruit and vegetable production as well as cattle ranching were dominated by agro-industrial capital in the *media luna*. Peasant production units in the altiplano could not compete with the agro-industry in the lowlands of Santa Cruz, and peasants lost land, credit and markets for their crops. Peasants had to seek seasonal labor and needed nonfarm income to sustain themselves, fostering an urbanization of rural labor, adding to the growing informal employment in towns and cities. Moreover, reductions or eliminations of subsidies to staple foodstuffs, utilities, fuel, and transport worsened the economic exclusion of swathes of society where poverty levels remained above 50 percent in urban areas and 77 percent in rural zones.

While the quality of democracy narrowed for popular sectors, it also became shallow as policymaking was dominated by the interests of capital, guided by supranational agencies, and decisions were taken in a technocratic and unaccountable manner. Excessive use of presidential decrees, scant legislative debate, and a lack of consideration for the interests, demands and priorities of subordinate social groups became the norm. As de Lozada admitted, the market reforms served the political aim of muzzling popular sector voices by weakening organized labor, especially the COB. Informalization, public sector downsizing, and the restructuring of COMIBOL atomized the labor movement and weakened the FSTMB, the mine workers union who were the militant core of the COB. While popular sector voices were excluded, beginning with the 1980s debt crisis, the influence of transnational actors and agencies including the IMF, the World Bank, and the US state in setting domestic Bolivian economic policy increased.

Monedero[15] critically summarizes this era, noting that "a small group of wealthy, light-skinned agribusiness and banking families" whose fortunes were based in the eastern lowlands around Santa Cruz controlled the state and policymaking. Indeed, as Monedero continues, despite the 1952 popular upheaval, the state that emerged from the Banzer dictatorship in the 1980s "reproduced the oligarchic features of the 19th century in liberal-democratic form ... Party coalitions—MNR, ADN, the formerly left MIR—colluded to select wealthy scions of the agro-financial elite, typified by Gonzalo Sánchez de Lozada." The Andean tin mines, a historic center of worker militancy, were closed while the oligarchic families enriched themselves by selling off state assets such as gas, oil, telecoms, electricity, railways, and water.[16] However, the efforts from the 1980s through the 1990s and 2000s to construct a market democracy did not go unchallenged by popular sector movements and organizations.

Resisting market democracy

From 1985 to 1993, urban labor in cooperation with largely indigenous peasantry mobilized against the New Economic Policy. The COB and other unions organized massive strikes, while the CSUTCB announced peasant roadblocks to support urban strikers. However, as noted above, the capacity of organized labor to challenge market democracy was debilitated by the neoliberal reforms. Indeed, reforms were adopted precisely to undercut the COB's capacity to lead anti-neoliberal resistance. In this scenario, the CSUTCB, led by militant coca-growers,[17] came to play a leadership role in organizing anti-neoliberal protest. Framing protest against the Bolivian state and US imperialism around coca policies allowed for an intertwining of cultural, identity, and economic motivations which became a key feature of future anti-neoliberal organizing. Furthermore, the coca growers' successes highlighted how "successful organization (as measured by capacity to mobilize and to force negotiation) had shifted from the factory and the mine … to territorially based forms."[18]

A second wave of contention erupted during de Lozada's first presidency (1993–97), with the CSUTCB organizing protests such as the March for Life, Coca, and National Sovereignty in 1995. The framing of the protests highlighted how neoliberal "commodification destroyed the economic, social and cultural conditions that supported life."[19] This represented a shift from the language of class struggle and attracted various social groups and identities. Authorities faced protests from multiple sectors in both rural and urban settings with teachers, the COB, and Chapare coca growers resisting neoliberal reforms.

It is important to note that neoliberal decentralization policies opened new spaces of participation at the local level. The Popular Participation Law of 1994 (LPP) fostered decentralization via the establishment of hundreds of municipalities and instituted direct elections for mayors and municipal councils. The LPP also encouraged some poor and indigenous groups to take on the idea that liberal institutions could be transformed to meet their needs, and one response was the formation of the *Movimiento al Socialismo* (Movement Toward Socialism—MAS)[20] which would go on to play a key role in Bolivia's post-neoliberal democratization process. While the LPP encouraged local participation, it further eroded the power of the COB and organized labor. The law recognized urban neighborhood councils and indigenous communities as Territorial Based Organizations (OTBs) whose task was to identify and supervise the construction and delivery of public work. The law specifically states, however, that "functional," that is class-based, organizations such as trade unions could not be recognized as OTBs, thereby excluding unions from a new important arena of decision-making.[21]

A third wave of protest erupted during the presidencies of Banzer (1997–02), de Lozada (2002–03), and Carlos Mesa (2003–05) as the presidents adopted economically exclusionary reforms without popular sector inclusion in decision making. During this period, sectors of the urban union movement forged ties with informal worker organizations and rural peasant movements. The cities of Cochabamba and El Alto/La Paz were the centers of massive anti-neoliberal urban protests between 2000 and 2005.

Following a water privatization scheme in 2000 in Cochabamba brokered by the government and the Bechtel corporation which "caused a 400 percent increase in the cost of water in local communities, a series of 'wars' broke out"[22] between the government and organized popular forces. Law 2029 which allowed for privatization of water distribution was rushed through Congress without discussion, publicity, or consultation with affected groups. Large private enterprises were to receive exclusive rights over water resources, forcing local cooperatives and neighborhood associations into contracts with private businesses to receive water. Once more, the political exclusion from policymaking of those sectors who were to suffer from the massive price increases drove a new wave of mobilization in which the regional factory workers union headed by Oscar Olivera played a central role. Drawing from traditional national-popular anti-imperialist discourse, water privatization was framed as part of a broader marketization of Bolivian society that began with the 1985 Decree 21060.[23]

Citizens of Cochabamba launched a mass protest against the company who won the concessions to supply water to the city, Aguas del Tunari, a subsidiary of the US Bechtel corporation by organizing themselves into a powerful social movement, the Coordinating Committee in Defence of Water and Life.[24] Coca growers, under the leadership of Evo Morales, joined the protests, blocking roads connecting Cochabamba to Santa Cruz. The CSUTCB also joined the protest, helping to generate national-level mobilization in support of the water protests by framing the issue as an extension of neoliberal expropriation of indigenous livelihoods. Beginning with protests in December 1999, "15,000 irate citizens kicked off the Cochabamba Water War"; the following February, a two-day street war left 175 injured; in April, "over 30,000 protesters shut down the city and forced the government to declare martial law as demonstrations spread to … La Paz and El Alto."[25] Despite, and indeed because of, government repression of protesters, the CSUTCB peasant organization redoubled their protests. In the face of such mobilization, and at a time when Bolivia needed to offer an ideal investment climate for foreign investment to consolidate neoliberal economic reforms, the government agreed that Aguas de Tunari would leave and changes to Law 2029 were adopted to reflect the demands of the Coordinating Committee including greater input into establishing rate structures, the blocking of monopolization of water distribution concessions, and recognition of customary water rights for local water committees and cooperatives.[26]

Before continuing with the discussion of the anti-neoliberal protests, the following section offers a discussion of Evo Morales' role in the coca growers union and the formation of the MAS because the new movement-party was to play an increasingly important role in calling for an end to the market model of democracy.

The emergence of the MAS and its move from the countryside to the city

Popular protest movements began to forge links with political parties during the Cochabamba Water War, particularly the MAS, as the historic roots of the MAS are in the coca-growing zone of Chapare, Cochabamba. Following the crash in tin prices and privatization of the mining industry, tens of thousands of jobless miners migrated, with many moving to Chapare to begin a new life as small-holding cocalero (coca growing) peasants. Given the militant Marxist history of the miners, when the government, at the behest of the US, launched the "War on Drugs," the cocaleros quickly began organizing resistance, eventually forging a social movement party called Assembly for the Sovereignty of the People (ASP). By 1998, however, disputes between the three main indigenous leaders in the country—Felipe Quispe, Alejo Véliz, and Evo Morales—led to the eventual disintegration of the ASP. Two new parties emerged, one led by Quispe, and, most importantly for Bolivia's post-neoliberal democratization process, the Instrumento Político por la Soberanía de los Pueblos (Political Instrument for the Sovereignty of the Peoples, IPSP) led by Evo Morales. Due to legal technicalities, the IPSP was required to change its name, assuming the moniker of the defunct Movimiento al Socialismo—MAS.

Morales had—and throughout his later presidencies retained—tight links with the cocaleros having risen through the ranks of the cocalero peasant unions in the El Chapare region, becoming secretary general of the Six Federations of the Tropics of Cochabamba—a coordinated council of coca growers' unions—in 1988. Indeed, the MAS essentially emerged from rural social movements. The genesis of the party was from the bottom-up; it was a movement party in that it was sponsored by social movements as their electoral vehicle. It represents a hybrid organization that straddles the line between party and movement; movements tend to challenge the state, whereas parties are participants in state institutions.[27] The MAS, at least up until the election of Morales as president, adhered to Roberts'[28] "organic model" of party development in the sense that it engaged in electoral politics and competed for office, while at the same time it engaged in extra-parliamentary struggles and bargaining in pursuit of a programmatic agenda.

The decentralization law LPP 1994 created the space at municipal levels for the MAS to compete electorally, and in the 1999 municipal elections, the MAS won 3.27 percent of the national vote, ten mayoralties, and 79 municipal council seats. The majority of MAS' vote share came in the Chapare region, and from this base, the MAS sought to pursue an electoral route to national power. The Water War gave the MAS a platform on which to launch itself from a regional to a national party. The MAS used the context of the Water War to adopt a "plural popular"[29] strategy of coalition building, in which "indigenous issues became the framing plank for successful political articulation."[30] Morales, via the MAS, played a key role in coordinating amongst multiple groups—peasant organizations, cocaleros, urban labor unions, and urban neighborhood organizations—by framing specific group or organization grievances as issues that emerged due to Bolivia's market democracy. The MAS, then, was built from the bottom-up via historical cocalero organizing (which in turn had developed due to the influence of the Marxist tin-miners), competed in local elections, before attempting to spread laterally from region to region, ultimately becoming a national party. This territorialized development and close linkages to popular organizations boosted the political and institutional strength of the MAS.

It is crucial to highlight however, that the MAS had both a core social coalition and a more autonomous bloc of movement organizations that engaged with it in a strategic alliance. As Silva[31] points out, the core was composed of an "inner circle" that included the cocaleros and the Six Federations of the Tropics unions, the Bartolina Sisa National Confederation of Campesino, Indigenous, and Native Women of Bolivia (CNMCIOB-BS), and the CSUTCB. Evo Morales had tight, organic links with these organizations. The second autonomous-strategic bloc included the COB (especially the traditional, salaried miners); public sector unions; urban informal sector workers organized in neighborhood associations—the *Federaciones de Juntas de Vecinales* (Federation of Neighborhood Associations—FEJUVE) —especially in El Alto; informal sector miners' unions, the so-called cooperativistas; and the CONAMAQ,[32] which represents highland Aymara and Quechua who inhabit marginal largely pastoral lands.

In the 2002 national election campaign, the MAS "eschewed exclusionary language and repeatedly emphasized that the party was open to all people."[33] Furthermore, the MAS sought to include left-leaning and nationalist intellectuals as well as urban indigenous and nonindigenous classes. Crucially however, expansion of their support base via electoral mobilization was accompanied by support of social protests, allowing the MAS "to forge a strikingly heterogeneous coalition that would challenge the established political class, the status quo, and neoliberalism."[34] In this scenario, Evo Morales and the MAS placed second with 20.9 percent of the vote to Gonzalo Sánchez de Lozada and the MNR'S 22.5. MAS also placed 27 deputies in the lower chamber, boosting its relevance as a major political party.

However, despite the MAS' active support for protesters in the Water War, the increasing focus on electoral politics by the MAS did see a decline in its association with extra-parliamentary activism from the 2002 elections on. Moreover, Webber[35] states that the party moderated economic demands to appeal to urban middle-class voters; the party leadership saw a diminishing role for anti-imperialist, anti-neoliberal cocaleros; while an urban middle-class intelligentsia played an increasing role. This is not to suggest that the MAS, and the groups it represented, did not pose an electoral challenge to the status quo. However, as it broadened into a catch-all party to compete electorally, more radical demands were increasingly sidelined.[36]

While the party became less radical as it shifted toward electoral politics, the shift in strategy also had a crucial impact on how it interacted with non-organic popular strategic organizations in urban settings whose influence over grassroots voters in courted. To gain a foothold in the cities it often had to insert itself on top of pre-existing political parties and organizations which led to top-down co-optation of urban movement leaders and politicians who were gatekeepers to grassroots electoral support.[37] The case of El Alto is emblematic of the process.

El Alto has a long history of community organizing which stems partly from the rural Andean community traditions brought by the migrants who make up the majority of the population.[38] In addition, the neoliberal structural adjustment during the 1980s that fostered the closure of many of the country's mines resulted in mass migration of Quechuan miners to El Alto who brought with them Marxist traditions of organizing. Two civic organizations in the city played a central role in organizing and mobilizing residents and workers against neoliberal policies, the *Central Obrera Regional-El Alto* (Regional Bolivian Workers—COR-El Alto) and the *Federacione de Juntas Vecinales* (Federation of Neighborhood Associations—FEJUVE-El Alto).

The COR, infused with militancy from the miners, was originally founded in 1985 to represent the demands of El Alto's workers and street traders.[39] In fact, the "COR was paradoxically a result of the neoliberal adjustment package implemented in 1985, because as more unemployed workers turned to the informal sector, guilds grew exponentially and founded the organization."[40] It was founded on the principles that it must retain autonomy and independence from all political parties. Indeed, its purpose was to perform a contestatory role representing worker demands in front of the state.

The FEJUVE can be traced to 1957 when the first inhabitants of the then seven zones of El Alto formed a neighborhood council to protest against discrimination faced by Alteños (residents of El Alto) at the hands of the leaders of the *Federación Departmental de Juntas Vecinales de la Paz* (Departmental Federation of Neighborhood Associations, La Paz) and to demand the state provide basic services such as water and electricity. Daniel Gutiérrez, the press officer for the FEJUVE, told me how the FEJUVE developed over time from a social movement that appeared at specific moments to focus on specific grievances, into a social organization with much more general demands regarding the development of the city and the country.[41]

In terms of structure, local barrios organize at the district level in which all of the *juntas vecinales* of the base of the district decide on and coordinate actions, while above the district level is the executive branch of the organization, that is, the FEJUVE. The members of the executive are selected by the 14 district-level organizations.[42] Fluid relations between the base and upper levels seek to provide a counterweight toward any tendency of top-down decision-making.[43] As discussed below, the nature of the structure gave the FEJUVE the capacity to mobilize enormous numbers during moments of anti-neoliberal resistance. Indeed, as Crabtree and Chaplin[44] state, the FEJUVE became the principal institution representing Alteños' interests, more so than the mayor or the elected city councillors. However, precisely because of these dual roles as representative and mobilizer, the FEJUVE, along with the COR, became strategic targets for the MAS as the party leadership sought to expand from the Chapare into the city.

As discussed previously, the Law of Popular Participation introduced in 1994 meant that municipal governments assumed greater roles and responsibilities, while also empowering the neighborhood committees because they were charged with overseeing municipal spending via "comités de vigilancia" (vigilance committees). However, the LPP also divided communities along territorial lines with local groups battling for their portion of the budget.[45] In this context, "the neighborhood associations became key mediators between the state and society, and increasingly formed a clientelistic relation"[46] whereby political parties offered public works contracts in return for the political support of the leaders of popular organizations.[47]

As such, while the COR and FEJUVE organizations represented their base, as Alfredo Cahuaya told me, there has always been a tendency for political parties to control them from above,[48] be that the right-wing MNR, the populist *Conciencia de Patria* (Conscience of the Fatherland—CONDEPA), or center-Left MIR under the guidance of José Luis "Pepelucho" Paredes. MAS' arrival to the city did not fundamentally alter these party-organization relations as the party sought to place loyalists at the head of the COR and FEJUVE to guarantee the electoral support of the organizations' bases.[49]

More neoliberalism, the gas wars, and El Alto's mobilization

Following the 2002 election of de Lozada, economic crisis weakened the new government. While de Lozada had no intention of fundamentally altering the neoliberal model, he had run on a moderately progressive platform promising to boost public spending and employment and to support demand-led economic growth. However, the international recession triggered by the Asian financial crisis reduced demands for Bolivian exports, leading to fiscal deficit of 9 percent of GDP. In this scenario, under IMF-direction, the government implemented economic stabilization policies including income tax rises and a moratorium on public sector pay rises. As Silva[50] summarizes,

> the economic and stabilization policies adopted in … 2002 sharply increased economic exclusion. Per-capita GDP shrank, unemployment rates climbed, informal employment jumped to almost 68 percent, and income concentration advanced unchecked. Despair and rage over Sánchez de Lozada's policy reversal, globalization, and IMF policies perceived to cause only misery fuelled an upsurge of mobilization.

The city of El Alto was at the epicenter of mobilization. The period of 2002–05 witnessed a fundamental reformation of how popular organizations engaged with the municipal state and political parties. The traditional clientelistic relations between parties—including the MAS—and popular organizations faced increasing scrutiny from the grassroots base. The announcement in mid-2003 by the mayor of El Alto, José Luis Paredes, to introduce a land registry system to regulate transactions in real estate in El Alto irked Alteños who saw the proposed regulations as a new tax to extract more money from the poor.[51] Locals argued that they had already paid property tax, labeling the new payment as "Maya Paya," an Aymara term meaning "once and twice." Sentiment amongst indignant locals that they had already paid too much in property charges was captured by the commonly heard slogan "it is impossible that they demand us to pay taxes even on our dog's kennels."[52]

The proposed tax led to local forums and debates centered on the notion of Alteño dignity, particularly in District 4 of the city. Initially, the FEJUVE, led by Mauricio Cori, did not support the District 4 calls for a forum due to the traditional *prebendalismo* (political parties giving perks to organization leaders) and party-FEJUVE links that still existed at that time. However, local leaders in District 4 contacted *dirigentes* across the city without the support of the FEJUVE executive and called on all Alteños to reject the Maya Paya tax. A forum was organized and in the face of widespread rejection of the tax, the FEJUVE executive accepted that all districts should protest until the proposed tax was completely rescinded. With the FEJUVE organizing massive protests, and despite the mayor's heavy-handed repressive tactics, the Maya Paya tax proposal was rescinded in September 2003.

In conjunction with events in El Alto, a series of peasant roadblocks in the town of Warisata organized by Felipe Quispe and the CSUTCB held a tourist bus convoy hostage, with Quispe calling for the liberation of imprisoned comrades, redress for peasant-related issues, as well as changes to natural gas policy. The government sent the army in on a "rescue" mission to free the tourists on 20 September, culminating in the deaths of six peasants and one soldier.[53] The "news that the military had killed civilians while assisting foreign tourists reinforced a view that the Sánchez de Lozada administration did not put the interests of the Bolivian people first,"[54] and further marches and protests erupted. Many of the Aymaras of the highlands who supported Felipe Quispe's ideals were "peasants with one foot in the countryside and one foot in the city of El Alto … El Alto was the bedroom of the migrants" who came to the city to sell their produce.[55] As such, the government response to the Warisata incident resonated deeply with the city's populace.

Furthermore, with El Alto's neighborhood organizations already mobilized against the proposed Maya Paya tax, in October 2003 Alteños "mounted massive demonstrations after the neoliberal president Gonzalo Sánchez de Lozada unveiled plans to give concessions to transnational corporations to pipe natural gas from the eastern lowlands to Chilean ports for export to the United States."[56] The "terms of the concession to foreign capital, framed as a giveaway, turned the issue into a symbol of the popular sector's exclusion from market society,"[57] and the wave of protests that engulfed El Alto and then spread across the country became known as the 2003 Gas War.

On October 8th, the FEJUVE-El Alto called for an indefinite "paro cívico" (general civil strike). Meanwhile, miners from Huanuni marched to

El Alto to join the struggle. The COR-El Alto also played a central role in the 2003 Gas War, in particular the *gremialista* sector of street traders who closed markets in concert with the general strikes called for by the FEJUVE and the COB. The students of the public university of El Alto, the UPEA also joined the protests.

The exact role of the FEJUVE and COR leaderships in organizing the Gas War mobilizations is however somewhat disputed. While Mauricio Cori, then president of the FEJUVE, maintained that the organization was always in control of the protests, others suggest that it was the *pueblo* that revolted whereby the neighborhood organization leaders had to follow the will of the grassroots base.[58] It is necessary to emphasize here the nature of the relations between the base, neighborhood organizations' leaderships, and the government before the Gas War of 2003. In many ways, "democracy had reached its limits in 2003 whereby the people, instead of being incorporated or included in the plans for the development of the city, they had been excluded" and the *dirigencia* (of the FEJUVE and COR) simply towed the political party line.[59] The parties in turn "adhered to the demands of foreign capital."[60] There was a sense among Alteños of both political and socioeconomic exclusion—that the city had been "forgotten" by successive governments that instead pandered to the demands of powerful national and foreign economic actors.[61]

It was in this scenario, whereby regular citizens were becoming increasingly agitated regarding the economic and political scenario in the country, yet where the organizations charged with defending their interests failed to offer a response that reflected the sentiment in the city that the base sought to rejuvenate the COR and the FEJUVE. Emanating from the successful Maya Paya resistance, there were local meetings that culminated in a conscientization of the base, whereby the people realized that they must "oblige their *dirigentes* to respond to the needs of the *barrio*, and not to the political parties."[62] As Luis Flores, a central actor in the FEJUVE leadership during the 2003–05 period told me, the head of the FEJUVE, Mauricio Cori, faced threats from the municipal government to quell the rising protests against the government and the selling of gas, but at the same time, Cori was facing threats from the FEJUVE *dirigencia* to listen to the base.[63] There was a change in mentality, both of the base and of their *dirigentes*, in terms of how the FEJUVE should interact with the government. They emphasized that *dirigentes* must be clean, that they must not be corrupted by the parties and that they must not "extend their hand looking for presents."[64]

In this light, the COR and the FEJUVE elected new leaders who were not beholden to any party. As Alfredo Cahuaya told me, "if ever there was a moment, it was in 2003 when the El Alto *dirigencia* didn't belong to any political party." Carlos Barrerra, the former vice president of the FEJUVE and central actor in the 2003–05 protest period, told me that the *dirigentes* were "completely united around one mission whose objective was to improve El Alto."[65] Furthermore, the *dirigentes* of the FEJUVE in 2003 held strong left-wing beliefs that had been formed over many years, and they ensured that the top level of the FEJUVE was held to account.[66] Indeed, with the *dirigentes* from district four leading the way, all of the districts united behind the idea of re-taking the FEJUVE from the parties and restoring it to a popular organization that would no longer fall prey to political co-optation. The FEJUVE even replaced the secretary and the doorman that were paid for by the municipal government so that the organization could ask "Well, what are we going to rely on the municipal government or the central government for … For nothing!"[67]

The new COR and FEJUVE executives, reflecting the concerns of the grassroots base, outlined a set of demands calling for wholesale nationalization and the reclamation of control over the extraction and industrialization of Bolivia's natural gas, state provision of non-precarious employment and basic services such as sewerage, drinking water, gas connections, and lighting. This set of demands became a unifying agenda that drove further waves of mass mobilization. Protest waves were driven not only by demands for more control over national resources and state provision of services but by the demand that the entire political structure be cleansed of corrupt parties and actors beholden to the interests of capital.

In response to the popular protests, the government ordered the military to break up marches, with troops killing scores of civilians in what came to be known as Black October. The repression backfired, with mass protests erupting across the country calling for the president's resignation and with miners and protesters from Oruro and Potosí, coca growers from Chapare, and peasants from the highlands converging in La Paz. Demonstrators from El Alto and working-class neighborhoods of La Paz were accompanied by intellectuals, middle-class personalities, NGO leaders, human rights advocates, and politicians, while waves of protests of tens and hundreds of thousands rocked the country. A set of demands emerged, calling for the ouster of the president and his neoliberal model, as well as the nationalization of gas. With an estimated 500,000 people in the streets, "Sánchez de Lozada and his closest supporters fled the country for exile in the United States on October 17," with vice-president Carlos Mesa taking over.[68] The Gas War protest which originated in El Alto due to a unified base re-taking control of their erstwhile co-opted neighborhood organizations had thus erupted into a national level movement which successfully removed a sitting neoliberal president.

The new leadership of the FEJUVE following the 2003 Gas War took on the mandate to advance the October Agenda—the set of demands that emerged during the tumultuous October of 2003. As Spronk[69] states, "not only was the FEJUVE working on local issues, but also on national political demands such as the call for a Constitutional Assembly and the nationalization of natural resources." Such a stance was considered vital because the Gas War of 2003 had "not lead to a revolutionary break with neoliberal capitalism" with Carlos Mesa adopting "a neoliberal reformist style of governance."[70] While Mesa initially sought to appease the mobilized popular sectors by speaking progressively in public, as the traditional economic elites increased their pressure on Mesa to avoid capitulating to the October Agenda demands, and with the TNCs, IMF, and US embassy allying behind the domestic elites, Mesa dropped any pretense of supporting popular demands and realigned with the elites of the *media luna*.[71]

The struggles around the 2004 Gas Referendum were emblematic of the tensions that had been simmering in the country since the adoption of the 1985 New Economic Policy. Gustafson[72] describes the referendum as a "tricky spectacle" aimed to calm a polarized society through the appearance of the expression of democratic collective will. However, "the questions favored the private fossil fuel industry" with each question designed to produce a "yes" answer that would actually facilitate the export of gas while giving the appearance that the state was asserting more control over the hydrocarbon industry and the money, without actually securing any real power.[73] The referendum only offered a 50/50 split of profits on gas via taxes and royalties, which would see the state's take increase, which was appealing to voters, but at the same time fell far short of the demands of the October protests which had called for wholesale nationalization.

While the referendum passed the popular vote, Mesa faced ongoing mobilizations and road blockades with demands focusing on formulating a new hydrocarbons law that would give the state a greater role in controlling the industry and profits. The MAS supported the protests, demanding a revision of contracts, absolute state ownership of hydrocarbons, state recovery of the privatized YPFB gas company, and state control over transport, storage, and commercialization of gas.[74] In May, both houses of congress passed a hybrid law that offered a diluted response to the demands of the protesters.

With the new FEJUVE-El Alto executives already mobilizing the grassroots base, Roberto de la Cruz of the anti-capitalist movement M-17 and Jaime Solares of the COB attended meetings of FEJUVE–El Alto in an attempt to build solidarity across different sectors of the working class and peasantry.[75] Popular sector organizations at the local, regional, and national levels co-ordinated protests, mobilizing hundreds of thousands of protesters, effectively shutting down the cities of La Paz and El Alto, and forcing Mesa to resign. Indeed, the Gas Wars ultimately completed what the Cochabamba Water War had started, transforming "demands from local, regional, or union-specific grievances … to national-level demands centered on sovereignty, state control of natural resources, pro-formal sector employment and worker's rights policies, agrarian reform, demilitarization of the drug war, and calls for a constituent assembly."[76]

However, while popular power from below had succeeded in removing two sitting neoliberal presidents, the Mesa presidency foreshadowed future power struggles between the state, popular organizations, the traditional elite, and transnational actors which would impact the path and outcomes of Bolivia's post-neoliberal democratization process. During Mesa's presidency, "Bolivia was characterized by a deepening political polarization along the axes of class, race, and region."[77] Two social blocs emerged. First, a left-indigenous bloc comprised predominantly of "indigenous urban proletarian and peasant forces" rooted

> primarily in the most heavily indigenous departments of La Paz, Cochabamba, Oruro, Potosí, and Chuquisaca, was solidified on the basis of a similar alliance as in the … gas war in 2003 that led to the overthrow of President Gonzalo Sánchez de Lozada.[78]

The demands of the bloc centered on adherence to the October Agenda demands of nationalization of hydrocarbon resources, land and wealth redistribution, and a revolutionary constituent assembly.

The second bloc that consolidated between October 2003 and June 2005 "was an eastern-bourgeois bloc led by the regional bourgeoisies of the hydrocarbons-rich departments of Tarija and Santa Cruz and their allies in Beni and Pando."[79] The bloc was represented by the Pro Santa Cruz Committee which was comprised of the Agricultural Chamber of Eastern Bolivia, the Federation of Ranchers of Santa Cruz, and the Chamber of Commerce, Industry, Service, and Tourism of Santa Cruz (CAINCO).[80] As Spronk and Webber[81] highlight, "the Spanish oil giant Repsol-YPF, Brazilian state-owned Petrobras, and Enron are members of CAINCO's board of directors." The Santa Cruz agro-industrial, petroleum, and financial elites, who were the most influential proponents of the neoliberal model, had enjoyed direct access to the central state via the MNR, ADN, and MIR parties. In response to the October Agenda of 2003, this bloc advanced the January Agenda of 2005 calling for greater "departmental autonomy, regional control over natural resources, department control over most tax revenue, departmental authority over all policies except defense, currency, tariffs, and foreign relations, 'free-market' capitalism, openness to foreign direct investment, racism, and state repression of left-indigenous protesters."[82]

With Mesa stepping down from the presidency, and with distinct social blocs cleaving around distinct ideas for Bolivian democracy, citizenship and development, the stage was set for critical elections in December 2005.

Party system breakdown and election of Evo Morales

Leading up to the December 2005 presidential elections, disenchantment with the performance of liberal democracy coupled with market-oriented policies was growing. Since 1985, traditional mainstream parties from across the political spectrum had played a role in implementing neoliberal structural adjustment policies. In 1985, the historic populist party that led the 1952 Revolution, the MNR were the first party to shift the country toward a marketized citizenship model. The liberalizing reforms were then deepened by the principal leftist (MIR) and conservative (ADN) parties "providing an example of neoliberal convergence *par excellence*."[83] Moreover, neoliberal reforms were adopted in a "bait-and-switch" manner by party leaders who had overtly campaigned against neoliberal orthodoxy. The convergence around structural adjustment policies by all the mainstream parties, and the backtracking on campaign promises by elected officials, meant that popular sector anger and aspirations were funneled into extra-systemic forms of social and electoral protest. By 2004, only 23.4 percent of the population reported confidence in the traditional parties.[84] Indeed, the 2005 elections "were defined by the utter exhaustion of the traditional neoliberal parties ... that had ruled the country through various coalitional governments since 1985."[85]

The MAS filled the void created by the decline of the traditional parties who were associated with neoliberalism, wooing "the support of disaffected voters with steadfast opposition to the government's policies and its strong nationalist and anti-establishment rhetoric."[86] Morales and the MAS easily won the 2005 elections in the first round with 53.7 percent of the vote to 28.6 percent for former president Jorge "Tuto" Quiroga and *Poder Democrático y Social* (Democratic and Social Power—PODEMOS).

MAS won with high support in rural areas, including Cochabamba (where the cocaleros' peasant unions dominate). MAS also garnered the support of the cooperative miners and the state-employed miners. In addition, MAS won in the cities, gaining support from the informal urban proletariat and working-class barrios.[87] In El Alto, in a scenario of severe *desgaste* (exhaustion) with the traditional parties, protester fatigue, and with a lack of local alternatives, the MAS and Evo Morales came to fill the vacuum. Despite the mobilization power that was built during the Maya Paya protests and the Gas Wars, and the re-claiming of the COR and FEJUVE by autonomous executives between 2003 and 2005, El Alto lacked a leader capable of harnessing the popular energy to take political power at the national level. While there was a fundamental questioning of the role and capacity of the existing model of democracy, as Carlos Rojas, a central actor in El Alto's wave of anti-neoliberal struggles and long-time activist in the city told me, the popular sectors were "not organized politically around a program or project that would allow us the possibility of truly taking power."[88] A strategic alliance between the MAS and the FEJUVE and the COR deepened around the 2005 elections. Local organization leaders saw in the MAS an opportunity to gain access to the state and to push toward achieving the October Agenda. The MAS meanwhile managed to infiltrate the leadership of these two organizations so as "to extend its influence and control throughout the territory and to recruit leaders who mobilize large numbers of voters."[89] As a result, Morales won the 2005 election with massive Alteño support.

PODEMOS, meanwhile, was essentially a coalition of major sectors of the MNR, ADN, and MIR parties who sought to rebrand themselves for the election. However, their primary social base remained those sectors who benefitted during the neoliberal era— "primarily the internationally oriented fractions of capital in the eastern department of Santa Cruz, including those in natural gas, agro-industry, banking, and illegal narcotics."[90]

While Morales and MAS easily won control of the executive, legislative, and departmental elections were a closer affair. The MAS won a 72-seat majority in the 130-seat lower house, with PODEMOS a close second, while the senate was almost evenly split between the two. In departmental (regional) elections, MAS won just three of nine prefectures, and regional destabilization efforts by right-wing opposition forces to Morales' government would become a prominent feature in the post-election era.

Fundamentally, Evo Morales was elected with the task of deepening and extending democracy. Morales was given a mandate to challenge the market model of democracy by restoring a degree of national and political autonomy from the IFIs, the US state and transnational capital, to (re)incorporate long-excluded leftist and popular sector voices into decision-making, and to advance a more protectionist state that would guarantee a minimum standard of social citizenship for all. The election of Morales after 20 years of neoliberalism thus represented "a critical break with the past."[91]

Summary of Bolivia's historical era: setting the scene for post-neoliberal struggles

Similar to the Venezuelan case, the turn to market democracy in Bolivia fostered extremely narrow and shallow forms of citizenship for popular sectors, fostering an unstable democratic equilibrium in which discontent with the traditional parties became untenable. Bait-and-switch adoption of neoliberal policies by parties across the spectrum, technocratic decision-making, and supranational agenda setting of Bolivian governments' policy space, alongside increasing inequality, precarity, and struggles for daily survival for popular sectors meant that democracy faced a legitimacy crisis by the early 2000s. With organized labor sidelined and no representative avenues for the incorporation of popular sector demands for protections from the excesses of the marketization of citizenship, waves of protest erupted. A tipping point was reached as the impacts of the Asian crisis and a fiscal crisis witnessed further bait-and-switch adoption of IMF-sponsored policies, while state forces brutally repressed protests. The acute realities of how neoliberal policies damaged the quality of life for popular sectors while benefitting traditional elite groups, as well as the nature of how these policies were adopted, delegitimized the political system and widened the space for a progressive-outsider to emerge in the form of Evo Morales and the MAS.

The election of Morales set the stage for new struggles between competing social blocs around competing notions of democracy and citizenship in which the new left-led government would confront a recalcitrant elite (domestic and transnational) willing to use an array of ideological, economic, military, and political resources to stymie the governments' capacity to respond to popular demands for improved socio-economic and political inclusion. The process that emerged was complex, with simultaneous democratization and de-democratization occurring at different junctures, while some sectors of the popular base witnessed substantially better-quality incorporation than others.

Moreover, given the crucial role of social movements and popular organizations in bringing Morales to power and in forging the MAS, the post-election process would witness complex party-base tensions. The party's movement origins and organic relations with powerful rural organizations capable of mass mobilization left an imprint on how the party would, at times, eschew top-down decision-making and incorporate voices from below into party discussions and agenda-setting. However, while the historical nature of the MAS' formation did encourage popular incorporation into decision-making, at the same time, the relinquishing of organizational autonomy by leaders of non-core organizations would trigger a series of tensions that would shape the direction of post-election sequencing. As government-elite struggles increased, leading to a moderation of policies, and when organization leaders who had lost autonomy by forging linkages with the MAS failed to protest such moderation, tensions would emerge not only between popular organizations and the government but between the grassroots and the executives of popular organizations themselves. These government-opposition, party-base, and internal popular organization tensions, whose origins lay in the historical period, would greatly impact the direction and outcomes of Bolivia's post-neoliberal process. In the following chapters, I discuss the post-election process in Bolivia.

Notes

1 For detailed analysis of the historical emergence of the COB see Jorge Trujillo and Susan Spronk, "Socialism without Workers? Trade Unions and the New Left in Bolivia and Ecuador," in Eduardo Silva and Federico Rossi (eds), *Reshaping the Political Arena in Latin America: From Resisting Neoliberalism to the Second Incorporation* (Pittsburgh, PA: University of Pittsburgh Press, 2018): 129: 156.

2 Jeffery Webber, *From Rebellion to Reform in Bolivia: Class Struggle, Indigenous Liberation, and the Politics of Evo Morales* (Chicago, IL: Haymarket Books, 2011): 18.

3 Dan Slater and Erica Simmons, "Coping by Colluding: Political Uncertainty and Promiscuous Power-sharing in Indonesia and Bolivia," *Comparative Political Studies* 46, no. 11 (2013): 1366–93.

4 Carlos de la Torre, "In the Name of the People: Democratization, Popular Organizations, and Populism in Venezuela, Bolivia, and Ecuador," *European Review of Latin American and Caribbean Studies* 95 (2013): 33.

5 Webber, *From Rebellion to Reform*, 18.

6 Ibid.

7 See Linda Farthing, "The New Underground," *NACLA Report on the Americas* 25, no. 1 (1991): 18–23; Merilee Grindle, "Shadowing the Past? Policy Reform in Bolivia, 1985–2002," in M. Grindle and P. Domingo (eds), *Proclaiming Revolution: Bolivia in Comparative Perspective* (London and Cambridge, MA: ILAS and David Rockefeller Centre, 2003). Trujillo and Spronk, "Socialism Without Workers," 135; Eduardo Silva, *Challenging Neoliberalism in Latin America* (New York: Cambridge University Press, 2009): 107.

8 Silva, *Challenging Neoliberalism*, 109.

9 Catherine Conaghan, James Molloy, and Luis Abugattas, "Business and the 'Boys': The Politics of Neoliberalism in the Central Andes," *Latin American Research Review* 25, no. 2 (1990): 9, 14, 15.

10 Grindle, "Shadowing the Past,"; Trujillo and Spronk, "Socialism without Workers," 135.

11 Bret Gustafson, *Bolivia in the Age of Gas* (Durham, NC: Duke University Press, 2020): 100–2.

12 Gustafson, *Bolivia in the Age of Gas*, 102.
13 Tom Kruse, "Trancisión Política y Recomposición Sindical: Reflexiones desde Bolivia," in Marco Calderón Mólgora, Willem Assies, and Ton Salman (eds), *Ciudadanía, Cultura Política y Reforma del Estado América Latina* (IFE Michoacán: El Colegio de Michoacán, 2002): 232; Webber, *From Rebellion to Reform*, 20–5.
14 The term "*media luna*," or "half moon," refers to the crescent shape formed by the boundaries of the departments of Santa Cruz, Beni, Pando and Tarija, where the most conservative sectors of the political and economic elite opposition are located.
15 Juan Carlos Monedero, "Snipers in the Kitchen: State Theory and Latin America's Left Cycle," *New Left Review* 120, Nov/Dec (2019): 18.
16 Ibid., 19.
17 Coca is a tea-like plant that has been used by indigenous communities to fight altitude sickness and surpass hunger, thirst, and pain. It is an important component of indigenous culture in Bolivia.
18 Silva, *Challenging Neoliberalism*, 115.
19 Silva, *Challenging Neoliberalism*, 122.
20 See Nancy Postero, "The Struggle to Create a Radical Democracy in Bolivia," *Latin American Research Review* 45, no. 4 (2010): 59–78; Raul Madrid, "Origins and Policies of the Movimiento al Socialismo," in Steven Levitsky and Kenneth Roberts (eds), *The Resurgence of the Latin American Left* (Baltimore, MD: John Hopkins University Press, 2011): 239–59.
21 Linda Farthing and Benjamin Kohl, *Impasse in Bolivia: Neoliberal Hegemony and Popular Resistance* (London: Zed Books, 2006); Trujillo and Spronk, "Socialism Without Workers," 136.
22 Amy Kennemore and Greg Weeks, "Twenty-First Century Socialism? The Elusive Search for a Post-Neoliberal Development Model in Bolivia and Ecuador," *Bulletin of Latin American Research* 30, no. 3 (2011): 269.
23 Willem Assies, "David versus Goliath in Cochabamba: Water Rights, Neoliberalism, and the Revival of Social Protest in Bolivia," *Latin American Perspectives* 30, no. 2 (2003): 14–36; John Crabtree, *Patterns of Protest: Politics and Social Transformation in Bolivia* (London: Latin American Bureau, 2005); Silva, *Challenging Neoliberalism*, 125.
24 Waltraud Morales, "Social Movements and Revolutionary Change in Bolivia," in Gary Prevost, Carlos Olivia Campos and Harry Vanden (eds), *Social Movements and Leftist Governments in Latin America* (London: Zed Books: 2012): 56.
25 Ibid.
26 Silva, *Challenging Neoliberalism*, 131; Assies, "David versus Goliath," 30.
27 Santiago Anria, "Social movements, Party organization, and Populism: Insights from the Bolivian MAS," *Latin American Politics and Society* 55, no. 3 (2013): 22, 23.
28 Kenneth Roberts, *Deepening Democracy? The Modern Left and Social Movements in Chile and Peru* (Stanford: Stanford University Press, 1998): 75.
29 Robert Albro, "The Water Is Ours, ¡*Carajo*!: Deep Citizenship in Bolivia's Water War," in June Nash (ed.), *Social Movements: An Anthropological Reader* (Oxford: Basil Blackwell, 2005): 249–71.
30 Anria, "Social Movements, Party Organization," 27.
31 Eduardo Silva, "Social Movements, Policy, and Conflict in Post-neoliberal Latin America: Bolivia in the Time of Evo Morales," *Research in Political Sociology* 21 (2013): 59.
32 Consejo Nacional de Ayllus y Markas del Qullasuyu (National Council of Ayllus and Markas of Qullasuyu).
33 Madrid, "Origins and Policies," 245.
34 Anria, "Social Movements, Party Organization," 27.

35 Webber, *From Rebellion to Reform*, 3, 44, 63.
36 Interview with Carloz Arze of the Centro de Estudios para el Desarollo Laboral y Agrario (CEDLA), La Paz, August 25, 2017.
37 Santiago Anria, *When Movements Become Parties: The Bolivian MAS in Comparative Perspective* (Cambridge, New York: Cambridge University Press, 2019).
38 John Crabtree and Ann Chaplin, *Bolivia: Processes of Change* (La Paz: OXFAM/CEDLA/Fundación PIEB, 2013): 67.
39 A.D. Mancilla, *Poder y Masacre en El Alto: La Mafia Sindical Alteña* (La Paz: Viejo Topo, 2016): 71.
40 Xavier Albó, "El Alto: Mobilizing Block by Block," *NACLA Report on the Americas*, Retrieved https://nacla.org/article/el-alto-mobilizing-block-block.
41 Interview with author, El Alto, August 9, 2017.
42 Ibid.
43 Carla Espósito and Walter Arteaga, *Movimientos Sociales Urbano-Populares en Bolivia: Una Lucha contra la Exclusión Social, Económica y Política* (La Paz: UNITAS, 2006): 63.
44 Crabtree and Chaplin, *Bolivia: Processes of Change*, 69.
45 Carlos Revilla, *Visibilidad y Obrismo: La Estrategia del Plan Progresso En La Ciudad de El Alto* (La Paz: UNITAS, 2007): 19.
46 Crabtree and Chaplin, *Bolivia: Processes of Change*, 72.
47 Revilla, *Visibilidad y Obrismo*, 19.
48 Alfredo Cahuaya was a resident of District 4 and an active participant in the protests. He is also a researcher at the UNITAS center in La Paz. Interview conducted in La Paz, August 18, 2017.
49 This view was shared by numerous leaders or ex-leaders of both the COR and Fejuve during interviews conducted in El Alto in 2017.
50 Silva, *Challenging Neoliberalism*, 133.
51 Juan Arbona, "Histories and Memories in the Organization and Struggles of the Santiago II Neighborhood of El Alto, Bolivia," *Bulletin of Latin American Research* 27, no. 1 (2008): 36.
52 Interview with Alfredo Cahuaya.
53 Sian Lazar, "El Alto, Ciudad Rebelde: Organizational Bases for Revolt," *Bulletin of Latin American Research* 25, no. 2 (2006): 184.
54 Arbona, "Histories and Memories," 37.
55 Interview with Carlos Arze.
56 Postero, "The Struggle to Create a Radical Democracy," 61.
57 Silva, *Challenging Neoliberalism*, 134–5.
58 Lazar, "El Alto, Ciudad Rebelde," 193.
59 Interview with Alfredo Cahuaya.
60 Interview with Carlos Arze.
61 Espósito and Arteaga, *Movimientos Sociales*, 79, 86.
62 Interview with Alfredo Cahuaya.
63 Interview, El Alto, August 23, 2017.
64 Ibid.
65 Interview, El Alto, June 27, 2017.
66 Interview with Luis Flores.
67 Ibid.
68 Susan Spronk and Jeffrey Webber, "Struggles against Accumulation by Dispossession in Bolivia: The Political Economy of Natural Resource Contention," *Latin American Perspectives* 34, no. 2 (2007): 36.
69 Susan Spronk, "Roots of Resistance to Urban Water Privatization in Bolivia: The 'New Working Class,' the Crisis of Neoliberalism, and Public Services," *International Labor and Working-Class History* 71, no. 1 (2007): 19.
70 Spronk and Webber, "Struggles against Accumulation," 37.

71 Gustafson, *Bolivia in the Age of Gas*, 113; Jeffrey Webber, "Carlos Mesa, Evo Morales, and a Divided Bolivia (2003—2005)," *Latin American Perspectives* 37, no. 3 (2010): 54.
72 Gustafson, *Bolivia in the Age of Gas*, 114.
73 Ibid., 114–6.
74 Ibid., 123.
75 Webber, "Carlos Mesa," 61.
76 Silva, *Challenging Neoliberalism*, 138.
77 Webber, "Carlos Mesa," 52.
78 Ibid.
79 Ibid.
80 Spronk and Webber, "Struggles against Accumulation," 37.
81 Ibid.
82 Webber, "Carlos Mesa," 52.
83 Roberts, "Changing Course," 274.
84 Mitchel Seligson, Daniel Moreno Morales, and Vivian Blum, *Auditoría de la Democracia: Informe Bolivia 2004* (La Paz: Universidad Católica Boliviana, 2004): 102.
85 Webber, *From Rebellion to Reform*, 44.
86 Madrid, "Origins and Policies," 244.
87 See Salvador Romero Ballivián, *El Tablero Reordenado: Análisis de la Elección Presidencial de 2005* (La Paz: Malatesta, 2006): 50–4.
88 Interview, El Alto, June 28, 2017.
89 Anria, "Social movements, Party organization," 33.
90 Webber, *From Rebellion to Reform*, 53–4.
91 Pía Riggirozzi, "Social Policy in Post-Neo-Liberal Latin America: The Cases of Argentina, Venezuela and Bolivia," *Development* 53, no. 1 (2010): 74.

6 Progressive and regressive centralization

the Evo Morales' years, 2006–14

In this chapter, I evaluate the efforts to move toward a post-neoliberal model of democracy in Bolivia during under the first two presidencies of Evo Morales from 2006 to 2014. In the following chapter, I examine the third presidency of Morales from 2014 to 2019 before discussing the 2019–21 period following his removal from power by a coup. The chapters trace the evolution of the process while accounting for the evolving ideological, economic, military, and political struggles between the Morales-led government and an opposition-bloc intent on maintaining/restoring a market model of democracy. The influence of organized popular sectors on the process is also accounted for, highlighting how early linkages between the MAS party and sectors of the base both opened and restricted avenues for bottom-up input into decision-making processes. The chapters highlight the impacts on the quality of liberal, participative, and substantive elements of democracy, with simultaneous democratization and de-democratization occurring.

The constituent assembly, opposition destabilization, and tightening party-base relations: 2006–09

As described in the previous chapter, during the market democracy era Bolivia's economic elites had enjoyed direct access to state decision-making via mainstream political parties. With the collapse of the party system and the emergence of the anti-neoliberal outsider MAS, elite access to the ruling party was partially impeded and popular social movements and organizations whose voices had long been excluded were brought into decision-making processes. This dramatic shift threatened elite interests and opened a complex power struggle between the government, opposition-bloc, and organized popular sectors that shaped the direction and outcomes of the Morales-led process.

In June 2006, the government presented the National Development Plan 2007 that called for a deepening and extending of democracy. The plan offered an alternative vision to that of market democracy, and called for *buen vivir*, an indigenous vision based on communitarian forms of living together.[1] The plan outlined that the state needed to intervene as "promoter

DOI: 10.4324/9781003262466-7

and protagonist of national development,"[2] whereby the state would act to transform society and the economy, but only if "all peoples and cultures are present in the economic and political decisions of the State."[3]

The plan was based on developing two sectors of the economy. The first comprised surplus-generating activities such as hydrocarbons, electricity, mining, and natural resources, and the second was made up of employment- and income-generating sectors such as tourism, agriculture, manufacturing, transport, and services. The plan called for revenues generated through increased state control over the surplus-generating sectors to be redirected toward the transformation of the employment-/revenue-generating sectors via state spending and redistribution, boosting internal demand and supporting social equality. Nationalization of primary commodity sectors was also to be used to develop the industrialization of primary materials.[4] Over time then, the aim was to utilize primary commodity rents to support a transition toward a diversified industrial development model.

In May 2006, Morales declared that Bolivia's hydrocarbon sector was to be nationalized so as to allow the state to increase the price of and rents from its natural gas exports. Via decree 28701, "the Morales administration recovered the state's right to commercialize its hydrocarbons and increased the prices it received from the sale of its natural gas."[5] Prices for gas exported to Argentina and Brazil were increased while the combined royalty and taxation rate that investing firms paid was increased from 18 to 50 percent. As discussed in detail below, while the "nationalization" was in fact moderate,[6] the changes did represent a fundamental shift in the state's role in the hydrocarbon sector and boosted the fiscal capacity of the government.

The NDP plans to deepen popular sector voices in decision-making and to extend democratic quality via increased state control over the economy, redistributive social policies, as well as indications there would be a reform of land ownership directly challenged elite interests, especially in the department of Santa Cruz.[7] The tensions would come to the fore during efforts to convoke a Constituent Assembly to rewrite Bolivia's constitution.

The constituent assembly struggles and powerful popular organizations

In response to the PND, and making use of their political, economic, ideological, and military power, eastern lowland elites in the *media luna* and the PODMEOS party began to struggle for regional autonomy in a bid to avoid the proposed changes to the status of private property rights, land reform, and redistribution of state revenue. Autonomy was understood as

> regional control over natural resources (e.g. land, timber, gas, and oil); the right to retain control over two-thirds of all tax revenues generated in the department; and authority to set all policies other than defence, currency, tariffs and foreign relations.[8]

In the political sphere, despite winning the presidential election while also capturing a simple majority in the Chamber of Deputies, MAS did not control the senate or the traditionally conservative judiciary.[9] Conservative opposition candidates also won six of nine departmental prefectures in the 2005 elections. In Santa Cruz, Rúben Costas was elected. Costas was a cattleman and a prominent leader of the autonomist movement. Autonomist leaders also won the governorships in the *media luna* departments Beni, Pando, and Tarija. The powerful business leaders of Santa Cruz "had created grassroots political allegiances through the hegemonization of a popular regional or *camba* identity associated with beauty, modernity, and prosperity in contrast to things Indian, backward, poor, and antidemocratic."[10] As Gustafson[11] describes,

> The autonomy project sought to carve out a regional space of hegemony distanced from the regulatory and electoral pressures of the national state. The cruceño autonomists revelled in locality and faux authenticity but their localism was a transnational effort supported by outside forces and interests, from multinational gas companies to Spanish and USAID advisors supporting the "autonomy" agenda.

The autonomists enacted racist violence under a veneer of claims of protecting regional democracy and identity, while in fact resisting national efforts to democratize resource distribution. USAID funded autonomy workshops in the eastern regions while Transredes, a Shell-Enron-Prisma pipeline company, financed autonomy workshops and supported pro-autonomy media.[12] The geographical concentration of opposition in the eastern lowlands allowed the formation of dense organizational networks, enabling governors to enlist societal support which they could mobilize in attempts to block reform efforts.[13]

Moreover, the country's wealthiest families with links to the traditional parties owned the major television networks and newspapers,[14] capturing 70 percent of the TV audience and 64 percent of print media circulation.[15] The families who dominated the private media were also major landholders in the eastern departments. According to Lupien, the traditional media's response to the MAS agenda was characterized by "disdain and fear," painting ideological enemies as illiberal extremists, and focusing attention on disruptive actions by certain sectors of government supporters while downplaying similar actions by opposition groups.

In response to government promises to adhere to popular protester demands, the opposition-bloc used their control over the media and the departmental governments, the judiciary, senate, and the state bureaucracy to impede the government where possible.[16] In the Constituent Assembly, PODEMOS politicians sought to torpedo reforms. In response to institutional efforts to block popular reforms, Morales decreed that rules governing the Constituent Assembly would be determined by a simple majority rather than by a two-thirds vote (the MAS enjoyed a majority, but not a super-majority of two-thirds). This illiberal, though popularly supported response by Morales, fostered a change of tactics on behalf of reform opponents. PODEMOS and the autonomist forces accused the MAS of attempting an *autogolpe* (self-coup) and subsequently boycotted the Constituent Assembly, sending it into indefinite recess. Furthermore, stoked by opposition-bloc media, autonomist forces across the *media luna* engaged in massive demonstrations and a civic strike.

When the economic power of the Santa Cruz elites who were mobilizing for autonomy and who maintained control over finance, and who had intimate ties with foreign capital (the department attracts more FDI than any other department) is considered in conjunction with the ideological and political power of the opposition bloc, we can see that the MAS faced resistance from a powerful adversary.[17] Moreover, the opposition-bloc wielded military power in the form of fascist mobs who could be called to take the streets and attack MAS-supporters, while in the transnational sphere there were powerful opponents to the MAS' post-neoliberal agenda. That is, across all spheres of power—ideological, economic, military, political, and transnational—the MAS government faced strong resistance from pro-market democracy forces.

Facing such opposition, MAS offered to accept a mixed voting system in the Constituent Assembly whereby particularly contentious issues would require two-thirds support to pass. However, PODEMOS and the autonomists rejected the offer and continued to mobilize. The extra-parliamentary activism of the autonomists influenced public perception of Morales, whose support fell from a high of 80 percent to 52 by the end of September 2006, while support for the Constituent Assembly declined from 69 percent in August to 45 percent in September 2006.[18] In the face of opposition-bloc power and their protests and threats to veto the entire process, Morales accepted that each article of the Constituent Assembly would require two-thirds support, and with this compromise, the assembly ended its seven-month impasse. In December 2007, the Constituent Assembly approved a draft constitutional charter which, while favorable to government aspirations, was also more moderate than the October Agenda set out during the anti-neoliberal protests.

Confronting a common enemy and the formation of party-base linkages

The opposition bloc's resistance toward MAS and the Constituent Assembly and the conflicts that emerged meant that a variety of organic-core and strategic popular organizations supported MAS in order to fight against the conservative opposition.[19] Early in Morales' first term, the Unity Pact, a coalition of popular movements, some of whom had organic links to the MAS, while others were more independent, was formed in order to fight firstly for the realization of the Constituent Assembly, and after that process had begun, to articulate and promote campesino and indigenous interests in the assembly.[20]

The Unity Pact worked closely with MAS representatives in the Constituent Assembly. Indeed, the Unity Pact represented a significant deepening of democracy as it acted as a space of corporative-collective deliberation and mobilization for the campesino and indigenous sectors outside of the MAS.

In response to opposition-bloc destabilizing tactics, in 2007, and stemming from the Unity Pact, Morales organized supporters from the top down into the Coordinadora Nacional por el Cambio (CONALCAM). Zuazo[21] states that Morales' creation of CONALCAM was part of a double strategy; on one side, to confront the opposition and to re-establish the power of the key movements from the anti-neoliberal protest era, "but this time under government direction"; secondly, it was an attempt to give content to the idea of a "government of the social movements" by establishing social movement forms of action as a part of the government repertoire.

Under the Unity Pact, the MAS was coordinated by the social movements. With the emergence of CONALCAM however, this relationship changed, as government leadership over rural and urban organizations emerged in order to confront the challenge of building a process of change from the street, indicating emerging centralization and top-down influencing of the base as a response to elite destabilization tactics. However, as Zuazo[22] notes, government control over the direction of CONALCAM was only one side of the process; the other side was "the increase in its convocation in the most serious moments of conflict" thereby fostering the belief in the social movements that they were part of the government and that the government of the MAS was in fact "their" government. An ally-type relation was thus forged between party and base who confronted a common enemy with the joint goal of advancing a post-neoliberal model. Linkages between the core organizations and the MAS were strengthened, while new linkages were forged between the party and strategically allied organizations.

In El Alto, for example, a strategic alliance was forged between the MAS, the COR, and the FEJUVE who were united in a common struggle to push forward with constitutional reform in the face of elite resistance. Having witnessed the mobilizational power of El Alto's organizations, Morales wanted to be sure he could count on the support of their leaderships not only electorally but also in defending against the conservatives' destabilization tactics. Meanwhile, FEJUVE and COR leaders saw in the MAS an opportunity to gain access to the state and push toward achieving both the October Agenda and El Alto's development via state provision of basic services and non-precarious jobs.[23] As a spokesperson for the COR told me, the organization was willing to support Morales because he was facing destabilization efforts by the "elites and their transnational allies who have always tried to keep us down and control our resources."[24] Positions in government or direct access to decision-making were exchanged for loyalty which entailed mobilizing the base for elections, engaging in defensive protests against elite destabilization efforts, and ensuring that large-scale protests against the MAS policies would not erupt.[25] The COR had had

> very good relations with the central government ever since the gas war of 2003. We supported the government in the Constituent Assembly; we supported them against the autonomists. The government and the COR, we were very close. We had to defend the process.[26]

Furthermore, a FEJUVE leader during Morales's first term told me,

> Look, Evo was not from here, he came here as an outsider, but we had to offer him support against the elites and the right. And we could, because we were all united around reclaiming democracy, reclaiming Bolivia from the neoliberals. When we called on the base to take to the streets, they responded.[27]

The long organizational and mobilizational histories, of both the core- and the strategically allied organizations shaped the nature of party-base relations in the early stages of the MAS government. Their capacity to engage in sustained, coordinated mobilization ensured not only that they could confront the opposition-bloc, but also that Morales actively sought to incorporate both their demands and leaders. The process was not a simple top-down co-optation of popular organizations. Given the strength of the base, MAS adopted proposals from below while opening new avenues of participation for organization leaders. These new linkages took both extensive and intensive forms, with organizations receiving funding from the executive for their respective needs, while leaders in turn were incorporated into the bureaucratic structure of the party. As discussed previously in regards the Venezuelan case, such linkages open avenues for both deepened democratic participation but also top-down control. However, in these early stages, given the historic power of the base as well as the need to confront a recalcitrant opposition, there were genuine avenues for bottom-up input into party decision-making processes.

In 2008, with the constitutional draft still being contested, and with the autonomist movement pushing further by carrying out an illegal referendum on autonomy, Morales "sought to break … the impasse that threatened his government, calling on all the prefects to run in recall referenda, including himself and his vice-president."[28] Morales easily won with 67 percent, up from the 54 percent of the 2005 elections, while MAS boosted its political power by recovering two of the regions from the opposition. As the relative balance of political power shifted in Morales' and the MAS' favor, the opposition-bloc increasingly sought to use extra-institutional powers to impede the reform process. The autonomist movement sped up its attempts to economically and politically disconnect from the Bolivian state and "by August 2008 there was an almost undeclared civil war in the east, especially in Santa Cruz."[29]

CONALCAM member-organizations,[30] whose mobilizational powers were at their height following the third wave of anti-neoliberal protest, called for mass protest when opponents sought to shut down the Constituent

Assembly process and force Morales' ouster.[31] The last resistance to the draft constitution rescinded in the face of the continued support of the armed forces for the government, the mobilization of member organizations of CONALCAM, and the Brazilian-led UNASUR intervention which stated that only electorally validated decisions would be recognized, thereby quashing autonomists' hopes of regional support.[32] In January 2009, voters approved the new Constitution by 61.4 percent to 38.6 percent.

The Constitution outlines various mechanisms that seek to both deepen and extend democracy. Adhering to the Unity Pact demands, the Constitution redefined the nation as "plurinational and communitarian." Bolivia's democracy is described in article 1.1 as "participatory, representative and communitarian." The "participatory form is associated with direct citizen participation in politics by means of mechanisms to include citizens' decisions in legislation and/or public policy."[33] In addition to standard liberal representative democracy, mechanisms of direct and participatory democracy include referendum, recall of public servants, prior consultation, and legislative initiatives of citizens. Furthermore, members of the judiciary, after preselection by the legislature, are to be elected by the populace.[34] Organized civil society is to participate in the design of public politics and to execute social control at all levels of the state.[35] New spaces for participation are to be opened whereby organized civil society may impact policymaking regarding health, education, economic, and environmental issues.[36]

In terms of extending democracy, echoing the 2007 NDP, the 2009 Constitution supports economic, social, and cultural rights for underprivileged groups, proclaiming its primary goal is to achieve *buen vivir,* the good life. To achieve this, the Constitution calls for "universalizing access to the surplus generated by the use of non-renewable natural resources."[37] Hence, democratic expansion was to be funded by the

> creation and/or strengthening of strategic state enterprises, the state's appropriation of the revenue generated by the oil and gas industry, and the redistribution of this revenue through transfers and royalties to subnational governments and conditional cash transfers to vulnerable groups, as well as the exponential increase in public investment.[38]

The structural power of capital, moderation of reforms and emergent party-base tensions: 2009–14

In the 2009 presidential elections, Morales won in the first round while the MAS won control of congress. In the 2010 departmental elections for governors, mayors, and departmental assemblies, the MAS won six of nine governorships, up from three in the 2005 election. The relative balance of political power between MAS and the opposition bloc swung decisively in favor of Morales. With the new-found dominance in the legislature, MAS sought to gain influence over the traditionally conservative judiciary by pushing through a reform authorizing Morales to appoint five Supreme Court justices, ten Constitutional Tribunal judges, and three members of the Judicial Council.[39] Despite critique from political opponents that Morales was centralizing power and that horizontal control over the executive was decreased, MAS and Morales retained enormous popular support from social movement leaders who felt that Morales was simply redressing a long history of elite capture of state institutions.[40]

The 2011 elections for judges to the high courts (Supreme Court, Constitutional Court, Judicial Council, and Agricultural Court) as stipulated in the 2009 Constitution were also interpreted differently by differing sectors. Once approved by two-thirds vote in the Legislative Assembly, candidates could be presented on the ballot for direct election. According to Driscoll and Nelson,[41] while meritocratic qualifications were eschewed in the selection process, which was opposed by the OAS and opposition politicians, ethnic qualifications were prioritized. As the authors continue, "despite the formal ban on party affiliation, many selected candidates had direct connections to the MAS as party organizers, legislative aides or legal advisors."[42] The elections radically transformed the ethnic makeup of the judiciary by stipulating that slates must include candidates of indigenous decent—a critical achievement in a country that is predominantly indigenous and yet had witnessed the almost complete exclusion of indigenous persons from representation in state institutions. However, over 60 percent of votes cast were spoiled indicating widespread critique of the judicial elections.

While opposition-bloc politicians pointed to the illiberal impacts of executive interference in the judiciary, Morales' relationship with the mass media also drew scorn. The MAS government sought to re-balance the opposition's dominance of the media landscape by boosting state media and by having supportive business interests buy confrontational media outlets such as TV stations ATB, PAT, Full TV as well as newspapers Extra and La Razón.[43] According to Peñaranda, there was a clear shift in the editorial line and content of the media, with critical reporting of the government declining. Between 2006 and 2009, the Morales government had faced a media bombardment as

> The directors of the media were part of the neoliberal elite. Carlos Mesa used to meet with the media directors every 15 days, and they would ask him what he thought about this and that. El Deber, Unitel, La Razón … The media were attacking Morales so forcefully that they were actually putting his ability to govern in doubt.[44]

Just as the pro-neoliberal parties had lost dominance over all the branches of government, the neoliberal media elite lost influence and political space with the arrival of Morales.[45] In conjunction with successful efforts to shift the editorial line of many of the major media outlets, Morales "wanted to have a direct interaction with the public. He gave talks all over the country, and the state media broadcast them. It was his version of Chávez' *Aló Presidente*."[46]

While there were successful efforts to tilt ideological powers in favor of the government, it should be noted that all the private media, including those whose ownerships changed hands, gave space to opposition voices. However, the space for opposition views was not equal to that of pro-government views. There was "never repression of journalists. It was not a dictatorial government."[47] Moreover, following the sale of La Razón, a new La Paz-based newspaper—Página Siete—was established. Página Siete took a critical stance toward the government and would over time become a key source of information for middle- and upper-class Bolivians. However, there is little doubt that from 2009 onward the Morales government re-shaped the media landscape. As discussed in the following chapter, this re-shaping was not permanent, and traditional opposition media figures would find their voices once again.

There was a shift in relations between the military and the civil leaders, with Morales becoming the first democratic president to meet weekly with the military high command. The MAS government boosted the budget for the armed forces which had been slashed during the preceding neoliberal years. Moreover, the armed forces recovered some of the businesses which had been privatized in the 1990s, and there was an increase in the number of military officers working in the diplomatic service and as ambassadors.[48]

While liberal democratic standards were being stretched as Morales sought to challenge opposition-bloc dominance over key sources of power, democratic quality was extended. The "Heroes of the Chaco" decree relating to the increased share of state company Yacimientos Petrolíferos Fiscales Bolivianos (YPFB) in gas activities and the establishing of new contracts regarding taxation with transnational companies meant that the state received eight times more income from gas, increasing from $673 million in 2005 to more than $5 billion in 2013.[49] Public expenditure, underpinned by a commodities boom and the increased taxes and royalties on hydrocarbon exports, increased by 500 percent between 2006 and 2013.[50]

There were significant investments in education and health, particularly in rural areas, while infrastructure projects across the country led to improving human capital indicators, falling transport costs and increased domestic commerce.[51] Transfers such as the Bono Juancito Pinto, which aimed at incentivizing school attendance, covered 1.8 million children; 100 percent of the population were eligible for Renta Dignidad, an old-age pension; and the Bono Juana Azurduy aimed to lower maternal-infant mortality rates and chronic malnutrition of children under the age of two. Programs aimed at zero illiteracy, malnutrition, and eye health were also introduced. From 1999 to 2011, average income rose 45 percent, and 182 percent among rural populations.[52] The real minimum wage increased by 87.7 percent from 2005 to 2014.[53] Inequality decreased, with the income of poorer sectors of the population growing much faster since 2006 than that of the higher-income households.[54] Poverty was reduced between 2005 and 2011 from 59.6 percent to 45 percent, and extreme poverty fell from 36.7 percent to 20.9 percent.[55] The percentage of Bolivians living on less than USD 2/day fell from 60 in 2006 to 30 in 2011.[56] Furthermore, Bolivia's build-up of international reserves, which topped 48 percent of GDP in 2013, acted as somewhat of a buffer against the global financial crisis while also allowing the country to avoid the restrictive conditionalities attached to IMF borrowing.[57]

Despite a clear movement toward a post-neoliberal model of development and democracy, and while Morales and the MAS presented their project as a radical alternative to neoliberalism which involved a diversification of the economy away from primary export-based development accompanied by a nationalization of Bolivia's natural resources, neither of these goals was fully achieved. Bolivia became more dependent on primary exports than ever before, with primary goods increasing from 89 percent of total export value in 2005 to 95 percent in 2012.[58] Hydrocarbons as a share of total export value increased from 35 percent before Morales' first election to 51 percent in the 2011–14 period.[59] Furthermore, the extent of nationalization and state control over natural resources was limited. PETROBRAS and REPSOL, two transnational companies, retained control over 75 percent of natural gas production.[60]

From Morales' perspective, he had been elected promising to overhaul the worst excesses of economic exclusion. However, he inherited an economy that was underdeveloped and reliant on commodity exports, with an underfunded and outdated state extraction company, where transnational extractive firms were contractually and infrastructurally embedded in the economy, and where TNCs had the extractive capacity and capital funds required to invest in new explorations. Hence, the government was heavily dependent on transnational extraction firms to exploit the resources with which social-economic policies were to be funded.[61] When Morales took power, "most transnational mining and hydrocarbon firms had 20-year contracts giving them access to the mineral and hydrocarbon reserves that bi- and multilateral-trade agreements legally guaranteed."[62] As such, transnational capital "had successfully embedded itself in Bolivia's natural resource sectors for decades to come."[63] In this scenario, Morales opted for a "neoliberal nationalization."[64] While taxes and royalties on TNCs were increased, wholesale nationalization was not attempted. The vast majority of the hydrocarbon value chain was not nationalized, while booming gas prices meant TNC profit levels were not drastically impacted despite the new tax and royalty contracts.[65]

In the mining sector, despite some nationalizations, private transnationals retained control. State mining company COMIBOL played a minor role, accounting for around 5 percent of total production by 2014, with private capital controlling around 70 percent.[66] In terms of agricultural policy and land reform, the structural power of large-scale agricultural and livestock producers from the *media luna* who produce essential foodstuffs for the domestic and export markets ensured they maintained influence in policy-making.[67] The power of international economic actors and agri-elites to influence government policy ensured that their privilege was protected, thereby limiting the possibility of adhering to more radical demands of protesters from the 2000–05 period. Indeed, agro-industrial elites from Santa Cruz, with support from the US government and Brazilian rural elites with ties to Sao Paulo and international financial capital, maintained influence over policymaking, preventing plans to implement a radical agrarian revolution where 90 percent of the land is owned by 1 percent of the population.[68]

While there were clear advances in terms of minimum wages, in urban sites the level of extremely precarious jobs as measured by income, access to social security, and job stability rose from 22.1 percent in 2001 to 51.6 percent in 2011.[69] Meanwhile, Quiroga[70] notes that while cash transfers had a positive impact, their benefits were severely undercut by a regressive tax system, while property and wealth taxes were practically non-existent. In sum, while increased state revenues from taxes and royalties on hydrocarbon exports funded increased social spending, there was little change in the structure of the economy, industrialization levels and land reforms were moderate, taxation remained regressive, and the number of quality jobs remained low.

As noted earlier, from 2006 to 2009 business groups took a fiercely confrontational stance toward the government, using their links to the conservative autonomist movement and their control of the media to attempt to destabilize Morales. These attempts failed, however, due to the governments' political strength and the defensive mobilization of allied popular organizations. Indeed, it was precisely because of the government's domination of the political sphere following the 2009 and 2010 elections that TNC directors, agri-industrial exporting elites and business associations from the Santa Cruz department came to realize that relying solely on an alliance with right-wing political parties to gain political leverage was futile.[71] Hence, they switched their tactics of dealing with the Morales government from confrontation to dialogue, and ultimately, outright cooperation.[72] As Weber[73] states, in August 2008, Rubén Costas was plotting Morales' ouster from office. By 2013, "he was regularly lunching with Morales." Morales regularly consulted business confederations such as CAO, ANAPO, CAINCO and the CEFB—the very business organizations that had supported the 2008 autonomy drive aimed at forcing Morales from power.

The new business-government relations re-opened channels for economic elites to shape policymaking. As Wolff[74] discusses, a key example of this rapprochement between the economic-elite wing of the opposition-bloc and the Morales government was a shared agenda for the expansion of agribusiness in the lowlands. The

> joint commitment to the Agenda Patriótica 2015, which the MAS government and key representatives of the economic elite from Santa Cruz ratified in December 2013, basically implied a private-public partnership to heavily increase investment in infrastructure in order to significantly expand agricultural production and export.[75]

Such plans required that the government roll back on any notion of land reform as well as efforts to limit food exports so as to prevent domestic food prices rising too rapidly. Land titling of productive lands favored cattle and extensive crop production while export quotas were determined by negotiation with respective producers and associations.

New government–business relations were the result of strategically oriented calculations made by both parties regarding given structural constraints. That is, with the autonomist movement defeated and the MAS dominating the political sphere, yet where the government's economic power was deeply reliant on TNCs and agri-business (high structural power of business), and where economic elite's traditional avenues to policymaking (pro-neoliberal parties) were in disarray, a pragmatic compromise was reached.

Such compromise, while allowing Morales to govern, restricted the space for a more radical agenda, thereby opening the possibility of government-base tensions. Relatedly, given the reduction in government-elite confrontations, Morales was less reliant on the support of strategic movements to defend the post-neoliberal process. Indeed, given the power balance between the government and the TNC and domestic economic elite, and his desire to economically advance Bolivia so as to have the capacity to engage in democratic extending, this phase of the post-neoliberal democratization project witnessed elements of "exclusionary and authoritarian tendencies ... directed against 'internal enemies' and former allies."[76] That is, despite popular sector support for a radical-substantive democratization project, the underlying development model adopted by MAS fostered tensions with some sectors of the popular base. The easy revenue from the commodities boom meant that social and welfare spending could occur without any major redistribution of private property in what Riofrancos calls a "hydrocarbon-fuelled-social-democratic bargain."[77] The moderation of the project in the face of the structural power of economic opposition triggered a re-calibration of party-base relations.

Party-base linkages, tensions, and limited participation: progressive-regressive centralization

Silva[78] expertly outlines the nature of the policymaking process under MAS governments. At a strategic-planning level of policymaking the MAS leadership sought relative autonomy from popular organizations. At the same time, the MAS was connected to its base because ministries were staffed with members of popular organizations and so popular concerns were likely to be incorporated. However, macro-economic policymaking was insulated from popular input and so the development model underpinned by tightening linkages to extractive and agro-industrial elites was not open to popular influence. Morales and his representatives met directly with popular-organization leaderships in assembly-style meetings via CONALCAM in order to foment consensual agreements. A further key measure of the popular base's ability to influence the MAS-government was its capacity to engage in informal contestatory interest intermediation.

While informal contestatory interest intermediation, ministerial appointments, and deliberative participation via CONALCAM offered a deepened quality of democracy that tethered executive power to popular sector organizations, the evolving power relationships between the government and the opposition-bloc re-shaped how such spaces of participation operated, and who was invited in. The easing of government-opposition tensions had two interrelated impacts. On the one hand, the government's survival was less reliant on the defensive mobilization of strategically allied organizations, and there was a clear distinction in the quality of democratic participation between core-organizations and strategic-organizations. Moreover, while the moderation of the project did trigger resistance from strategic groups, the continued support of core groups (whose demands were generally met) as well as the use of intensive and extensive linkages to curb the contestatory mobilization of strategic groups meant that Morales did not face regular mass contestatory mobilization. In fact, popular organizations that did seek to challenge the new government-economic elite relations via contestatory mobilization faced a hostile scenario in which executive power was used regressively to co-opt organization leaderships. While the emergent power factors shaped the nature of democratic deepening, historical factors were also key. It was the core movements who founded the MAS who were most directly incorporated into decision-making. Moreover, the early historical formation of intensive and extensive linkages between MAS and strategic-organizations during the allied confrontation against the autonomists shaped how party-base tensions evolved.

In return for their support, Morales gave core-supporters and some leaders from strategic-organizations privileged positions in ministries, as well as power to nominate "personnel for positions of medium and low importance in the executive branch at the national, departmental, and local levels of government."[79] There was a dramatic increase in representation of formerly excluded sectors with the social and demographic profile of elective representatives shifting to incorporate more women, peasants, indigenous groups and urban-popular groups. Furthermore, Morales regularly consulted with CONALCAM. While CONALCAM was not entirely a bottom-up vehicle, the interactions between Morales and CONALCAM on policy decisions, laws, and long-term strategies did increase member movements' power to influence decision-making processes.[80] Once CONALCAM approved a proposed law, it was sent to the National Assembly where MAS representatives sought its approval. Given the considerable presence of members of core social movements in both the National Assembly and MAS, CONALCAM decisions were guaranteed to be taken into account by the legislative body.[81]

While core movements certainly achieved access to the political decision-making channels, the nature of the relationship between Morales and the organizations raises concerns. Given the economic power of the government to redistribute resources, some observers question whether autonomous deliberative and participatory space exists for core organization members to challenge the government. For example, many observers state that the CONALCAM has in fact "primarily served to channel and constrain the autonomy of member groups and movements into support for the government."[82] Schilling-Vacaflor[83] meanwhile describes how the unwavering support of leaders of the Six Federations coca-growers organization for the government has inhibited the scope of the base to express grievances resulting from negative socio-environmental impacts of hydrocarbon activities and the lack of mitigation measures. As Schilling-Vacaflor[84] states, "before Morales became president ... protest activities, or at least the threat of blockades against the ... extraction companies, were quite common." However, today the cocaleros, the municipal government, and community members do not wish to challenge "their" government, even if government supported extraction policies negatively impact the well-being of some of the base. The organic nature of the relations between government and the core organizations has thus hindered democratic deepening in some instances.

However, while there certainly appears to have been some instances of co-optation of organic movements, given their historical mobilizational powers, they have at times shown sufficient autonomy to critique and mobilize against Morales when they are not included in decision-making processes that have an impact on their livelihoods. For example, after the decree to cancel fuel subsidies in December 2010 that led to an estimated 83 percent increase in fuel prices, popular revolts against the policy that came to be known as the *gasolinazo* forced the government to backtrack. While the COB organized mass protests, as Balderacchi[85] notes, what was interesting about the protests is that core support groups including the cocaleros and CSUTCB leaders were also involved. It was not simply the increase in gas prices that upset core supporters. It was the exclusionary method of decision-making that irked these groups.

In sum, core-organization opportunity and agency to influence a range of issues that resonate with movement demands was built, albeit through informal, un-institutionalized channels in return for active government support. The organizational composition of CONALCAM—it is comprised almost entirely of organic movements supportive of the government—and its privileged position in accessing political decision-making channels raises a further concern regarding the deepening of democracy in Bolivia's post-neoliberal process. While the power of organic groups has prevented top-down decision-making by holding the government to account, their very power prevents Morales from engaging fully with popular sector opponents of his regime.

While land reform was moderated by agro-industrial elite powers, there was more scope for core organizations such as the CSUSTCB to influence policymaking and for their organization members to take positions within the Ministry of Rural Development and Lands.[86] Non-core organizations who strategically allied with the MAS such as the lowland CONAMAQ and CIDOB increasingly saw their concerns side-lined. The TIPNIS case is emblematic of such issues. Government plans to build a highway to connect two lowland Bolivian departments and Brazil on indigenous protected territory, without prior consultation, fostered tensions between the government and strategic-allies the CIDOB and CONAMAQ. The government argued that the highway was needed to boost access to markets for agricultural goods produced in the region. Strategic-groups in the region however mobilized marches to La Paz, gaining significant support and media attention, forcing the government to postpone the TIPNIS plans in 2011. Core-constituency groups such as the coca-growers, the Bartolina-Sisa, and the Interculturales however, mobilized in support of the TIPNIS project, highlighting the tensions within the support base of MAS. Concerted pressure from core-groups means that the TIPNIS plan has not entirely been removed, yet strategic-bloc mobilizations have prevented the project from advancing to date.

What we see here is the MAS government was caught between demands of strategic popular organizations, core-organizations, and an economic elite whose power to dictate policy had not been broken. In response, the government sought to weaken contestatory organizations via a divide-and-conquer strategy. This process developed over time, beginning with the MAS insertion into areas where it had no organic base, but required electoral support, particularly in urban areas. By incorporating militant leaders into the party structure, MAS leaders sought to ensure a calm governing environment. Co-opted organization leaders were required to show political loyalty if they wished to receive a cut of the public funds which they require in order to respond to the demands of their base.[87] As a central actor in the El Alto FEJUVE leadership of 2003 notes,

> from the moment the government of Evo Morales was elected, the FEJUVE, the social organizations ... they became corrupted ... the new *dirigencias* (leaderships) just entered the organizations to rob. And they didn't even rob for the benefit of El Alto, but for their own personal benefit.[88]

The result of this co-optation of erstwhile contestatory organizations was a monopolization of power in the MAS to the "detriment of the exercise of concurrent and progressive powers of citizens with levels of autonomy and independent decision-making," whereby participation that aims to transform living conditions "has been reduced to simple and uncritical support of the government."[89]

In conjunction with co-opting, the government fostered *paralelismo*, that is, the creating of parallel organizations to existing contestatory organizations. The government fostered divisions in existing organizations by identifying sectors of the leaderships who would support the MAS and refrain from contestatory mobilization against MAS policies. It used its economic power to direct funding to this "loyal" section, while using its ideological power and media influence to side-line elements of the organization who sought to retain autonomy. If confrontations emerged with core-allies, the government framed these as "creative tensions within the revolution," but where strategic groups' mobilizations directly challenged the underpinning development model and government-business relations they were labeled "counterrevolutionary."[90] The outcome was a divided and confused base whose collective power was diminished, while social movements, indigenous communities, and former allies turned against each other. These processes of co-optation, division, and *paralelismo* were evidenced, amongst others, in the cases of the CONAMAQ, CIDOB, urban popular organizations such as the FEJUVEs, and the Assembly of Guaraní People (APG).[91] The COB faced similar problems as the upper echelons of the labor bureaucracy were incorporated into the MAS via intensive and extensive linkages, becoming increasingly distanced from the grassroots workers, thereby weakening the organization's contestatory capacity while also triggering intense internal debate regarding organizational autonomy from the MAS.[92]

In the case of El Alto, for many Alteños who had taken to the streets between 2003 and 2005, the government pacts with business elites represented a reneging on Morales's earlier promises to adhere to the October Agenda. As one executive committee member of the 2003 FEJUVE said, "the MAS gave a few little crumbs, a stadium and other trinkets, but this is not what we fought for in 2003."[93] According to Alteños drinking tea at a stall in La Ceja, El Alto, "Nothing changed here. Evo forgot us once he became president. We still have no jobs, no security. We are still poor." As another member of the FEJUVE executive committee during the 2003 protests put it,

> The October Agenda demanded complete nationalization, not a negotiation on the price TNCs pay. The government has not demanded that the TNCs leave. This is not nationalization. All the TNCs and businesses have actually been given even more help by the government. The elites, now more than ever, have grabbed hold of the government. They have it in their hands; it is simply at the service of the TNCs.[94]

Despite such sentiment among the people I spoke with in El Alto, the central vehicles for contestatory interest intermediation, the COR and the FEJUVE, in general did not call for mass demonstrations against government policy.[95] According to a member of the FEJUVE leadership during the gas war, COR and FEJUVE leaders were offered political positions in the MAS, thereby using the popular organizations as "trampolines to become deputies, senators, city-councillors, to run for mayor."[96] The leaderships of the popular organizations who allied with the MAS claimed that it was necessary to support the government as it was the best buffer against the neoliberal parties. As the spokesperson for the COR told me,

> as an organization for the workers, we cannot align with governments or parties of the right. We did not have any relationship with Tuto Quiroga, Doria Medina or any of the right-wing parties ... We are leftists, and so we have to continue on the side of Evo Morales because the MAS is a party of the left.[97]

While such a stance may be understandable, it opened space for tensions between the popular organizations and their bases. Despite sentiment among members of the grassroots base that Morales had ceded too much ground to economic elite interests, with the leaderships of the organizations forging intensive and extensive linkages with the MAS, contestatory mobilization did not erupt. That is, via linkages forged during Morales' first term, the executive used state powers to curb popular power and prevent mass contestatory mobilizations from erupting in response to his new capital-friendly policies and exclusionary decision-making processes.

Anria[98] expertly analyzes the nature of MAS candidate selection, highlighting that in districts where civil society is densely organized, autonomous, and aligned with the party, the grassroots organizations are more likely to impose their choices of candidates for the MAS and resist top-down selection. However, there is a central issue with MAS-organization linkages. While candidate selection may offer new avenues for participation from below, if the candidates selected come from the popular organizations themselves, then the very autonomy needed to direct the party from below is sacrificed. Moreover, there is a tension between retaining autonomy from the party and aligning with the party. For those popular organizations who did not align with the MAS agenda, they could retain autonomy but they were side-lined. Conversely, those branches of the popular organizations who did align with MAS sacrificed their autonomy but retained access to decision-making channels. Hence, while a powerful COR-El Alto may have been able to impose its choice of candidate for local elections, it could do so precisely because a sector of its leadership aligned behind Morales and the MAS. Problems with such an arrangement become apparent, however, when the leadership of the popular organizations aligns with the MAS, but grassroots members do not. In fact, as discussed in the following chapter, such arrangements may foster such deep tensions that the organizations split into competing factions.

In 2013, the Law of Participation and Social Control was passed and the government created the National Mechanism for Participation and Social Control as part of the Ministry of Transparency. The law states that "participation is a right, condition, and fundamental element of democracy" and that as such, social organizations should oversee the functioning of state organs and politicians, formulate and elaborate public policies and laws, and have independence to take decisions. However, the government determines which organized sectors should be recognized, and each government ministry convokes meetings with a pre-established agenda.[99] Hence, while core- and allied-strategic organizations may see increased avenues for bottom-up participation, the agenda is set prior to participation. Moreover, the new law also increased the ability of the government to exclude those popular organizations who challenged the MAS. Participation was increasingly managed from above, with the scope for successful contestatory interest intermediation restricted.

In sum, while the MAS and economic elites strategically selected to form "pacts of non-aggression" given the existing balance of powers, the flipside of these structurally guided selectivites was the need for the party to confront/co-opt formerly powerful constituent organizations whose grassroots rejected government-business pacts. While booming commodity prices managed to lubricate a social peace—between business interests, core-organizations, and "loyal" strategic organizations, the 2014–18 period would reveal the problems of preventing contestatory mobilization from emerging as internal tensions lead to strategic organizations splitting apart, opening a new stage in Bolivia's post-neoliberal process. In the following chapter, I evaluate this phenomenon, as well as the re-emergence of the political-wing of the opposition-bloc, before turning to an analysis of how such party-base tensions and increasing oppositional political power impacted business-MAS pacts and, ultimately, the direction of the process between 2019 and 2021.

Notes

1 Nancy Postero, "Bolivia's Challenge to 'Colonial Neoliberalism,'" in Mark Goodale and Nancy Postero (eds), *Neoliberalism, Interrupted: Social Change and Contested Governance in Contemporary Latin America* (California: Stanford University Press, 2013): 34.

2 Bolivian Ministry of Planning and Development, *Plan Nacional de Desarrollo: Bolivia Digna, Soberana, Democrática y Productiva para la construcción del Vivir Bien. Lineamientos Estratégicos 2006–11* (La Paz: 2007): 4.

3 Ibid., 15.

4 Luis Arce Catacora, *Modelo Económico Social Comunitario Productivo Bolivian* (La Paz: Ministry of Economy and Public Finances, 2015).

5 Brent Kaup, "A Neoliberal Nationalization? The Constraints on Natural-Gas-Led Development in Bolivia," *Latin American Perspectives* 37, no. 3 (2010): 129.

6 Carlos Arze Vargas and Javier Gómez, "Bolivia: ¿El 'Proceso de Cambio' nos Conduce al Vivir Bien?" in Carlos Arze, Javier Gómez, Pablo Ospina, and Víctor Álvarez (eds.), *Promesas en su Laberinto. Cambios y Continuidades en los Gobiernos Progresistas de América Latina* (La Paz: CEDLA, 2013): 45–176.

7 George Gray Molina "The Challenge of Progressive Change under Evo Morales," in Kurt Weyland, Raúl Madrid, and Wendy Hunter (eds), *Leftist Governments in Latin America: Successes and Shortcomings* (Cambridge: Cambridge University Press, 2010): 57–76.

8 Kent Eaton, "Backlash in Bolivia: Regional Autonomy as a Reaction against Indigenous Mobilization," *Politics & Society* 35, no. 1 (2007): 74.

9 Steven Levitsky and James Loxton, "Populism and Competitive Authoritarianism in the Andes," *Democratization* 20, no. 1 (2013): 117.

10 Íñigo Errejón and Juan Guijarro, "Post-Neoliberalism's Difficult Hegemonic Consolidation: A Comparative Analysis of the Ecuadorean and Bolivian Processes," *Latin American Perspectives* 43, no. 1 (2016): 46.

11 Bret Gustafson, *Bolivia in the Age of Gas* (Durham, NC: Duke University Press, 2020): 150.
12 Gustafson, *Bolivia in the Age of Gas*, 265.
13 Kent Eaton, "Recentralization and the Left turn in Latin America: Diverging Outcomes in Bolivia, Ecuador, and Venezuela," *Comparative Political Studies* 47, no. 8 (2014): 1130–57.
14 Erick Villanueva "The Media in Bolivia," in Jairo Lugo-Ocando (ed.), *The Media in Latin America* (New York: McGraw-Hill/Open University Press, 2008): 29–45.
15 Pascal Lupien, "The Media in Venezuela and Bolivia: Attacking the 'Bad Left' from Below," *Latin American Perspectives* 40, no. 3 (2016): 228.
16 Raul Madrid, "Origins and Policies of the Movimiento al Socialismo," in Steven Levitsky and Kenneth Roberts (eds), *The Resurgence of the Latin American Left* (Baltimore, MD: John Hopkins University Press, 2011): 257; Benjamin Kohl and Linda Farthing, "New Spaces, New Contests: Appropriating Decentralization for Political change in Bolivia," in Victoria Beard, Faranak Miraftab, and Christopher Silver (eds), *Planning and Decentralization: Contested Spaces for Public Action in the Global South* (London and New York: Routledge, 2008): 69–85.
17 Waltraud Morales and Annabelle Conroy, "New Social Movement Governance in Bolivia: Contention in a Multi-Ethnic Democracy," in Harry Vanden, Peter Funke, and Gary Prevost (eds), *The New Global Politics: Global Social Movements in the Twenty-First Century* (London and New York: Taylor & Francis, 2017): 32.
18 Jeffery Webber, *From Rebellion to Reform in Bolivia: Class Struggle, Indigenous Liberation, and the Politics of Evo Morales* (Chicago, IL: Haymarket Books, 2011): 96.
19 Almut Schilling-Vacaflor, "Bolivia's New Constitution: Towards Participatory Democracy and Political Pluralism," *European Review of Latin American and Caribbean Studies* 90, no. 3 (2011): 12.
20 Moira Zuazo, '¿Los Movimientos Sociales en el Poder?" *Nueva Sociedad* 227 (2010): 129. Initial members of the Unity Pact included, amongst others, the CSUTCB; La Confederación de Pueblos indígenas de Bolivia (Confederation of Indigenous Peoples of Bolivia - CIDOB; CONAMAQ; La Confederación Sindical de Colonizadores de Bolivia (CSCB); La Federación Nacional de Mujeres Indígenas, Originarias y Campesinas de Bolivia Bartolina Sisa (FNMCB-BS).
21 Ibid., 130.
22 Ibid.
23 Franklin Troche, international press officer for the COR, interview with author, El Alto, July 13, 2017.
24 Interview with author, El Alto, July 13, 2017.
25 Former vice-president of the FEJUVE, interview with author, El Alto, June 27, 2017.
26 Spokesperson for the COR, interview with author, El Alto, July 13, 2017.
27 Interview with author, El Alto, July 13, 2017.
28 Errejón and Guijarro, "Post-Neoliberalism's Difficult Hegemonic Consolidation," 46–7.
29 Ibid.
30 The CONALCAM was expanded in 2008 with the addition of various urban social organizations such as the COB, neighborhood associations, unions, students, and miners' cooperatives.
31 Eduardo Silva, "Reorganizing Popular Sector Incorporation: Propositions from Bolivia, Ecuador, and Venezuela," *Politics & Society* 45, no. 1 (2017): 100–01.
32 Errejón and Guijarro, "Post-Neoliberalism's Difficult Hegemonic Consolidation," 46.
33 Walter Arteaga, "Building Citizenship in the Context of the Debate on the Post-2015 Agenda in Bolivia," *Community Development Journal* 50, no. 4 (2015): 579.

34 Art. 182, 188, 194, 198 of the Constitution.
35 Art. 240, 241 of the Constitution.
36 Art. 40, 78–93, 309, 343 of the Constitution.
37 Arteaga, "Building Citizenship," 579.
38 Ibid., 573.
39 Madrid, "Origins and Policies," 252.
40 Interview with executive committee member of the COR-El Alto, El Alto, July 13, 2017.
41 Amanda Driscoll and Michael J. Nelson, "The 2011 Judicial Elections in Bolivia," *Electoral Studies* 3, no. 31 (2012): 629.
42 Ibid.
43 Raúl Peñaranda, *Control Remoto: De cómo Evo Morales Creó una Red de Medios Paraestatales y un Plan para Acosar a la Prensa Independiente* (La Paz: Plural, 2–14).
44 Interview with Fernando Molina, March 2021. Molina is a Bolivian writer and journalist.
45 Fernando Molina y Susana Bejarano, "La Transformación Restauradora del campo Mediático: El Alineamiento de los Medios de Comunicación con el Bloque de Poder Postevista en Noviembre de 2019," in Jan Souverein and José Luis Exeni Rodríguez (eds.), *Nuevo Mapa de Actores en Bolivia: Crisis, Polarización e Incertidumbre (2019–2020)* (La Paz: FES Bolivia, 2020): 165–200.
46 Interview with Fernando Molina, March 2021.
47 Ibid.
48 Fernando Molina, "Patria o Muerte: El Orden Castrense de Evo Morales," *Nuevo Sociedad* 278, Nov-Dec (2018): 119–129.
49 Pablo Solón, "Algunas Reflexiones, Autocríticas y Propuestas Sobre el Proceso de Cambio en Bolivia," *Hoy es Todavía*, February 2 (2016): Retrieved https://pablosolon.wordpress.com/2016/02/25/algunas-reflexiones-autocriticas-y-propuestas-sobre-el-proceso-de-cambio/.
50 Arteaga, "Building Citizenship."
51 Jean-Paul Faguet, "After Riding Commodities Boom, Bolivia Faces Stress of Falling Prices," interview in *World Politics Review*, October 15 (2015): Retrieved https://www.worldpoliticsreview.com/trend-lines/16958/after-riding-commodities-boom-bolivia-faces-stress-of-falling-prices#:~:text=Faguet%3A%20Bolivia%20is%20highly%20susceptible,huge%20stress%20on%20regional%20budgets.
52 Ibid.
53 Jake Johnson and Stephan Lefebvre, "Bolivia's Economy under Evo in 10 Graphs. *CEPR*, October 8 (2014): Retrieved http://cepr.net/blogs/the-americas-blog/bolivias-economy-under-evo-in-10-graphs.
54 Ibid.
55 Ibid.
56 CIA Factbook (2011): Retrieved https://www.cia.gov/library/publications/the-world-factbook/geos/bl.html.
57 Johnson and Lefebvre, "Bolivia's Economy."
58 ECLAC, *Statistical Yearbook for Latin America and the Caribbean* (Santiago, Chile: United Nations, 2013): 111.
59 Carlos Arze, *Una Década de Gobierno. ¿Construyente el Vivir Bien o un Capitalsimo Salvaje* (La Paz: CEDLA, 2016).
60 Solón, "Algunas Reflexiones."
61 Brent Kaup, "Transnational Class Formation and Spatialities of Power: The case of Elite Competition in Bolivia," *Global Networks* 13, no. 1 (2013): 101–19.
62 Ibid., 114.
63 Ibid.

64 Kaup, "A Neoliberal Nationalization," 135.
65 Diego Andreucci, "Resources, Regulation and the State: Struggles over Gas Extraction and Passive Revolution in Evo Morales's Bolivia," *Political Geography* 61 (2017): 170–80.
66 Arze, *Una Década de Gobierno*, 16.
67 Kent Eaton, *Territory and Ideology in Latin America: Policy Conflicts between National and Subnational Governments* (Oxford: Oxford University Press, 2017).
68 Nicole Fabricant and Bret Gustafson, "Socialism from Below? Bolivia in the age of Extractivism," *New Politics* XVI, no. 3 (2017); For a detailed analysis of land retitling under the Morales' governments see Chapter 7 of Jeffrey Webber, *The Last Day of Oppression, and the First day of the Same: The Politics and Economics of the New Latin American Left* (London: Pluto Press, 2017).
69 Bruno Rojas Callejas, Carlos Arze Vargas, and Silvia Escóbar de Pabón, *País sin Industrias, País con Empleos Precarios: Situación de los Derechos Laborales en Bolivia, 2011–12* (La Paz: CEDLA, 2014): 182.
70 UNITAS, *Desafíos Para la Implementación de los Objetivos de Desarrollo Sostenible en Bolivia* (La Paz: UNITAS, 2017): 13.
71 Jonas Wolff, "The Political Economy of Bolivia's Post-Neoliberalism: Policies, Elites and the MAS Government," *European Review of Latin American and Caribbean Studies* 108, July-December (2019): 115.
72 Jonas Wolff, "Business Power and the Politics of Postneoliberalism: Relations between Governments and Economic Elites in Bolivia and Ecuador," *Latin American Politics and Society* 58, no. 2 (2016): 137.
73 Webber, *The Last Day of Oppression*, 223.
74 Wolff, "The Political Economy of Bolivia's Post-Neoliberalism," 118.
75 Ibid.
76 Schilling-Vacaflor, "Bolivia's New Constitution," 13.
77 Linda Farthing and Thea Riofrancos, "The State of the Left in Latin America: Ecuador and Bolivia after the Pink Tide," *NACLA*, June 2 (2017).
78 Eduardo Silva, "Social Movements and the Second Incorporation in Bolivia and Ecuador," in Eduardo Silva and Federico Rossi (eds), *Reshaping the Political Arena in Latin America: From Resisting Neoliberalism to the Second Incorporation* (Pittsburgh, PA: University of Pittsburgh Press, 2018): 46–9.
79 Silva, 'Social Movements, Policy, and Conflict," 67.
80 Claudio Balderacchi, "Participatory Mechanisms in Bolivia, Ecuador and Venezuela: Deepening or Undermining Democracy?" *Government and Opposition* 52, no. 1 (2015): 1–31.
81 Ibid., 18.
82 Morales and Conroy, "New Social Movement Governance," 33.
83 Almut Schilling-Vacaflor, "'If the Company Belongs to you, How can you be against it?' Limiting Participation and Taming Dissent in Neo-Extractivist Bolivia," *The Journal of Peasant Studies* 44, no. 3 (2017): 658–76.
84 Ibid., 666.
85 Balderacchi, "Participatory Mechanisms," 23.
86 For discussion see Santiago Anria, *When Movements Become Parties: The Bolivian MAS in Comparative Perspective* (Cambridge and New York: Cambridge University Press, 2019): 145–7.
87 Luis Tapia, *El Estado de Derecho como Tiranía* (La Paz: CIDES-UMSA, 2011); Sian Lazar, *El Alto, Rebel City: Self and Citizenship in Andean Bolivia* (Durham, NC and London: Duke University Press, 2008).
88 Interview with author, El Alto, August 10, 2017.
89 Arteaga, "Building Citizenship," 583.

90 See Trujillo and Spronk, "Socialism without Workers."

91 The nature of co-optation, divisions, and *paralelismo* differ from case to case, requiring in depth analysis to comprehend outcomes. I focus on urban organizations in El Alto and La Paz here and in the following chapter. For an excellent analysis of the APG struggles see Schilling-Vacaflor, "If the Company Belongs to you." For discussion of the TIPNIS conflict and the splits in the CONAMAQ and CIDOB see Waltraud Morales, "The TIPNIS Crisis and the Meaning of Bolivian Democracy under Evo Morales," *The Latin Americanist* 57, no. 1 (2013): 79–90.

92 See Angus McNelly, "Labour Bureaucracy and Labour Officialdom in Evo Morales's Bolivia," *Development and Change* 50, no. 4 (2018): 896–922; Trujillo and Spronk, "Socialism without Workers."

93 Interview with author, El Alto, August 8, 2017.

94 Interview with author, El Alto, August 24, 2017.

95 Carlos Arze, interview with author, La Paz, August 25, 2017.

96 Interview with author, El Alto, August 9, 2017.

97 Interview with author, El Alto, July 13, 2017.

98 Anria, *When Movements Become Parties*, Chapter 3.

99 Zuazo, '¿Los Movimientos Sociales en el Poder?" 134.

7 Splits in the popular base, the return of the opposition, and the removal of Evo Morales, 2014–21

In this chapter, I evaluate the third presidency of Evo Morales between 2014 and 2019 before discussing his removal from office in 2019 and the aftermath period. Building on the analysis in the preceding chapter, I trace the shifting ideological, economic, military, and political balances of power as well as the evolving party-base relations, identifying how the quality of democracy changed in liberal, substantive, and participative terms.

Regressive centralization, fractures in the base, and the re-emergence of the political opposition: 2014–19

In the 2014 presidential elections Morales won 61 percent of the vote, the MAS won a two-thirds supermajority in both houses, while also winning eight of the nine provinces, including "three of four in the eastern lowlands—leading him to proclaim the 'defeat' of the political Right, and the replacement of the *'media luna'* by the *'luna llena'* (full moon) of a united Bolivia."[1] At the inauguration of his third term, Morales outlined an ambitious ten-year development plan—the "Agenda Patriótica 2025" (Patriotic Agenda 2025). The Patriotic Agenda 2025, like the Economic and Social Development Plan of 2016–20, outlined plans to continue using extraction to finance development. As vice-president García-Linera stated in August 2016, "we are going to use extractivism for at least two decades more" in order to develop and protect society. Moreover, with "no other strong national leadership in the wings, MAS party logic held that a fourth presidential term for Morales was critical to accomplish this mission."[2] These two decisions—to continue to use primary commodity exports to fund the reformist development project as well as to seek a constitutional reform to allow Morales run for a fourth term influenced the nature of party-base relations, opposition-bloc—government relations and, consequently, economic elite-government relations in the 2014–19 period.

In the 2014 elections, MAS gained support in the *media luna*, but lost ground in former Andean strongholds and urbanized zones in La Paz, Oruro, and Potosí, highlighting both Morales' efforts to woo voters in erstwhile enemy territory and the rural nature of his continuing support. Core-organizations

DOI: 10.4324/9781003262466-8

continued to actively support Morales and mobilized their grassroot bases to vote for him. For example, CSUTCB leaders openly admitted that communities would be sanctioned according to the "norms of community justice" if they failed to support the MAS[3] while in the Chapare municipalities, over 95 percent voted for Morales.

Meanwhile, the MAS and Morales' successes in the eastern lowlands—the traditional home of the most conservative elements of the opposition-bloc—partly reflected the increasingly cooperative relations between the government and agri-business elites in the region. Furthermore, "600 militants from the conservative Democratic National Action Party (ADN) of Santa Cruz, formed by ex-military dictator Hugo Banzer" were "welcomed by the MAS leadership after renouncing their party affiliations."[4]

The 2015 subnational elections followed the trend of the 2014 elections, with the MAS consolidating its electoral power, but losing ground in the urban zones where it lost in eight of the ten principal cities, the departmental capitals, along with El Alto. Core-organizations who had been included in decision-making channels retained support for Morales, though Nelson Condori, the Aymara representative on the executive of the CSUTCB, warned that "we will only continue to support Evo only for as long as he listens to our demands."[5] The government tactics of courting conservatives and economic elites and moderating the extent of the democratization project, combined with the efforts to meddle in formerly autonomous organization leaderships and to select MAS candidates from the top-down cost the government legitimacy amongst some urban popular voters. Indeed, vice president García Linera admitted that "the population accompany the project, but they were not in agreement with the candidates we selected."[6] Carlos Calle, head of the Central Obrero Departmental-La Paz (Departmental Workers' Union of La Paz, COD), told me that interactions between popular organizations and the MAS, and the interactions between the base and their organization leaders were guided by money and political favors, whereby *dirigentes* asked the grassroots members "What party are you with? If you support this party I will listen to your demands, if you are of the other party, I won't."[7]

The case of El Alto offers a useful insight into the evolving party-base relations in urban zones and between the MAS and strategic-organizations more generally. In 2015, Soldedad Chapetón from the right-wing *Unidad Nacional* (UN) party was elected mayor, while six of the 11 city councillors elected were also from UN. The party was formed in 2003 by Samuel Doria Medina, a businessman educated in economics in the United States and the United Kingdom who owns the franchise rights for all of Bolivia to Burger King and Subway amongst other ventures. Medina formed the party after breaking from the MIR. The electoral results should not be read as support for UN per se, but rather as a castigating vote against the MAS. In light of the perceived failure of the MAS to adhere, at the national and local level, to the October Agenda, combined with a corruption case against former MAS mayor Edgar Patana who "failed to provide works … or projects for the base" Alteños decided that they wanted a change.[8] Soledad Chapetón took advantage of the *desgaste* with Patana's corruption[9] as well as MAS co-opting tactics of local organization leaders.[10] In this light, some *dirigentes* began to ask themselves "why am I obeying this person if they are corrupt."[11] Internal tensions regarding how the popular organizations should relate with the MAS that had been growing in the 2009–14 period became more pronounced, culminating with organizational schisms into allied- and contestatory-blocs.

Divisions within the FEJUVE leadership led to a scenario in 2016 in which two congresses were organized simultaneously to select a new leadership, one based in the original site of the FEJUVE on Avenida 6 de Marzo and recognized by the MAS and a second based in Villa Dolores and recognized by Mayor Chapetón. Likewise, the result of the MAS linkages to "loyal" COR leaders fostered a schism in the organization that was encouraged by UN, which supported and financed the development of a parallel COR.[12] A central concern regarding the COR-*original* (the bloc allied with the MAS) was the lack of rotation of leadership which the statute calls for every two years, leading to the issue of *prorroguismo*, or "extensioning."[13] In terms of

> the duration of executives in their roles, the situation is chronic, because some *dirigentes* have held their positions for more than fifteen years, and in some cases, even twenty. For example Remigio Condori and Sebastián Condori, who since 2000 have continued to be *dirigentes* in the COR.[14]

For critics, these leaders tow the party line. Indeed, a central figure in the MAS-aligned FEJUVE-*original* admitted that

> the COR has been completely co-opted by the government. The *dirigentes* who now seek roles in the organization all have the notion that when they finish their time as a COR *dirigente* they will become a senator or deputy, or minister or vice-minister.[15]

After Remigio Condori relinquished his position as secretary-general of the COR so as to take up his position as a city-councillor for MAS, he was replaced by Eliseo Suxo who had been the first secretary of the COR. Suxo was a MAS deputy for the La Paz department before returning to head the COR. Such intensive and extensive party-organization linkages allowed allied organizations to receive much-needed funding, while the MAS could continue to advance the reform process without facing contestatory mobilization. However, they also had a deleterious impact in terms of popular organization legitimacy. Indeed, a member of the COR-*original* executive committee told me, under the condition of anonymity, that Suxo was deeply damaging the organization because

> One minute he is openly supporting Evo Morales, the next he is not. The COR has been sullied and dirtied, and it must be purged, but this could

> take a generation. We should have kept our autonomy. I do not agree with how the COR has been directed. We have lost all legitimacy. We are working on the problem that is Eliseo Suxo. Perhaps after supporting the government during the constituent assembly, we got too close to be critical.[16]

The issue of autonomy and scope to critique the government is at the center of the demise in legitimacy of the COR and FEJUVE. In conversations with Alteños, I heard complaints on a daily basis from a range of citizens who felt the organizations had become spaces "for the swapping of political favors" (bus driver in El Alto) … "Those guys don't want change, they are happy so long as the government keeps paying them to be happy" (tea-stall owner, El Alto). Even Daniel Ramos, the regional director of the MAS, highlighted the issue of Eliseo Suxo having been a MAS deputy, stating that

> When you have occupied a political position, you do not have credibility before the population. And I could talk of other organizations here in El Alto where ex-deputies, ex-councillors have taken over. It gives a bad signal. I have said many times that there must be a renovation of these organizations. But the issue is that these people are old and astute, they are cunning and they do not allow new leaders to emerge. This is the issue facing us today, and this error has been taken advantage of by the right.[17]

The formation of extensive and intensive linkages with the parties meant that the popular organizations could not act as a funnel for informal contestatory interest intermediation as they did in the 2003–05 period. Co-opted organizations "must walk a tightrope, responding to popular needs and avoiding open confrontation with their benefactor parties."[18] Indeed, a leading figure in the FEJUVE–6 de Marzo stated,

> We may not be in full agreement with the MAS all the time, and neither is our base. But neither can we organize a big mobilization against it, because this would mean that we would no longer receive support for other projects. Unfortunately, this is how politics works. If you go against the party, the government doesn't help you.[19]

The

> problem with the divisions and co-opting in FEJUVEs and CORs is that today in El Alto there is no popular force. What can the organizations do when they are in the service of the parties? Nothing! What are they going to demand? Nothing![20]

There is "*desgaste* with the social organizations, such a change from October 2003 when everyone was unified."[21] The "*pueblo* is sick, its leaders are sick and are simply ambitious for power, and so the organizations are also sick."[22]

The decapitation and division of organizations in El Alto, and across Bolivia, in conjunction with the "the integration of significant portions of the eastern lowlands agribusiness and conservative political elite into the MAS project" fostered the "political and social realignment of the MAS—and its transformation from a 'government of the social movements' to a 'big tent' hegemonic power."[23] In a scenario where the opposition-bloc had weak political power, and where Morales retained support from the core-organic organizations and their members, as well as the allied-blocs of strategic organizations, regressive centralization guaranteed MAS and Morales continued electoral success. The cracks in the once unified popular-bloc would prove decisive, however, once the opposition-bloc's political power began to grow from 2016 onwards.

The 2016 referendum and the rebalancing of power

Morales sought a referendum on modifying the Constitution so as to allow a third re-election of the president and vice-president. A "No" coalition formed around traditional right-wing politicians, along with the new mayor of El Alto, Soledad Chapetón and the mayor of La Paz, Luis Revilla. Completing the coalition "were ex-MASistas and representatives of alienated left-popular sectors seeking to rehabilitate what they perceive as a stagnating 'process of change', who constituted themselves as the 'popular No' bloc."[24]

The calling of the referendum acted as a rallying cause for the ideological and political wings of the opposition-bloc who had remained muted as Morales and the MAS continued to dominate elections with high levels of support. The right-wing of the "No" coalition focused media attention on a series of scandals,[25] with Página Siete running daily editorials seeking to challenge the credibility of Morales and MAS.[26] The referendum was narrowly defeated by 51.3 percent, thereby blocking the possibility of re-election for Morales. However, in September, the MAS asked the Constitutional Tribunal to rescind limits on elected authorities seeking re-election, arguing that they violate human rights. The Constitutional Tribunal ruled that all elected officials could run for office indefinitely. The use of presidential power to meddle in judicial affairs alongside the court's decision to allow re-election galvanized the divided political opposition, while further de-legitimizing Morales in the eyes of some former allies.

The referendum defeat re-ignited the dispute over the meaning of democracy with opposition protests focusing on the defense of democratic norms such as alternation of leaders, pluralism, and the rule of law. As Mayorga[27] states, the MAS responded to such critiques of its democratic credentials by focusing on the participative and substantive components of democracy, highlighting that there is an equivalence between democracy and justice. Democracy was considered synonymous with equality and institutional norms were of secondary importance to the social and economic achievements of the post-neoliberal process. Defense of democracy was the rallying call of both MAS and opposition-bloc figures, with each rallying around differing conceptions which they claimed to be more democratic than their opponents.

On December 3, judicial elections were held which "became a litmus test of the country's political climate … due to an effort spearheaded by a coalition of former presidents, vice-presidents, governors, and political party leaders to urge Bolivians to cast null votes."[28] While 84 percent of the electorate voted, 51 percent of the ballots cast were nullified. Opposition-bloc political and media figures framed the results as evidence that support for Morales was declining. Samuel Doria Medina Tweeted that "The citizens have defeated Evo Morales, a leader who is trying to impose re-election on Bolivia, along with corruption and the manipulation of the justice system."

While the 2016 referendum and judicial decision to overrule its results re-vitalized the opposition-bloc's political and ideological wings, in light of MAS efforts to co-opt and meddle in the leaderships of popular organizations, and with a moderation of the project in the face of economic elite structural power, it was not only the traditional opposition who critiqued Morales. That is, as centralization slid from a progressive to a more regressive form, popular organization leaders and their grassroots bases that were sidelined, and who had in earlier stages accepted a bending of liberal norms as necessary to overcome opposition-bloc resistance to post-neoliberal reforms, increasingly scrutinized the illiberal actions of Morales.

Before discussing popular critique, it is essential to highlight that while some popular organizations rejected Morales' re-election and the Constitutional Tribunal's ruling, the 2016 referendum was only just defeated, and Morales retained the backing of core-organizations as well as the allied-blocs of strategic organizations. For example, on February 21, 2018—the second anniversary of the original referendum vote—CONALCAM successfully called on constituent organizations across the country to march in defense of Morales, with the Fejuve 6 de Marzo and the COR-original in El Alto taking to the streets. While the MAS retained the backing of CONALCAM organizations, there was a growing bloc of poplar organizations who withdrew support for Morales. However, popular opposition to Morales' plans for re-election should not be confused with allegiance with the traditional opposition-bloc who advocated a return to market democracy. Popular challenges to Morales and the Constitutional Tribunal's ruling to allow him to run for office again were underpinned by beliefs that the substantive and participative elements of the post-neoliberal project had contracted.

A leading activist in the 2003 El Alto Gas War noted that until 2016–17, people did not want to criticize the government because they felt that "it is from our class, it is of our people."[29] However, as the activist notes,

> people are now realising that the government of MAS has failed to adhere to grassroots demands and a new phase of popular mobilization will erupt waving the flag of October 2003 as a reminder of what we are capable of when we are united.[30]

The spokesperson for the Trotskyist La Paz Federation of Educational Workers emphasized to me that "the unions and organizations that were controlled by MAS and that fought for MAS" were beginning to "break with the politics of MAS … The notion of *paralelismo* will not bear fruit."[31]

While some popular leaders were calling for autonomy, others remained supportive allies of Morales leading to confusion and divisions within the organizations. The case of the COR-El Alto demonstrates the issues during this period. The COR-*original* was aligned with the COB, headed by Guido Mitma, and the COD headed by Carlos Calle. While COR-*original* executives had forged tight linkages with the MAS, both the COD and the COB had begun to take a critical stance toward the MAS government for interfering in popular organizations. At the end of a massive march from El Alto to La Paz organized by the COD and the COB on June 12, 2017 in response to the government's plans to raise the electricity tariff by 3 percent, Guido Mitma shouted to the crowd that

> we cannot allow the government to continue with these neoliberal policies. We cannot continue with this dictatorship of a government who make decisions that affect workers without even engaging with the COB and the base. With *paralelismo* they have tried to fracture the COB. The entire *proceso de cambio* has been a betrayal.

Carlos Calle of the COD suggests that the protest was important, as it showed that the base was

> waking up … it has been asleep while it received some crumbs of benefit. Seven years ago, to come out and protest against this government was a big deal because everybody would whistle at you, you couldn't protest. But now we are seeing the reality, and the new perspective of the people.[32]

Indeed, as the march wound its way down from El Alto to the city of La Paz below, I spoke to dozens of protesters from student groups, neighborhood councils, and unions. While the proposed tariff increase was the frame for the protest, a more general sense of frustration with the government was apparent, with many protesters expressing the belief that the government had forgotten about El Alto despite "the vital role we played and the blood we shed so that all of Bolivia could be free" (female protester from district 4 of El Alto). The sentiment that insufficient change had been achieved under Morales was tied to the issue of co-optation and *paralelismo*. During the protest and amidst the near constant cacophony of exploding homemade fireworks, I interviewed Jaime Solares, ex-leader of the COB and central figure in the 2003–05 anti-neoliberal protests. Solares emphasized that the "COB lost its way, it became servile to the Morales government. The COB must be contestatory. It is time for all our popular organizations to re-claim their autonomy from the government."[33] Echoing Solares' sentiments, a protester chanted over a megaphone "this is a demonstration against this government, this lying government which has tried to undermine the workers' protests." As the protest reached a conclusion in the Plaza San Francisco in the heart of La Paz, an effigy of Evo Morales was set alight to chants of "*Fuerza fuerza fuerza, fuerza compañeros, que la lucha es dura, pero venceremos* (Don't give up comrades, though the struggle is tough, we will overcome)."

The relationship between the COR-*original* and the union hierarchy, the COD and COB, on one hand, and the central government and the MAS on the other appeared to leave the COR in an awkward position. Franklin Troche of the COR-*original* states, however, that "it is not the case that we are in the middle, and when we want to, we support the government. We have our own line of thinking and we are going to keep this."[34] As Troche explains, "we have to do what our base tells us to. They didn't like the increase in electricity prices, and so we had to take the streets to block it." Indeed, the COR-*original* has in some instances confronted the central government. For example, Eliseo Suxo stated that the COR would join the marches organized by the COB due to the lack of government engagement with the unions regarding the retirement fund for workers, modification to the Pensions Law, and the increases in electricity and gas prices. However, the COR-*original* generally sought to avoid open criticism of Evo Morales as they were concerned as to who would be in a position to replace him as president. As a central figure in the COR-*original* leadership explains,

> What would happen if we were to push Evo and he was to fall? … The right would return, the military governments would return. As such, this must be part of our thinking. We can, and do, critique the government. But there must be a successor. A leftist successor from the *pueblo*. Someone who is with the workers. But at the moment, such a person does not exist. So for the moment, we cannot push too quickly.[35]

Such a sentiment highlights the difficult tightrope balancing act facing popular organizations regarding how to critique a progressive leader from a leftist position without opening space for the opposition to take advantage. At the same time, failure to call for contestatory mobilization if the grassroots disagree with MAS candidates or policies leads to friction between organization leaderships and their bases.

The 2014–19 period saw a more vociferous ideological and political opposition re-emerge, while Morales faced protests from both middle-class and popular sectors as cracks within the popular bloc became more pronounced. The economic and transnational spheres also became less favorable for the government in this period; 2015 witnessed a steep fall in prices for Bolivia's primary commodity exports, signaling an end to the resource-boom that fuelled Morales' democratic extending programs. From April 2014 to April 2015, the collection of Direct Tax on Hydrocarbons decreased by 16 percent.

However, prudent economic management during the boom provided a safety net that prevented social spending from coming to a complete stop. I stress here that it was not simply declining economic resources available for redistribution that led to popular discontent. Popular discontent had been rising due to exclusion of critical bottom-up participation and top-down meddling in popular-organization affairs. However, it is also the case that as socio-economic spending slowed and as the availability of resources to distribute to allied-organization leaderships declined, popular questioning of the depth of the reform process that had long existed amongst more critical groups bubbled to the surface. Moreover, key ally Venezuela was mired in a deep economic and political crisis leading to a reduction in funding to Bolivia, further weakening the economic power of Morales' government. The regional scenario also fundamentally shifted, with the return of pro-neoliberal presidents in Argentina and Brazil reducing ideological support for a post-neoliberal project in regional organizations such as the *Mercado Común del Sur* (Common Market of the South—MERCOSUR).

In the 2009–14 period, the economic elite forged a pact with Morales because the MAS not only dominated the political sphere, but also had ideological legitimacy and was capable of limiting popular sector mobilization. However, over the course of the 2014–19 period, the balance of powers shifted, and it became apparent that Morales was losing his capacity to manage competing demands. With the economic boom coming to an end, the political wing of the opposition-bloc finding its voice, and with popular protests growing more vociferous as the grassroots bases of some organizations rejected leaderships who allied with the MAS, the scenario which encouraged economic elites to pact with the Morales government appeared to be coming to an end. Morales' participation in controversial elections in 2019 and the opposition-bloc's rejection of their results would prove to be a tipping point for the Morales-led process.

Contested elections, the removal of Morales, and the beginning of a new MAS-led era: 2019–21

Election rejection, coup, and the return of the right to state power

Following the "no" vote in the 2016 referendum and the judicial decision to allow Morales run, in the lead up to the 2019 elections the opposition-bloc pushed the narrative that an authoritarian, illiberal MAS government would do anything to stay in power. According to early polling, the main rival to Morales' re-election bid was former president Carlos Mesa of the Comunidad Ciudadana party. To avoid a second-round run-off required winning a simple majority or more than 40 percent of the vote plus a 10 percent margin of victory over the nearest rival candidate. With almost 84 percent of the votes counted, and with Morales leading with 45.3 percent to Mesa's 38.2, the unofficial online counting system (*trep*) stopped live transmission of the quick-count ballots. The following day, following a request from the Organization of American States (OAS) Electoral Observation Mission for a resumption of the *trep*, updated results were presented reflecting 95 percent of tally sheets. Morales' margin of victory had narrowly exceeded the 10 percent required to avoid a second-round run-off. The OAS immediately stated their "deep concern" about the "change in trend," creating the impression that fraud had taken place, an opinion quickly reproduced in domestic news sources such as Página Siete whose sensationalist headlines sought to induce their readers to believe that the Electoral Tribunal's results were falsified.[36]

However, a report by researchers at MIT's Election Data and Science Lab suggests "that Morales's victory can be explained by his voter support before the preliminary vote count halted." The report's authors go on to state that "the final result can be explained by a pattern in the vote count prior to the cut-off of the *trep*. Therefore, we cannot find quantitative evidence of an irregular trend as claimed by the OAS."[37] The difference in the vote count before and after the *trep* blackout was consistent with the later reporting of rural votes where Morales has traditionally garnered almost twice as many votes than in earlier reporting urban centers. The OAS has long been considered a strategic ally of Washington and, as Webber and Hylton state, the OAS "performed its appointed role of undermining Bolivian sovereignty" with OAS general secretary Luis Almagro stating, "In Bolivia there was a coup on October 20 when Evo Morales committed electoral fraud … The military has to act in accordance with its mandate."[38]

Following the Electoral Court's announcement of the results in favor of Morales, with the OAS casting doubts over their legitimacy and with opposition-bloc media stoking beliefs that fraud had occurred, large-scale protests erupted in urban areas. While the initial protesters were middle class voters angered by perceived fraud, and the fact the elections had gone ahead in the first place given the results of the 2016 referendum, there was a belief amongst diverse social classes that the government would use power illiberally to remain in power. Formerly allied groups who had faced co-optive efforts to restrict their autonomy such as lowland indigenous groups, coca growers in the Yungas who felt Morales favored core-organization cocaleros in the Chapare, cooperative miners in Potosí, CONAMAQ, and factory-worker unions in Cochabamba amongst others first rejected the electoral results, and later demanded Morales' renunciation.[39] It is vital to remember, however, that Morales won the election with high levels of popular support, and that there were also marches from supportive popular organizations. Indeed, while opposition-bloc media gave in-depth focus to anti-Morales protests, they almost entirely ignored the pro-Morales marches which were occurring at the same time.[40]

While middle-class and some former strategically allied popular organizations protested against the election results/the fact Morales was seeking re-election, the crisis moment was ultimately captured and dominated by far-right conservative elements of the opposition-bloc who sought to take advantage and reclaim their "rightful" place at the head of the Bolivian state. Since April 2019, Luis Camacho had taken control of the Civic Committee of Santa Cruz and had been vehemently opposing Morales' re-election bid. The Civic Committee of Santa Cruz had long been the

> institution responsible for aggregating the interests of reactionary lowland elites and various sections of agrarian, financial, commercial, industrial, and narco capital in that part of the country, which was systematically favored by military dictatorships in the 1960s and 70s as well as the subsequent neoliberal partidocracia in the 1980s and 90s.[41]

Camacho openly called for the removal of Morales from power. Evangelical and Catholic Church leaders supported Camacho's calls for a return of God and the Bible to the presidential palace—a clear rejection of indigenous belief systems. Right-wing paramilitary groups took to the streets echoing Camacho's anti-indigenous slogans.

Camacho reached out to the president of the Potosí Civic Committee (Comico) headed by Marco Pumari. Representing urban civil society interests in the city, Comico had been mobilizing against the Morales government since 2016, demanding that the central state give the department a greater share of revenues earned from extracting lithium in the region. The powerful Potosí miners openly rejected Morales. This was crucial because the miners had a strong voice in the COB. Juan Carlos Huarachi, a close ally of the MAS who had replaced the more critical Guido Mitma as head of the COB, called on Morales to "reflect" on his position and to resign if it were necessary to pacify the country. The COB's withdrawal of support greatly weakened Morales' position.[42]

Morales' declining capacity to curb contestatory popular mobilization as well as the re-emergence of the political wing of the opposition bloc triggered a shift in economic elite relations with the government. The earlier rapprochement between business associations and the government was underpinned by the relative MAS dominance of political power vis-à-vis traditional opposition parties post-2008, as well as Morales' capacity to limit continuous popular protests. However, with the re-emergence of popular contestatory mobilization alongside the coalescence of opposition political power, and with commodity prices falling, thereby threatening profit margins, business groups gradually ended their tactical support for MAS. Business elites sought a political ally willing to more aggressively confront popular opposition to the development model underpinned by a neoliberal nationalization of extractive industries and expansion of agro-industry.[43] For example, business organizations from the eastern lowlands representing industrial and commercial interests such as CAINCO and the Agricultural Chamber of Eastern Bolivia representing agribusiness interests, sensing Morales' weakness, indicated their support for the removal of the president.[44]

With Camacho and allied racist figures inciting violence and with protests continuing across the country, Camacho called on the police to "stand on the side of the people." Police mutinies followed in Cochabamba, Santa Cruz, and Sucre while the police mingled with protesters in La Paz. General Williams Kaliman "suggested" Morales step aside. While Morales had enjoyed good relations with the military, the high command came from the white middle-classes and in many ways their support for Morales was tactical, just like the government-economic elite relations. Indeed, military, media, political party, and business support for the removal of Morales was heavily shaped by resentment of the fact that the traditional racial hierarchy that existed prior to Morales' election had been challenged during the post-neoliberal process.

With a loss of military power, with ideological powers in the form of church leaderships, the OAS, and traditional and social media aligned against him, with business associations withdrawing their support, with a re-emerging political opposition, and with a popular base that was divided and unwilling to engage in mass-defensive mobilization, Morales and MAS representatives were forced from office. Donald Trump's administration was quick to voice its backing for the change in leadership. While there is no doubt that Morales was ousted from power by the combined oppositional-bloc, the processes of top-down co-optation and *paralelismo* dealt a double-blow to Morales. On the one hand, a once powerful and unified base was fractured and weakened and incapable of mass-defensive mobilization. On the other, it was precisely in response to efforts to curb popular organization autonomy that contestatory-sectors of popular organizations engaged in offensive-mobilization *against* Morales.

Jeanine Añez, market democracy, and state-sponsored repression: 2019–20

With the ouster of Morales, Jeanine Añez, former deputy leader of the senate (and also a former TV host and long-time critic of Morales from the *media luna*), with a bible in her hands, was declared caretaker president. Despite winning just 4 percent of votes in the general election, Añez, from the Democratic Unity[45] party headed by ultra-conservative Rubén Costas, governor of Santa Cruz province, immediately installed a new cabinet with deep ties to Bolivia's right-wing sectors from the *media luna*. Camacho influenced the makeup of the cabinet, with three ministers selected who had links to the Civic Committee of Santa Cruz. When Áñez was named interim president, she immediately received the backing of major business organizations who stated their support for the "return to democracy."[46] Several of the new ministers including Economy and Finance, Environment and Water, Productive Development and the Rural Economy came from the Santa Cruz business sector. Just as during the market democracy era, economic elites and business interests had a direct link to state decision-making channels.

The interim government's Constitutional role was to convene new elections. However, it recognized right-wing leader Juan Guaidó as legitimate president of Venezuela, persecuted MAS leaders and intimidated supporters, arbitrarily detained outspoken critics of the coup-government, shut down critical media outlets and arrested journalists, called members of the MAS "animals" and deployed the armed forces to repress indigenous anti-coup protesters at Sacaba and Senkata killing at least 22 and injuring several hundred.[47] Opposition-bloc media backed the government, offered limited coverage of anti-Áñez protesters who were labeled as being part of a "hoard," and even supported the government's false claims that the repression and killing of unarmed protesters at Senkata was a response to "terrorists" using dynamite to attack a gasoline plant.[48]

While the opposition-bloc had always been comprised of differing groups with their own distinct interests, there was a shared belief that they were the rightful rulers of Bolivian society. As Mayorga[49] stresses, the interim government had oligarchic characteristics as it sought to return the white business and political elite actors who had been displaced by the MAS. Seeing an indigenous, campesino government direct the country "made them sick in their stomachs."[50] As the oligarchic elites re-took the reins of state power, they sought to end the statist MAS model that saw benefits directed toward popular-indigenous sectors and return to the preceding market model of democracy that benefitted the conservative, white elite.[51]

Confronting a common enemy and the return of the MAS: 2020–21

With the interim government postponing elections, indigenous and campesino groups in the Unity Pact began organizing their bases, firstly to demand new elections, and then to vote for the MAS presidential and vice-presidential ticket of Luis Arce and David Choquehuanca. The COB, whose leader Juan Carlos Huarachi had suggested Morales step aside to pacify the country, apologized for failing to defend the president and gave the interim government an ultimatum; fresh elections or "social upheaval." While there were tensions between the MAS and sectors of its constituent base around 2018–19, as well as tensions *within* popular organizations, the behaviors of the interim government provided a common enemy which acted as spur to re-unify divided organizations. For example, over the course of 2018–20, the FEJUVE-El Alto had fractured into three blocs; the contestatory bloc aligned with UN which lost relevance, as well as two blocs that contested control over the FEJUVE 6 de Marzo. One wing headed by Fernando Condori sought to reclaim organizational autonomy from the MAS, while the other bloc headed by Basilio Villasante retained tight linkages with the MAS. These struggles were pushed aside temporarily, however, as the leaders of both factions called for mass demonstrations demanding immediate presidential elections while also encouraging grassroots members to vote for the MAS candidates.

When the elections were finally held in October 2020, the MAS ticket of Arce and Choquehuanca won over 55 percent of the vote, with Carlos Mesa winning 28.5 and Fernando Camacho just 14 percent. In the first elections without Morales, and without state powers which critics had long-accused the MAS of abusing to help guarantee success, the party easily defeated the opposition candidates. Moreover, the MAS candidates won more of the vote share nationally than Morales achieved in the 2019 elections, while winning in six of nine departments. The MAS also won a majority in both chambers of the legislature, though not a two-thirds majority as they achieved in the 2014 elections. There was also an increased MAS vote in some urban areas compared to the 2019 elections, including in El Alto. The results dispelled any notions that the MAS was simply a party whose success depended on Morales. In fact, given the increased vote share for the MAS in the 2020 elections compared to 2019, it appears that while Morales' candidacy may have been unacceptable for some voters, the MAS and the post-neoliberal model it advocated retained popular legitimacy. It is important to stress, however, that part of the 2020 success for the MAS was based on its status as the only party capable of competing on a national level and defeating the pro-neoliberal, racist opposition parties. Tensions between the party and constituent organizations that had been simmering under Morales' presidencies, while pushed aside to confront a common enemy, had not disappeared.

MAS-base tensions and major challenges ahead for Arce

The scenario in El Alto is a useful lens through which to view party-base relations in Bolivia more generally. Shortly after Arce's electoral victory, the two blocs of the FEJUVE 6 de Marzo called for a unification of the popular organization. Condori stated that "I am not part of the MAS, but I am part of the process of change, and because of this, we have decided with Villasante to unify this emblematic institution." Meanwhile, Villasante, echoing earlier statements by FEJUVE leaders aligned with the MAS, highlighted that the only party who would work with the FEJUVE for El Alto's development was the MAS, and so the FEJUVE would work together with the MAS. However, this pact of unity did not last, and the old issue regarding the nature of linkages and autonomy between the FEJUVE and the MAS re-emerged, with Condori accusing Villasante of seeking to use the organization to gain political positions with the party.[52]

The divisions within El Alto's organizations were also apparent with the two blocs taking differing sides in support for mayoral candidates in March 2021 elections. Eva Copa was a MAS senator from El Alto, and during the interim government she had remained as the president of the senate. However, Copa, with the backing of the Condori-led wing of the FEJUVE, split from MAS to run for El Alto's mayorship on the new Jallalla La Paz ticket, stating that she was responding to demands from the grassroots of local popular organizations to reclaim organizational autonomy from the MAS. Evo Morales, who was still the leader of the MAS, verbally berated Copa and claimed that the MAS candidate for El Alto's mayor, Zacarías Maquera, would easily win. Copa, however, was elected with 68.7 percent of the vote.

The scenario in El Alto reflects the wider issue regarding the MAS and constituent organizations and the demands from below for a renovation of how the party interacts with strategically allied popular organizations. That is, while confronting a common ally at the national level may have seen a unification of party and popular organizations, building on their long histories of autonomous mobilization, there was the beginning of a push from below for a re-formulation of the intensive and extensive linkages that had ossified over the duration of post-neoliberal project.

In the face of the COVID-19 pandemic, and with no commodity boom to support easy social spending, Arce faces a tough balancing act going forward. While the discovery of a major new gas field by YPFB and multinationals may ease some of the economic tensions, the continued reliance on hydrocarbons and agro-industry will mean that his presidency will be fraught with frictions as the government tries to appease structurally powerful economic elites as well as the demands from myriad popular actors for increased incorporation. Furthermore, with financial reserves in decline, without a two-thirds majority in the legislature, with a military and police force imbricated in the massacres under the interim government, and with the judiciary in need of an overhaul in order to boost public trust in it, Arce faces a tough scenario.

As Bolivia enters the post-Morales era, the legacies of his presidencies will be defined by the capacity of organized popular sectors to re-group and overcome internal divisions fostered by the MAS, to reclaim and strengthen participatory spaces opened under the MAS and, via these spaces, to defend and advance the socio-economic gains achieved during Morales' presidencies. In short, the future pathways of Bolivian democratization or de-democratization processes will depend on the strength of the organized popular base to act as a counterweight to domestic and transnational elite demands, just as they always have.

In the next chapter, I compare the Bolivian and Venezuelan cases, discussing the conjunctural historical and emergent factors which shaped the emergence, development, and outcomes of the post-neoliberal processes. The long-term legacies of the cases are outlined before the broader lessons regarding anti-neoliberal processes are discussed.

Notes

1 Emily Achtenberg, "Evo's Bolivia at a Political Crossroads: Taking Stock of Bolivia's Changing Political Environment after Evo Morales' 2016 Referendum Defeat," *NACLA Report on the Americas* 48, no. 4 (2016): 374–5.

2 Ibid.

3 Emily Achtenberg, "Bolivia: Elections in the Time of Evo," *NACLA Rebel Currents* 29 September (2014): Retrieved https://nacla.org/blog/2014/10/12/bolivia-elections-time-evo.

4 Ibid.
5 Interview with author, La Paz, July 2017.
6 Cited in Fernando Molina, "La oposición boliviana gana espacios clave en las elecciones regionales," *El País,* 30 March (2015): Retrieved https://elpais.com/internacional/2015/03/30/actualidad/1427673912_141810.html.
7 Interview with author, La Paz, July 2017.
8 Daniel Ramos, regional coordinator for the MAS in El Alto, interview with author, El Alto, August 10, 2017.
9 Daniel Gutiérrez, international press officer for the FEJUVE, interview with author, El Alto, August 9, 2017.
10 Alfredo Cahuaya, researcher at UNITAS, interview with author, La Paz, August 18, 2017.
11 Daniel Gutiérrez, interview with author.
12 Ibid.
13 AD Mancilla, *Poder y Masacre en El Alto: La Mafia Sindical Alteña* (La Paz: Viejo Topo, 2016): 77.
14 Ibid.
15 Anonymous interview with author, El Alto, 2017.
16 Interview with author, El Alto, 2017.
17 Interview with author, El Alto, August 10, 2017.
18 Carlos Arze, interview with author, La Paz, August 25, 2017.
19 Anonymous interview with author, El Alto, August 12, 2017.
20 FEJUVE executive committee member 2003, interview with author, El Alto, August 24, 2017.
21 Daniel Gutiérrez, interview with author.
22 Luis Flores, interview with author.
23 Achtenberg, "Evo's Bolivia at a Political Crossroads."
24 Ibid.
25 For a discussion of allegations against high-ranking MAS politicians of mismanagement and corruption of the public funds see Carla Alberti, "Bolivia: La Democracia a una Década del Gobierno del MAS," *Revista de Ciencia Política (Santiago)* 36, no. 1 (2016): 27–49; See Achtenberg "Evo's Bolivia at a Political Crossroads" for overview of the "Zapata" affair in which false allegations emerged regarding Morales and Gabriela Zapata and an alleged "love-child," as well as the directing of multi-million dollar no-bid contracts from the MAS government to the Chinese company in which Zapata held a high-level post. Furthermore, an arson attack on the El Alto municipal building which left 6 dead was blamed on MAS party militants further eroding support for the re-election reform campaign.
26 Fernando Molina and Susana Bejarano, "La Transformación Restauradora del Campo Mediático: El Alineamiento de los medios de Comunicación con el Bloque de Poder Postevista en Noviembre de 2019," in Jan Souverein and José Luis Exeni Rodríguez (eds.), *Nuevo Mapa de Actores en Bolivia* (La Paz: FES, 2020): 165–200.
27 Fernando Mayorga, "El MAS-IPSP ante un Nuevo Contexto Político: De 'Partido de Gobierno' a 'Instumento Político' de las Organizaciones Populares," in Jan Souverein and José Luis Exeni Rodríguez (eds), *Nuevo Mapa de Actores en Bolivia* (La Paz: FES, 2020): 6.
28 Linda Farthing, "Bolivia Says Goodbye to Term Limits," *The North American Congress on Latin America* 15 December (2017): Retrieved https://nacla.org/news/2017/12/20/bolivia-says-goodbye-term-limits.
29 Luis Flores, interview with author, El Alto, August 2017.
30 Ibid.

31 Interview with author, La Paz, July 2017.
32 Interview with author.
33 Interview with author, La Paz, June 12, 2017.
34 Interview with author, El Alto, July 13, 2017.
35 Anonymous interview with author, El Alto, July 13, 2017.
36 Molina and Bejarano, "La Transformación Restauradora del Campo Mediático."
37 Jack Williams and John Curiel, "Analysis of the 2019 Bolivia Election," *Center for Economic and Policy Research* 27 February (2020): Retrieved https://cepr.net/report/analysis-of-the-2019-bolivia-election/.
38 Jeffrey Webber and Forrest Hylton, "The Eighteenth Brumaire of Macho Camacho," *Verso Blog* 15 November (2019): Retrieved https://www.versobooks.com/blogs/4493-the-eighteenth-brumaire-of-macho-camacho-jeffery-r-webber-with-forrest-hylton-on-the-coup-in-bolivia.
39 Alejandro Schneider, "Algunos Elementos para Comprender el Golpe de Estado en Bolivia," *CEDLA Blog* 13 November (2019): Retrieved https://cedla.org/cedla-en-los-medios/47243/.
40 Molina and Bejarano, "La Transformación Restauradora del Campo Mediático."
41 Webber and Hylton, "The Eighteenth Brumaire of Macho Camacho."
42 Though it is difficult to state with assurance, it seems likely that Juan Carlos Huarachi's withdrawal of support was also influenced by pressure from other sectors of the COB and former leaders such as Jaime Solares who had been demanding greater organizational autonomy from the MAS for several years.
43 For more see Schneider, "Algunos Elementos" and Wolff, "The Political Economy of Bolivia's Post-Neoliberalism."
44 Jonas Wolff, "Las Élites Económicas en la Bolivia Contemporánea," in Jan Souverein and José Luis Exeni Rodríguez (eds.), *Nuevo Mapa de Actores en Bolivia* (La Paz: FES, 2020): 139–64.
45 Democratic Unity is also the party of Óscar Ortiz, a Santa Cruz businessman who is perhaps Bolivia's most influential neoliberal ideologue. He is part of the transnational neoliberal think tank network. He is on the board of directors for the International Foundation for Liberty (FIL) while he heads the Atlas-partnered New Democracy Foundation. For more on Atlas and FIL see the discussions in the Venezuelan chapters regarding their support for the radical wing of the Venezuelan opposition-bloc. Ortiz was named Minister for Economy by Añez.
46 Wolff, "Las Élites Económicas en la Bolivia Contemporánea."
47 International Human Rights Clinic and University Network for Human Rights, "They Shot us like Animals: Black November and Bolivia's Interim Government" (2019): Retrieved https://www.humanrightsnetwork.org/bolivia; Emily Achtenberg, "MAS Party under Threat as Bolivia Moves Towards New Elections (without Evo)," *NACLA Rebel Currents* 10 January (2020): Retrieved https://nacla.org/blog/2020/01/10/mas-party-under-threat-bolivia-new-elections-without-evo.
48 Fernando Molina, "Los Medios tras la Salida de Morales del Poder," *LaRazón* 11 November (2020): Retrieved https://www.la-razon.com/voces/2020/11/15/los-medios-tras-la-salida-de-morales-del-poder/?amp=1&__twitter_impression=true.
49 Fernando Mayorga, "Derrota Política del MAS y Proyecto de Restauración Oligárquico-Señorial," in Fernando Mayorga (ed.), *Crisis y Cambio Político en Bolivia. Octubre y Noviembre de 2019 en Bolivia : La Democracia en una Encrucijada* (La Paz: CESU-UMSS, 2020): 2.
50 Interview with Fernando Molina, March 2021.
51 Fernando Molina, "Bolivia: Un Nuevo Bloque de Poder," *Nueva Sociedad* January (2020): Retrieved https://nuso.org/articulo/Bolivia-derecha-Evo-Morales/.

52 ElAltoDigital, "La Fejuve de El Alto Avanza Rumbo a la Unificación," *ElAlto-Digital* 21 October (2020): Retrieved https://www.elaltodigital.com/politica/la-fejuve-de-el-alto-avanza-rumbo-a-la-unificacion/; ExitoNoticias, "Se Rompe el Pacto de Unidad entre Basilio Villasante y Fernando Condori," *ExitoNoticias* 11 December (2020): Retrieved https://exitonoticias.com.bo/index.php/2020/12/11/se-rompe-el-pacto-de-unidad-entre-basilio-villasante-y-fernando-condori-se-toman-instalaciones-de-la-fejuve-de-el-alto/.

8 Venezuela and Bolivia in comparison

Toward a typological theory of outsider-led, post-neoliberal democratization

In this chapter, I compare the emergence, development, and outcomes of the post-neoliberal democratization processes in Venezuela and Bolivia. The chapter begins with a brief review of the shared scope conditions which opened space for anti-neoliberal outsiders to emerge, while also highlighting variations in the nature of anti-neoliberal protests and the early form of party-base linkages between the cases. Next, utilizing the relative power framework developed in Chapter 1 to explain the similarities and variations in the democratic outcomes in both cases, I develop a typological theory for analyzing anti-neoliberal, outsider-led, post-neoliberal democratization processes. I offer a periodized, internal case comparison of the process in Venezuela and Bolivia as well as a cross-case comparison. To allow for such comparison and typological theory development, the summaries and comparisons are kept at a general level. For more detailed specifics, readers may return to the individual case study chapters.

The chapter not only specifies how independent and emergent variables impact the nature of democratic outcomes (in terms of progressive, regressive, and authoritarian centralization) but, more importantly, offers contingent generalizations on how configurations of these variables produce effects on democratic quality. That is, the chapter seeks to specify the pathways through which specific combinations of historic and emergent factors influence the quality of democracy in liberal, participatory, and substantive forms. Such analysis acts as a springboard to discussions in the concluding chapter regarding how we can think productively about the concept of deepening and extending democracy in the 21st century in the face of intensifying conflict over competing solutions to the crisis of representation in contemporary democracies.

Venezuelan and Bolivian historical factors in comparison

Market democracy in Venezuela and Bolivia entailed a narrowing and shallowing of democratic quality for popular sectors at the same time that traditional elite blocs, with the backing of the IMF, retained control over policymaking. In a scenario of dualized labor markets, and indeed, dualized

DOI: 10.4324/9781003262466-9

social lives between those with a formal place in society and those excluded to the margins, austerity and socio-economic precarity, flexible labor, and rising inequality became entrenched while decision-making became a distant, elite-led, technocratic process. In both cases, there was a common perception amongst popular sectors that democracy had been hijacked by unelected elites and supranational bodies representing the interests of capital and that national sovereignty had been eroded.

As satisfaction with the economically and politically exclusionary market model of democracy sagged, spillovers from the 1997 Asian crisis, falling commodity prices, and IMF-backed austerity triggered waves of mass anti-neoliberal mobilization. Eruptions of popular discontent were often brutally repressed by state forces, further undermining the legitimacy of the democratic system, unifying protesters, and boosting the support for progressive anti-system outsiders. In both cases, mainstream labor-based and center-left parties were at the forefront of adopting neoliberal policies, leaving popular sectors with no representative alternative to policies that damaged their livelihoods and wellbeing. In this scenario, Hugo Chávez in Venezuela and Evo Morales in Bolivia emerged to the left of mainstream party systems, offering an electoral alternative to popular sectors who had become disillusioned with the traditional electoral options.

The anti-neoliberal outsiders in both cases attacked market democracy and its neoliberal underpinnings, advocating instead a post-neoliberal model of democracy that would better respond to the concerns of long-excluded marginalized groups. The emergence of Chávez and Morales and their calls for a post-neoliberal model of democracy thus directly challenged the status quo and the interests of traditional elites. Elite opposition-bloc actors began to organize around the idea of defending the market model of democracy which had allowed them to dominate political and economic affairs in the countries over the previous decades.

While the cases share similar scope conditions that opened space for anti-neoliberal outsiders to the left of traditional party systems, the capacity of protest leaders to bind together myriad groups into a unified protest movement varied between the two cases. In Venezuela, though there were instances of coordinated mobilization in zones with long histories of organization, more generally protests were ad hoc eruptions of discontent with market democracy. Given the (generally) ad hoc nature of protests in Venezuela (due to weak union power resulting from atomized labor conditions and a national union embedded with a mainstream party adopting neoliberal policies, as well as state repression of left-wing popular organizations), Chávez emerged somewhat independently of popular movements, playing a vanguardist-type role. Chávez acted as a focal point for voices who critiqued the mainstream parties, challenged domestic and transnational elite dominance of wealth and resources, and who called for a more inclusionary model of citizenship to that offered by market democracy. While a popular-bloc began to form around ideas of a post-neoliberal democracy, traditional elite groups continued to advocate a market model of democracy, setting the stage for post-electoral power struggles. The weak organizational history and the vanguardist leader-base relations would later feedback onto the process, fostering issues regarding a lack of internal party democracy and an incapacity of the base to direct the process from below once the project faced restrictions set by the opposition-bloc and veered from a post-neoliberal path.

In the Bolivian case, Morales emerged organically from the anti-neoliberal protests at the head of a movement-based party, acting as the political expression of groups in civil society with decades of experience in militant protest organizing. The genesis of the party was from the bottom-up, with core-organizations such as the cocaleros unions playing foundational roles. Morales' background in coca growers' unions and his connections to anti-neoliberal mobilization more broadly ensured that the party initially fostered spaces for bottom-up inclusion in decision-making. However, as the party spread beyond its geographical origins in the coca-growing region of the Chapare and sought to gain a foothold in urban areas, it brought local organizers into the party machinery. While such incorporation initially boosted popular sector capacity to participate in decision-making, issues of the loss of autonomy of popular sector organization leaders, particularly non-core, strategically allied organizations, would become apparent when post-election struggles between an opposition-bloc who coalesced around a market model of democracy and a popular bloc who supported a post-neoliberal democracy emerged (Table 8.1).

Summary of the Venezuelan case: progressive, regressive, and authoritarian centralization

Venezuela, stage 1 (1999–2004): progressive centralization (from above)

Following the collapse of the traditional Punto Fijo party system and the de-legitimation of the market model of democracy, Chávez came to power with ideological scope to advance an alternative, post-neoliberal democracy. The passing of the referendum which enshrined the new Bolivarian Constitution furthered his plans to deepen and extend the quality of democracy for marginalized sectors. In elections in 2000, Chávez, his party, and allied parties boosted their political power, retaining control of the executive with an increased vote share, while also winning a majority in the National Assembly. However, over the course of 2001–04, an intense struggle emerged between the government who sought to utilize its political power to advance a popularly backed radical-substantive democratization process and an opposition-bloc comprising the beneficiaries of the market model of democracy.

In 2001, the National Assembly passed an enabling law, allowing Chávez to rule by decree for one year. Chávez issued 49 legislative decrees, including new laws that directly challenged the interests of traditional elite actors. The

Table 8.1 Historical factor comparison, Venezuela and Bolivia (author's own elaboration)

Historical Factors:	*Venezuela*	*Bolivia*
Dualized labor market and society	Yes	Yes
Democratic shallowing	Technocratic decision-making; IMF agenda-setting; weakened unions; left-right programmatic convergence and bait-and-switch neoliberalism	Technocratic decision-making; IMF agenda-setting; weakened unions; left-right programmatic convergence and bait-and-switch neoliberalism
Democratic narrowing	Austerity; socio-economic precarity; labor flexibilization; unemployment; withdrawal of state protections (subsidies, price controls); regressive taxation; rising inequality	Austerity; socio-economic precarity; labor flexibilization; unemployment; withdrawal of state protections (subsidies, price controls); regressive taxation; rising inequality
Unstable democratic equilibrium	Legitimacy crisis of party system	Legitimacy crisis of party system
Trigger factors	Asian Crisis spillover; sudden fall in commodity prices; second IMF-led austerity, adopted in bait-and-switch manner	Asian Crisis spillover; sudden fall in commodity prices; second IMF-led austerity, adopted in bait-and-switch manner
Protests	Ad hoc	Coordinated
Protester repression	Yes	Yes
Anti-neoliberal outsider-popular base relations	Vanguardist, though some organic relations with pre-existing organizations	Organic, though alliances with non-core groups more strategic
Popular/opposition-bloc cleavages	Forging of popular bloc around post-neoliberal democracy; hardening of opposition bloc around market democracy	Forging of popular bloc around post-neoliberal democracy; hardening of opposition bloc around market democracy

laws called for land redistribution and taxation, partial nationalization of the oil industry, redesign of existing royalty and taxation rates on hydrocarbon extraction, and banking regulation to encourage lending at preferential interest rates to projects with social benefits. The use of decree laws, an illiberal action, was justified as necessary to allow the government to respond to long-standing grievances and exclusion.

While the opposition-bloc's political power had been weakened following the electoral victories by Chávez and his allies, they retained influence in the traditionally conservative judiciary. They also dominated ideological (media, church) and economic (unions, oil company management, control of imports) sources of power, while they retained the allegiance of some of the military top-brass. Given the balance of power, the opposition-bloc engaged in extra-institutional destabilization efforts aimed at protecting their interests—and preventing the left-led government from governing from the left, as was their mandate. The opposition-bloc unions called for general strikes, private companies south to create shortages by ceasing production or curbing imports of essential goods, oil managers shut down production, private media channels rallied middle-class groups to take to the streets, snipers shot protesters, media misreported realities to encourage further protests and splits in the military, the Catholic Church hierarchy joined the ideological assault of the government, and sectors of the military forced Chávez from office in a coup. Furthermore, in the transnational sphere, the US government supported (via funding, guidance, and ideological backing) the opposition-bloc and the coup.

Following the extra-institutional resistance by the opposition-bloc and the Supreme Court's refusal to rule that the April 2002 events constituted a coup, the Chávez-led government bent liberal norms by using presidential decrees and powers to intervene in civil society organizations and branches of the state filled with staunch opponents. The government sought to rebalance the media landscape by restricting the powers of the four principal private television stations. There were efforts to replace the management of PDVSA, the state oil company, with allied leaders who would not utilize the inherent structural power of the country's most important source of wealth to limit the capacity of the government to advance a post-neoliberal democracy. Likewise, the government also sought to break the economic power of the opposition-bloc by working with factions of capital who would continue to produce and import essential goods. Chavista loyalists replaced members of the armed forces who participated in the coup. While such actions and use of centralized powers clearly challenge liberal conceptions of democracy, Chávez argued that it was necessary to combat the opposition-bloc's capacity to resist by any means necessary a democratization processes that benefitted marginalized groups while also challenging entrenched elite privileges. The recalcitrant opposition, with the backing of the US government, established themselves as the defenders of a model of democracy that meant a protection of the pre-Chávez status quo—that is, a market democracy in which popular sectors are excluded politically and socio-economically. As such, despite the illiberal nature of the actions by the executive, the government retained popular support as it was seen to be confronting long-standing inequalities of power, as well as US meddling in sovereign affairs.

While liberal norms were bent in order to challenge the array of opposition-bloc powers, the government simultaneously sought to adhere to its popular electoral mandate to deepen and extend democracy by boosting the quality of political and socio-economic incorporation for sectors of Venezuelan society who were excluded during the market democracy era. The early formulation of party-base relations entailed democratic extending via social spending (such as the *misones*), democratic deepening via new avenues of participation in local planning, alongside a protagonistic role in electoral mobilization in support of Chávez and the Bolivarian process. Given the nature and tactics adopted by the opposition to impede the democratization process, an ally-type relationship was forged between the government and popular sector members who engaged with the new state-sponsored spaces of participation. Moreover, the historical weakness of the popular sectors' organizational ties and capacity to engage in sustained, coordinated mobilization shaped the nature of relations that emerged between Chávez and the popular base. The government actively supported the construction of an organized popular power. That is, a popular power capable of engaging in bottom-up mobilization at times of acute confrontation with the opposition was fostered from above by the left-led government. Extensive linkages were established and political ties forged via government payments to participatory spaces for sectors whose livelihoods and health had been ravaged during the market democracy era. Moreover, linkages took an intensive form whereby members of the new participatory spaces were integrated into the formal bureaucratic party structure, making them more dependable allies for the party and the Bolivarian process.

The historical conditions of weak popular sector organizing, however, meant this new deepening and extending had in-built tensions regarding party-base autonomy. The power of the popular base depends upon its capacity to engage in mass mobilization, which in turn is dependent upon the organizational strength and unity of purpose of the base. The early stage of the Bolivarian post-neoliberal process witnessed a significant development in these areas. Receiving state funding to improve living conditions and capacity to engage in democratic organizing was clearly a substantial advancement from the exclusionary market democracy where popular sectors were ignored by the state and the political parties. Moreover, incorporation into the party itself allows popular sector voices to shape internal decision-making.

At the same time, mobilizational power and the capacity to engage in informal contestatory interest intermediation is also dependent on autonomy from a governing party. Autonomy requires that popular organizations are not reliant on a particular party's funding for survival and that organization members can avoid co-optation by the party. While the extensive and intensive linkages forged between base and party boosted the quality of democracy for popular sectors, the lack of autonomy of new state-sponsored spaces of participation meant that they could be managed from the top-down toward the defense of the revolution at times of serious threat.[1] This is not to suggest that popular sectors did not want to defend the process. However, given the active role of the government in helping to build this popular organizational power, the ally-type relationship between government and base, and the formation of extensive and intensive linkages, base-party autonomy was restricted.

Top-down building of popular power was required given the generally weak organizational capacity of the base and the destabilizing power of the opposition. Indeed, while both party and base confronted a common enemy, issues of limited popular sector autonomy were not an issue. The differentiation in terms of the quality of the two components of popular sector mobilizational power—organizational capacity/unity of purpose on the one hand, and autonomy on the other—would, however, trigger an abrasive and paradoxical process of popular sector incorporation in later stages as the intensive and extensive party-base linkages forged during confrontations with a recalcitrant opposition would be used to curb autonomous contestatory mobilization from erupting.

In sum, the (top-down) progressive centralization of the first stage of Venezuela's post-neoliberal process which witnessed simultaneous bending of liberal norms as well as democratization in substantive and participative terms—albeit with in-built tensions regarding party-base autonomy—emerged as a result of the given configuration of popular power, government power, and opposition-bloc power (see Tables 8.2 and 8.3 for summary of outcomes and for conjunctural typological factors). That is, it was the specific conjuncture of historical exclusion under market democracy and the fragmented nature of organized popular power, in a scenario where a pro-market democracy opposition dominated ideological and economic spheres, had transnational backing from the regional hegemonic power as well as domestic military support, while the government dominated the political sphere, that democratic quality was deepened and extended (with top-down sponsoring of organization) at the same time that liberal norms were bent. Developments in this early stage of Venezuela's post-neoliberal process would shape the future direction and outcomes of the process.

Venezuela, stage 2 (2004–13): progressive centralization (from above) to regressive centralization

The 2004–13 period witnessed an intensification of IEMP power struggles between the government and the opposition-bloc, which, on the whole, culminated in a relative balance of power across the four spheres that was more favorable to the government than at the outset of the period. Chávez' party dominated the political sphere (executive, national assembly, regional, and municipal) from 2004 onward, restricting the space for the opposition-bloc to utilize institutionalized sources of political power to curb the post-neoliberal process. With oil prices booming on the back of Chinese demand (and the increased state share of hydrocarbon revenues), the US administration focused on the Middle East, ideologically aligned parties winning elections in the region, and Russia and China seeking new trading partners in Latin America, Chávez encountered a favorable transnational environment with little external leverage over his agenda-setting capacity. Moreover, following the post-2002 coup and purge of the military, Chávez had the backing of a supportive top-brass in the armed forces. Given the relative power distribution, and with his dominance in the political sphere, Chávez sought to radicalize the deepening and extending process, while also utilizing executive powers to both fracture the opposition-bloc's ideological and economic power and to further boost the government's military, economic, and ideological powers.

As discussed in detail in Chapter 3, there were efforts to limit the power of the opposition-bloc media which had participated in the 2001–04 destabilization efforts via new laws such as the Law of Social Responsibility in Radio and Television and the establishment of CONATEL. Government-funded community and radio stations were promoted. While such measures certainly impacted the relative balance of ideological power, private media supportive of the opposition-bloc's agenda retained dominance in terms of viewership figures. In the economic sphere, given the dominance of the governing party across all branches of political power, and with the opposition-bloc parties in disarray, there was a shift in the relations between the government and some economic elites. Despite the boosted economic power of the government given the changes in the hydrocarbon sector, private sector enterprises continued to import essential goods including foods and medicines not produced in Venezuela. The government in turn controlled access to the supply of dollars necessary for such imports. Given this mutual reliance, strategic ties were forged between the government and some importers and financial institutes, especially non-FEDECAMARAS businesspeople who comprised the core economic wing of the opposition-bloc. There were also a series of nationalizations aimed at fracturing opposition-bloc (domestic and transnational) economic power. In the military sphere, the 2008 Organic Law of the Bolivarian Armed Forces sought to invoke a defense of the post-neoliberal project. With no political opposition in the National Assembly, progovernment rectors were installed in the electoral authority, furthering the PSUV's dominance of political power.

Post-2010, the opposition-bloc, having failed to unseat Chávez via extra-institutional means, and with the ruling party partially weakening their economic and military power, the opposition switched strategy and sought to re-forge their capacity to compete for political powers by forming the MUD coalition. The MUD, with the support of the transnational neoliberal think tank network and a US administration whose focus was shifting back to regional developments, framed themselves as defenders of democracy and liberty against an illiberal government. There is no question whether the Chávez government engaged in illiberal actions. Indeed, for Weyland[2] "the core of the Chávez method is to use plebiscitarian mass support in order to transform established institutions, dismantle checks and balances, concentrate power in the hands of the president, and promote immediate re-election." According to Corrales,[3]

> during Chávez' presidency, Venezuela became the paradigmatic Latin American case of competitive authoritarianism. The ruling party … competes in elections against a legal multiparty opposition, as one would expect in a democracy. At the same time, the PSUV helps the executive branch to weaken checks and balances, treat the opposition unfavourably, and reduce the autonomy of civil society.

"Autocratic" laws boosted the power of the executive over other branches of the state, such as enabling laws that allowed Chávez to rule by decree in 2007 and 2010. According to this narrative, with comprehensive control over the political institutions by Chávez and PSUV, opposition voices were pushed to the sidelines, opposition media independence was challenged, and executive control over oil funding was used to boost electoral support.

For example, the 2007 enabling law allowed Chávez to pass 26 laws by decree. One of these was the Law on Public Administration which created "regional authorities" that could directly distribute resources without governors or mayors directing their usage. Other laws expanded the duties of the communal councils to participate in agro-industrial-policy and the development of a popular economy, while there were efforts to advance the communes (see below). Though these laws clearly challenge liberal norms, both in how they were adopted and in how they sought to bypass local branches of the state, their content was aimed at radically redistributing power to an organized popular base who would play a more proactive role in designing and implementing policies that directly influenced their standard of socio-economic citizenship. However, it must be noted that while the laws represented efforts at deepening democratic quality, many of the new laws had been rejected in the 2007 referendum. Moreover, in 2009, Chávez held and won a referendum eliminating term limits for all politicians. Ending presidential term limits was part of the defeated the 2007 referendum. Such actions may be described not only as illiberal, but as containing authoritarian traits.

In 2010, the outgoing PSUV-controlled National Assembly passed an enabling law allowing Chávez to rule by decree for 18 months. Chávez stated he needed the powers to deal with the national emergency caused by massive flooding that drove 140,000 people from their homes. He said that he would use the powers to increase the sales tax to raise funds for reconstruction following the floods. Chávez also pushed through a new banking law that forced banks to give 5 percent of their profits every six months to community groups. Such use of executive powers can hardly be said to be undemocratic and, in fact, represent efforts to redistribute wealth to vulnerable sectors. The use of decree laws was, however, also a response to the 2010 electoral gains made by MUD candidates in parliamentary elections. By winning over 40 percent of the seats, the opposition minority could limit the future granting of decree powers which requires support from a supermajority of assembly members. With the enabling law granting executive decree powers, reduced from 18 to 5 months by Chávez, the president could bypass the political opposition and radicalize the Bolivarian process. Indeed, Chávez openly stated that one of the intentions of the enabling law was to prevent the new opposition-bloc in the assembly from impeding the passage of laws pertinent to the project of 21st-century socialism.

In addition to the use of decree laws, and as discussed in detail previously, the media wars and the struggle over ideological power sources also clearly challenged liberal norms. However, the opposition-controlled media demonized the president and actively spread disinformation, while opposition-bloc civil society organizations with the backing of the transnational neoliberal think tank network and the US government incessantly delegitimized the post-neoliberal project as crude authoritarianism, regardless of its levels of popular support. While liberal scholars equate the use of executive powers to challenge opposition-bloc dominance of ideological sources of power as autocratic actions, given the pre-existing balance of ideological power that was so heavily skewed toward opposition-bloc interests, such appraisals fail to acknowledge the paradoxical potentiality that illiberal actions by a powerful executive may contain democratizing features. Indeed, failure to assess how a small clique of opposition-bloc elites dominated ideological and economic sources of power which they in turn used to try and upend a process that aimed to respond to popular sector needs, but challenged elite interests, is precisely what makes an analysis of the Bolivarian process via a strictly liberal-institutionalist lens so myopic.

While the government engaged in illiberal actions—some of which may clearly be described as undemocratic while others may be described as efforts to redress long-standing inequalities in terms of control of power sources—the illiberal actions were accompanied by efforts to deepen and extend democratic quality. Chávez' and the PSUV's electoral victories were not due to fraud. Jimmy Carter described Venezuela's electoral system as the best in the world. Public opinion data repeatedly highlighted strong popular support for Chávez and his policies. There was a dramatic upturn in "support for parties" over the course of the Chávez presidencies, "interest in politics" rose and turnout in presidential elections rose following the calamitous decline during the 1980s and 1990s.[4]

While critics describe Chávez as a big-spending populist who bought votes, the fact remains the Chávez' policies had great success in extending the quality of democracy for the country's most vulnerable citizens while decreasing levels of inequality. Booming oil prices alongside partial nationalization of the oil sector and reforms to the collection of tax and royalties on hydrocarbons paved the way for a doubling of social spending as a percentage of GDP from 11.3 percent of GDP in 1998 to 22.8 percent in 2011.[5] According to national statistics, poverty levels were decreased from 50 percent in 1999 to 31.9 percent in 2011 while extreme poverty levels were reduced across the same period from 19.9 percent to 8.6 percent. The state sponsored effective literacy campaigns, health care extensions, access to university for poor students, and housing-subsidies; unemployment levels decreased and there was an increase in formal sector jobs and wages compared to informal jobs.[6] The number of Venezuelans receiving a pension increased from 500,000 to 2 million. Child malnutrition of under-5s declined from 7.7 percent in 1990 to 2.9 percent in 2011.[7] According to the United Nations Development Program, Venezuela's Human Development Index ranking rose from medium to high between 2000 and 2012 while ECLAC figures show that Venezuela, alongside Uruguay, had become one of the two countries with the lowest levels of inequality in Latin America.[8]

In addition to efforts to extend the quality of democracy, democratic quality was deepened during the second stage of Venezuela's post-neoliberal process. The promotion of the communal councils and the communes provided new spaces for popular participation in local budgeting and development plans, while also helping to strengthen organizational ties within and across popular sector neighborhoods. The PSUV party was forged with the aim of providing more opportunities for bottom-up input form organized popular groups. The new party structure envisioned a tight leader-base relation that would allow such participation to actually shape policy without falling to issues of bureaucratization, clientelism, and corruption. Extensive linkages were forged as grassroots organizations received funding from the executive to carry out local development projects. Moreover, intensive linkages were forged as PSUV members were drawn directly from the popular organizations.

State-sponsored spaces of participation such as the CCs and communes became the key spaces of party-base interaction. There were many positive experiences of popular sector groups that took advantage of the organizational and financial impetus from above to participate in local decision-making, as well as to foster new connections between formerly disconnected groups. The level of popular organizing, financed and encouraged from above, far outstripped any historical precedent.

The dual process of extending and deepening democracy during the 2004–13 period, however, faced several challenges. Despite the impressive gains in extending the quality of democratic citizenship, they were not premised on a structural transformation of the Venezuelan economy away from a rentier state model, with oil's share of total export values rising from 68.7 percent in 1998 to over 95 percent in Chávez' final year in power. Moreover, many of the nationalizations of private enterprises were driven by political rather than economic logic as the state's fiscal and technical capacity was overextended, leading to insufficient investment for the upkeep and technological upgrading of state-run companies. Oil revenues were needed to keep many state companies afloat. Costly arbitration proceedings from expropriated private owners alongside declining oil prices post-2009 worsened Venezuela's fiscal position.[9] To maintain capacity to fund social spending, Chávez increased levels of international borrowing, from China and Russia principally, and made more onerous demands on PDVSA, with the company channeling US$49 billion in 2012 to the government.[10] The company was left with insufficient funds to maintain exploration, drilling and shipping activities that had been historically performed by transnationals.

Moreover, while wage rises and oil-funded social spending boosted the purchasing power of popular sectors, there was little increase in domestic production meaning that gaps between demand and supply were filled by increasing the level of imports. As imports are so critical to the Venezuelan economy, there is a tendency to overvalue the currency (thereby making imports cheaper, but exports more expensive). The result is that any efforts to promote domestic production are undercut on the one hand, while subsidized foreign currency earned from oil sales is funneled to pay for imports of food, basic consumer goods, intermediate inputs, and luxury goods.[11] As mentioned above, in this scenario, with Chávez seeking to weaken the economic power of the FEDECAMARAS-bloc, while still requiring that private enterprises maintained supply and distribution chains, a strategically selected compromise was reached between the government and some businesses who received preferential access to contracts, exchange rates, and credit. However, this scenario opened avenues for gross levels of corruption. Edmeé Betancourt, president of the Venezuelan Central Bank in 2012, said that of a total of US$59 billion in subsidized foreign exchange allocated in that year, US$20 billion was siphoned into shell companies or "artificial demand" "unrelated to productive activities."[12] Thus, the continuation of a rentier model of extractivism to fund democratic extending produced enormous inefficiencies and corruption, allowing well-placed civilian and military bureaucrats and strategically allied capitalists—the so-called *boliburguesías*, to line their pockets.[13]

While one may argue as to whether the strategic compromise with factions of capital was required, the pacts and the attendant corruption irked radical sectors of the organized base who wanted a more rapid transformation of the economy, as well as more space to participate in setting the development agenda of the process. However, several factors limited the capacity of critical voices from below from gaining influence or from fomenting contestatory interest intermediation that challenged party decision-making. The nature of a deepening process built around redistribution of oil wealth from a rentier petro-economy had in-built tensions. First, with oil rents financing imports, efforts to construct a socialist economy never received the full backing of the PSUV leadership. Second, while it is inaccurate to describe the state-sponsored spaces of participation as clientelistic hubs that simply towed the party line, there was clearly an issue regarding levels of autonomy of the popular base from the left-party. The extensive linkages forged through state funding, and the intensive linkages whereby CC and commune members were also PSUV members were a double-edged sword. Certainly, the quality of democracy was advanced as popular sector voices were incorporated into decision-making channels and the party structure. But the reality is that the scope for bottom-up, informal contestatory interest intermediation that sees popular organizations engage in demonstrations that challenge party-decisions was severely restricted.

Given the issues regarding organizational autonomy, one can question whether Chávez should have funded spaces of participation. At the same time, however, Chávez was responding to the desperate needs of communities who had been devastated by decades of neoliberal reforms, while he was simultaneously seeking to foster the development of a well-organized and connected popular base who would mobilize in defense of the reform process in the face of incessant opposition-bloc destabilization tactics. That is, the historic nature of (weak) popular sector organizing, in conjunction with an aggressive opposition-bloc, influenced the (top-down) nature of party-base relations. An ally-type relation was forged between party and base to confront a universal enemy in the form of an opposition seeking a return to market democracy by any means necessary. However, given the historic conditions of weak organization backgrounds, the ally-relationship and the extensive and intensive linkages meant that many popular organizations placed loyalty to the party ahead of loyalty to the post-neoliberal process. Consequently, those popular sector organizers who did raise concerns regarding the direction of the process were easily side-lined as they lacked capacity to mobilize sufficient numbers to engage in successful contestatory interest intermediation.

The 2004–13 period of the Bolivarian process thus witnessed the beginning of a move from progressive centralization toward regressive centralization (see Table 8.2 for outcomes), a process whose direction and outcomes were shaped by historical factors (nature of popular organization histories and early party-base relations), by events in the 1999–2004 period (aggressive opposition destabilization and the emergence of an ally-type party-base relationship), the evolving IEMP power relations between the governing party and the opposition-bloc, as well as the transnational sphere (see Table 8.3 for conjunctural list of historical and emergent factors). The creeping illiberalism and the slide toward regressive centralization continued to impact the direction of the process, with dire consequences under Chávez' successor, Nicolás Maduro.

Venezuela, stage 3 (2013–21): regressive to authoritarian centralization

The Maduro regime, particularly post-2015, moved toward authoritarian centralization as elections were not free and their results were not respected; state security forces were used to silence dissent from both the opposition-bloc and critical sectors of the original popular base of Chavismo; and the executive's control over scarce resources was used to guarantee that some popular sectors refused to actively challenge the government's rule. However, while Maduro's legitimacy was dramatically eroded within popular barrios by 2021, opposition-bloc parties did not automatically benefit. Their association with the exclusionary market democracy era preceding Chávez, as well as the radical sector's efforts to foment a coup and their calls for US support to overthrow Chávez meant that they remained, in the eyes of the most vulnerable, representatives of a different type of Venezuelan. The upshot was an entrenched political impasse. To help frame why the process under Maduro moved from regressive centralization to authoritarian centralization, we need to grasp the evolving government-opposition IEMP power struggles and international conditions over the 2013–21 period.

Briefly summarizing, in the political, economic, and ideological spheres, Maduro's government lost power relative to the Chávez era, while the election of Trump in the United States and right-wing victories in former Pink Tide states saw increased international efforts to isolate the Bolivarian project. Oil prices fell dramatically, compounding inefficient exchange and price control policies, while US sanctions hobbled Maduro's economic power further. The 2015 National Assembly election loss fractured Maduro's and the PSUV's political power. Maduro's response to the 2015 defeat and the formation of the ANC, as well as the Supreme Court's blocking of a recall drive, in conjunction with the shifting international scenario, emboldened the radical wing of the MUD to take the lead in pushing for Maduro's exit. Guaidó decreed himself "interim president" and was recognized instantly by the United States, the OAS, the Lima Group, and many EU states.

While violent opposition protests in 2014 did not galvanize mass popular support (and in fact triggered divisions within the MUD over how to best remove Maduro), the heavy-handed response by state security forces to the protests allowed the United States, first under Obama and later under Trump, to "reframe the critique of Venezuela around a human rights discourse — a narrative that has allowed alliance building with Canada, the EU and the OAS to address the Venezuela 'problem'."[14] This was precisely what the radical opposition, who encouraged the violent protests, wanted to happen. They repeated the tactic in 2017 as they knew that it would further tarnish Maduro internationally and allow for harsher sanctions and possibly foreign military intervention. Though Trump refrained from such military tactics, the drastic ramping up of sanctions hobbled the economic power of the government.

Lacking economic power, facing an alternative political power in the form of Guaidó, internationally delegitimized—though with China and Russia offering vital economic life support, and with foreign sanctions on doing business with Venezuela as well as on high-ranking PSUV officials and military officials, Maduro entrenched himself in power with the backing of the top brass of the armed forces. Seeking to overcome the deteriorating economic conditions, Maduro eased tensions with some sectors of domestic capital. However, it became increasingly clear that the military elites were involved in corruption, especially in trafficking medicine, food, and foreign currency, which directly affects popular sectors. Moreover, the deals with sectors of capital involved rolling back protective labor policies, maintaining currency policies that benefitted importing capitalists and wealthy Venezuelans but did nothing for vulnerable sectors, while new extractive projects undertaken by transnational capital were to be carried out along neoliberal lines.

While institutional-focused analyses on democratic backsliding in Venezuela correctly detail how a weakening of political power vis-à-vis opposition-bloc political power increased the likelihood that the ruling party would engage in authoritarian actions,[15] it was the conjunctural shifts in the prevailing balance of ideological, economic, military, and transnational powers, as well as in the political sphere, that ultimately pushed the process toward authoritarian centralization.

While the prevailing balance of IEMP powers and transnational conditions influenced the direction of the process, opening the way for a move to authoritarian centralization, the power scenario also shaped the relations between the PSUV leadership and the constituent base. Extra-institutional tactics by the opposition and the international efforts to isolate and strangle the Venezuelan economy meant that popular constituent members of Chavismo were in a difficult position as they were urged to show unity against elite and imperial aggressors. However, the establishment of the ANC to bypass the 2015 electoral defeat, corruption, bureaucratization, militarization, top-down decision-making, co-opting of participatory spaces, and the withholding of financing and foodstuffs from organizations that did not show fealty were challenged by some elements of Chavismo.

This critical position was sidelined and repressed, however, and was generally unable to impact the behaviors of the party leadership. While government-opposition power struggles pushed the PSUV in an illiberal, undemocratic and, paradoxically, neoliberal direction, the critical autonomous wing of the Chavista base was not powerful enough to hold the party to a post-neoliberal democratic agenda. Maduro accepted corruption, militarization, and neoliberalization because he was unable to confront the opposition destabilization tactics without the backing of the military and facets of domestic capital; and the critical Chavista bloc who rejected the corruption, militarization, and neoliberalization lacked sufficient support from an autonomous popular base capable of engaging in mass contestatory mobilization against government actions.

The limited backing for, or participation in, contestatory mobilization against the PSUV by large portions of the Chavista base was in part due to historical factors. The exclusionary nature of market democracy before Chávez and the fact that the opposition-bloc seeking to dislodge Maduro were considered to represent this market democracy meant that there was a reluctance to mobilize against Maduro and potentially help usher in a return to the past. A further issue relates to the historical lack of autonomous popular sector organization and mobilization at a mass scale before the election of Chávez as well as the ally-type party-base relation established to confront the opposition destabilization. While extensive and intensive party-base linkages boosted popular sector political and socio-economic incorporation, there was a fuzzy line between party and participatory spaces in terms of personnel and purposes. The extensive and intensive linkages ossified over time and became impediments to contestatory mobilization against Maduro and the PSUV leadership when, in response to opposition-bloc powers, the process slid toward authoritarian centralization with accompanying anti-popular economic policies. Lacking mass popular support, the critical Chavistas that did challenge the PSUV leadership's authoritarian and anti-popular turn were easily ignored and repressed. Ultimately, it was the particular combination of government-opposition IEMP and transnational power relations in

Table 8.2 Democratic outcomes of Venezuelan and Bolivian post-neoliberal processes (author's own elaboration)

Case	*Liberal Democracy*	*Deepened Democracy*	*Extended Democracy*	*Centralization*
Venezuela 1 (1999–2004)	Free elections; use of decrees with redistributive agenda; replacement of some military leaders; judicial purge; executive firing of oil managers; control of media licensing	Space for participation in local planning, linked to executive funding	Constitutional guarantee to protection of social citizenship; *misiones*; increased social spending; land tax; expropriation of unused land/property; partial nationalization of oil industry; increased hydrocarbon tax and royalties	Top-down progressive
Venezuela 2 (2004–13)	Free elections; use of decrees with redistributive agenda; "media war"; bypassing of mayors/local government with direct executive-base linkages; decrees to bring in elements of rejected 2007 referendum, including holding 2009 referendum for repeated re-election; corruption in state bodies	Communal councils; communes; PSUV formed; extensive linkages (executive funding to local participatory spaces); intensive linkages (positions within PSUV for popular-organization members); limited scope for internal critique and blocking of contestatory mobilization	Increased social spending (literacy, health, education, housing); rising formal employment and wages; increasing pension coverage; declining poverty rates; decreasing inequality; nationalizations (though some driven by political rather than economic reasoning)	Progressive-regressive
Venezuela 3 (2013–21)	Unfree elections; electoral outcomes not respected (ANC bypasses National Assembly); state repression of opposition protest; extra-judicial arrest of critical popular sector organizers; corruption in state bodies	Repression of contestatory mobilization; top-down control of state-sponsored spaces of participation	Rollback of pro-labor reforms; neoliberal-style hydrocarbon extraction deals; economic crisis and hyper-inflation erode quality of social citizenship; currency shortages; food shortages; use of state-controlled scarce resources to manage participatory spaces	Regressive-authoritarian

Bolivia 1 (2006–09)	Free elections; executive efforts to reform judiciary; confrontations with opposition-bloc media	Unity Pact (bottom-up incorporation); CONALCAM (partial top-down incorporation); Constituent Assembly process; intensive linkages (popular organization leaders offered positions within MAS and within state institutions)	Constitutional guarantee to protection of social citizenship; increased social spending; partial nationalization of hydrocarbon sector; increased hydrocarbon tax and royalties	Bottom-up progressive
Bolivia 2 (2009–14)	Free elections; executive efforts to reform judiciary; tightening executive-military relations	Core sectors of popular base retain bottom-up influence on executive via participatory spaces; successful contestatory interest intermediation by core organizations; some efforts to co-opt popular leaders; strategic bloc contestatory interest intermediation weakened via top-down meddling in organization leaderships; no bottom-up influence over economic and public financing	Increased social spending (universal pensions, education, nutrition, health); wage rises; declining inequality; limited land reforms; regressive taxation; limited creation of new formal sector employment	Progressive-regressive
Bolivia 3 (2014–19[b])	Free elections; refusal to adhere to referendum results and judicial backing of illiberal undemocratic executive actions; opposition-led coup	Core organizations retain scope for participation in party decision-making; strategic organizations split as "loyal" blocs recognized by MAS, contestatory blocs sidelined	Maintenance of hydrocarbon-funded redistributive model, but with moderation of social spending; weak formal sector job creation	Regressive-progressive[a]

a The "regressive-progressive" conceptualization indicates that while participation channels for core-organizations remained open, issues facing contestatory strategic organizations such as co-optation and promoted parallelism became increasingly problematic.

b I outline the outcomes of the process up to October 2019, the point at which Morales was forced from office.

Table 8.3 Typological table of historical and emergent factors, democratic outcomes (author's own elaboration)

Case	*Historical Factors*	*G: I*[a]	*G: E*	*G: M*	*G: P*	*O: I*	*O: E*	*O: M*	*O: P*	*Popular Power*	*Transnational*	*Outcomes*
Ven-1	Democratic legitimacy crisis; ad hoc protests; vanguardist party-base relations	W[a]	W-M	M	M-S	S	S	M	W-M	W	M-S	Progressive centralization, but strong party influence on base
Ven-2	Aggressive opposition destabilization; vanguard, ally-type party-base relations with intensive and extensive linkages	W-M	M	M	S	M-S	M-S	W	W	W-M	W-M	Progressive centralization edging toward Regressive Centralization
Ven-3	Creeping regressive centralization	W	W	S	M	S	M-S	W	M	W-M	S	Regressive-authoritarian
Bolivia 1	Democratic legitimacy crisis; co-ordinated protests; organic party-base relations	W	W	W	S	S	S	M	M	S	W	Progressive centralization-strong base influence on party
Bolivia 2	Aggressive opposition destabilization; ally-type party-base relations with intensive and extensive linkages	W	W-M	M	M-S	M	S	W-M	W-M	S	W	Progressive-regressive
Bolivia 3	Ossifying extensive and intensive linkages	M	W	W	M	S	S	M	M-S	M	M-S	Regressive-progressive

a The letters G and O in the column headings refer to "Government" and "Opposition-bloc." The letters I, E, M, and P refer to "Ideological Power," "Economic Power," "Military Power" and "Political Power." The letters W, M, and S stand for "weak," "moderate," and "strong".

conjunction with the weak autonomous mobilization capacity of the popular base vis-à-vis the PSUV that fostered a move away from post-neoliberalism to an authoritarian neoliberalism masquerading as a progressive project.

Summary of the Bolivian case: progressive and regressive centralization

Bolivia, stage 1 (2006–09): progressive centralization (from below)

Following the collapse of the traditional party system and the de-legitimation of the market model of democracy, in conjunction with the waves of anti-neoliberal protests coordinated by powerful popular organizations, Morales was elected to office with the ideological scope and popular backing to advance an alternative, post-neoliberal democracy. However, an opposition-bloc cleaved around protection of the status quo and market democracy. In the political sphere, despite winning the presidential election and a simple majority in the Chamber of Deputies, MAS did not control the senate or the conservative judiciary. Furthermore, opposition-bloc politicians won the control of the majority of departmental governments, including those regions where key sources of economic power lay (finance, agro-industry, and hydrocarbons). They also dominated the ideological sources of power (media and churches) and wielded control over fascistic mobs (a form of military power) who engaged in violent repression of government supporters.

As the government outlined plans to respond to popular demands to move away from a market model of democracy, utilizing their array of IEMP powers, the opposition-bloc adopted institutional and extra-institutional tactics to impede the MAS government, culminating in the autonomist drive aimed at blocking the Constituent Assembly process. While the opposition-bloc pressurized the MAS from the right, powerful popular organizations pushed the MAS from below to advance the process. In the tug-of-war between the opposition-bloc and popular demands, with the government located in between, MAS was heavily reliant on defensive-mobilization by the popular base to prevent elite destabilization tactics from succeeding. In fact, in "the opening phase of post neoliberalism the organic connection between the MAS and its social movement base ensured an alignment between them and Morales' government."[16] Squeezed between powerful popular organizations pushing for reforms and a powerful opposition-bloc resisting the post-neoliberal agenda, the Morales government engaged in illiberal actions to escape the bind.

To combat the conservative bias in the judiciary, the MAS pressurized some sitting judges, including the chief justice of the Supreme Court, by filing criminal charges against them. He was accused of participating in a plot to send Bolivian missiles to the United States and was replaced by a "loyalist."[17] According to Sánchez-Sibony,[18] the MAS-government denounced the judiciary publicly, claiming it was corrupt, and mobilized supporters to demand the resignation of members of the Constitutional Tribunal and the Supreme Court. Moreover, "the MAS government … jump-started impeachment processes against specific members of the Supreme Court" in an effort to remove pro-opposition judges. There were also frequent confrontations with the traditional media, with Morales describing them as a principal enemy of the post-neoliberal project.

Such illiberal behavior, however, retained popular support as it was considered part of the struggle against a pro-neoliberal opposition-bloc intent on restraining the MAS' attempts to adhere to electoral promises to move toward a post-neoliberal model of democracy that deepened and extended the quality of citizenship for long-excluded groups. Facing a common enemy, an ally-type party-base relationship developed and intensive linkages were forged between the MAS, core-organizations, and strategically allied organizations. Indeed, during this first stage of the post-neoliberal process, via the Unity Pact, CONALCAM, the Constituent Assembly process, the promulgation of the new Constitution, and the appointment of movement/organization leaders to ministry positions, the quality of democracy for popular sectors who had been excluded in the preceding market democracy era was deepened and extended. While Morales took decisions in an illiberal manner to confront the opposition-bloc, participatory spaces were opened to powerful popular movements that were capable of guiding the process from below in what may be termed a period of progressive centralization. That is, adherence to liberal norms weakened and executive power was boosted. However, Morales' executive powers and agenda-setting capacity were tethered to new spaces for popular participation and used to push forward popular reforms in the face of political, ideological, economic, and military forms of resistance from the opposition-bloc.

The international sphere also provided opportunities for a project that challenged market democracy. Thanks to the global commodities boom, which saw the price of Bolivia's principal exports dramatically rise, Morales had the economic power to extend democracy, with public investment increasing from 6.3 percent of GDP in 2005 to 10.5 percent in 2009. Furthermore, the availability of financing from the ideologically aligned Hugo Chávez-led Venezuela liberated Bolivia to experiment in alternatives to market democracy. Debt forgiveness under the IMF's 2005 Heavily Indebted Poor Country's (HIPC) initiative reduced the leverage of the financial institution over Morales' government by releasing the country from rigid conditionalities. With US overreach in the Middle East, and the ideological rejection of neoliberalism across much of the Latin American region, the Morales-led government appeared to be in a prime position to advance a "post-neoliberal" democratization project. However, the 2009–14 period would witness the emergence of tensions between the government and sectors of the popular base. To grasp why such tensions emerged, it is necessary to outline the nature of government-transnational corporation relations post-2010 and how these shaped state autonomy.

Bolivia, stage 2 (2009–14): simultaneous progressive and regressive centralization

The 2009–14 stage of Bolivia's post-neoliberal process contained elements of both progressive and regressive centralization. Liberal norms were bent as the MAS government sought to use its boosted political power via dominance in the legislature and the executive to weaken opposition-bloc control over the judiciary and mainstream media. These illiberal moves were justified as necessary to combat opposition-bloc capacity to destabilize the post-neoliberal process. Moreover, there was a tightening of relations between the executive and the military as Morales boosted the defence forces budget, created state positions for retired army personnel, and met with the high command on a regular basis. With a commodity-funded economy booming, a weakened oppositional ideological sector, electoral dominance in national and regional spheres, a more favorable judicial makeup, and a quiesced military, the 2009–14 period represents an apogee in terms of MAS hegemony across key sources of power. Moreover, in the transnational sphere, external leverage over the government was reduced, allowing Morales to push forward with the reform project. The boom in primary commodity prices, decreased external debt, and high levels of international reserves in the Central Bank meant that Morales was free from IMF or World Bank conditionalities, while regionally supportive governments in Argentina and Brazil provided sites for exportation while Venezuela offered oil on friendly terms.

Despite such a favorable balance of power, and even with the economy booming, Bolivia's continued reliance on primary commodity exports and agro-industry meant that the structural power of transnational and domestic economic elites could not be fractured. The upshot was that the post-neoliberal process could advance, but within structural limitations set by powerful economic agents. Hence, while the project sought to deepen and extend democratic quality for those excluded under the market model, the MAS leadership had to strategically select which popular groups' demands would be listened to, and whose would be excluded. Such strategic selectivities were shaped by the historical relations between the MAS and base organizations as well as the nature of the demands and whether or not they clashed with economic elite interests.

Democratic quality was extended for popular sectors. The scope of social citizenship was dramatically boosted as spending increased in the areas of universal pensions, education, nutrition, and health. Wages rose and inequality levels declined. However, taxation remained regressive. Growth in the number of non-precarious jobs was limited, promised land reforms fell short, and as mentioned above, nationalizations of mining and hydrocarbon industries were more moderate than anti-neoliberal protest movements had demanded. Moreover, the nature of deepening—and consequently the quality of democratic extending—varied across the constituent organizations as a segmented popular interest intermediation regime emerged.[19]

Core organization leaders tended to gain access to ministries more than strategic organizations; their choices for MAS candidates to fill representative roles in the legislature were accepted more often; their voices carried more weight in participatory spaces such as CONALCAM; following the 2013 Law of Participation and Social Control, core groups were more regularly invited to participate, while the informal contestatory mobilization by core groups forced the government to adhere to demands from below. As such, the 2009–14 period witnessed a radical deepening of democratic quality for members of core-organizations.

The historical emergence of the MAS from these core-organizations meant that voices from the core-constituent base always had an influence on policymaking. The nature of the relationship between Morales and the core-organizations and the power they retained due to their capacity to influence the electorate (as witnessed in the 2009 elections when organization leaders rallied massive grassroots electoral support for Morales); to mobilize in defense of the government—against elite opposition from 2006 to 2009 and against former allies post-2009; or to mobilize against MAS policies as witnessed during the *gasolinazo*, ensured that early experiences of bottom-up participation were reinforced over the 2009–14 period.

The historical organizational powers of the core organizations and their instrumental role in forging the MAS shaped how they interacted with the party in office. They retained a capacity for autonomous contestatory mobilization even as intensive and extensive linkages were forged, thereby allowing democratic quality to deepen while avoiding the inherent dangers of such close-knit party-base relations. However, the intensive and extensive linkages between core-organization leaderships and the executive meant that leaders at times failed to call for contestatory mobilization or to veto policies via their representatives in the legislature, even when the policies were not supported by the grassroots. More generally, however, core-organization voices were influential as legislative representatives, ministry officials, and the executive bargained with and incorporated their demands, even when they directly clashed with demands of strategic organizations.[20]

While democratic quality deepened for core-organizations, the Ministry of the Economy and Public Finance was generally sealed off from pressure from below, though the COB did have some impact in shaping the 2010 pensions reform. While popular sectors were excluded from the ministry and economic policymaking, dominant business interests were invited in. Furthermore, for strategic-organizations the post-neoliberal project contained elements of regressive centralization. It is true that policymaking under Morales was a "highly negotiated process" and that "when grass-roots social actors are strongly organized and can mobilize large groups of people in the streets autonomously, they can put real constraints on the government's agenda and steer policy in their desired direction."[21] However, a problem emerged when the grassroots of popular organizations that had demonstrated such mobilization capacity disagreed with the MAS in areas where the government confronted the structural powers of capital. In fact, it was precisely because of their historic capacity to engage in mass mobilization that the MAS leadership sought to co-ordinate organization leaderships via intensive and extensive linkages, linkages forged during the prior ally-type relation and struggle against opposition-bloc destabilization efforts.

Those organizations who sought to challenge the MAS' agro-industrial, primary-commodity focused development plan—either because it was considered too moderate and ceded too much ground to domestic and transnational economic elites or because it relied on a continual encroachment into indigenous lands—were weakened via top-down co-optive efforts. "Loyal" blocs of leaderships were recognized by the MAS, received funding for projects, and were incorporated into the party bureaucracy as they were selected from above as acceptable candidates for local elections. While those leaders who were allied to the MAS certainly sought to represent the interests of their grassroots, the issue was that if and when grassroots members did not agree with the direction of the process or the MAS-selected candidates, their organizations could not engage in autonomous contestatory mobilization—a key input to and outcome of radical democratization processes.

Bolivia, stage 3 (2014–21): regressive centralization and undemocratic illiberalism

The third stage of Bolivia' post-neoliberal process contained elements of both progressive and regressive centralization, though the process took an increasingly steep slide toward regressive centralization as formerly allied strategic organizations became targets of top-down manipulation. Such top-down meddling in popular organizations, in conjunction with the illiberal, undemocratic behaviors around the refusal to accept the 2016 referendum defeat on re-election, proved decisive in preventing Morales from remaining in office for a fourth term.

While the core-organizations that played a foundational role in the MAS retained voice in internal party discussions, as the linkages forged between the MAS and strategically allied organizations during early stage confrontations with a common enemy became impediments to critical contestatory mobilization, those same organizations witnessed intense internal tensions. That is, as the post-neoliberal process moderated in response to structural limitations set by powerful economic actors, the MAS leadership increasingly sought to maintain control over a "loyal" bloc in the leadership of powerful popular organizations. With some grassroots and "non-loyal" sectors of the leaderships disagreeing with the direction of the process, with the top-down meddling in popular organizations, and with the "loyal" bloc impeding contestatoty mobilization from occurring, internal organization friction increased. Ultimately, as the organizations lost capacity to engage in successful contestatory interest intermediation, they split apart into parallel "loyal" and "contestatory" organizations.

Meanwhile, though the MAS project had faced opposition-bloc resistance from the outset, from 2016 the relative balance of power shifted. The re-forging of the political and ideological wings of the opposition-bloc around the "No" campaign for the re-election referendum, alongside shifting international conditions—the crisis in ally Venezuela, declining international gas prices, the return of pro-neoliberal presidents in the region, and the strident OAS critique of Morales—allowed the opposition-bloc to take a more assertive confrontational stance that garnered middle-class support.

In conjunction with such shifts in the ideological, political, economic, and transnational spheres, Morales' efforts to remain in power for a fourth term resonated with many popular sector organizations whose statutes are founded on the idea of *rotatividad*, the need for rotation and renovation of positions of leadership. Re-election efforts, in addition to the regressive efforts from above to control powerful organization leaders and to foment loyal parallel organizations, meant that Morales faced a legitimacy crisis amongst some key popular organizations. In such a scenario, not only did Morales fail to elicit popular sector defensive mobilization to combat the opposition-bloc, but he faced demands from formerly allied organizations to step down from the presidency.

With the end of the economic boom, as the political wing of the opposition-bloc re-found its voice after a period of relative marginalization, and with Morales no longer able to contain popular protests, the conditions that encouraged economic elites to forge strategic pacts with the Morales government were shifting. Facing mass middle-class and popular protests, with far-right elements of the opposition bloc fomenting violence, and with opposition-bloc politicians, economic elites, and media figures demanding that Morales step aside, the police and military also withdrew their backing for the president.

Hence, in the ideological, economic, military, political, and transnational spheres, the balance of power shifted unfavourably for the Morales government. With popular sector organizations somewhat split over whether to defend the government from destabilizing pressures, Morales was forced from office. While opposition-bloc forces were crucial to removing Morales, the willingness of popular sector organizations to withdraw their support for Morales when he sought to remain in power beyond Constitutionally bounded limits was a critical component that prevented the Bolivian process sliding in a dangerously illiberal direction whereby an elected leader seeks to use the courts to overturn the results of electoral outcomes (as in the case of the 2016 referendum). That is, by protesting against the government, popular organizations signaled to the military that they would not defend the government, thereby reducing the risk of violent confrontations between the armed forces and powerful popular organizations if and when the military withdrew their backing for Morales.[22]

Even though Morales represented a barrier against the return of the opposition to state power, and a consequent return to market democracy, these popular sector organizations rejected the notion that the post-neoliberal project could not advance without Morales as president. In fact, given the moderation of the project, there was a belief that the best path forward for the project was a renovation of party-base relations and a renovation of party leadership. This willingness to confront a party of the left by demanding a tighter adherence to popular sector demands and to reject illiberal behavior that was not used to deepen and extend democratic quality was a key component in shaping the outcomes of the Bolivian case.

While historical autonomous mobilization histories engendered the willingness and capacity to challenge the MAS from below and to the left, this did not equate to a wholesale rejection of the MAS or of the post-neoliberal project. Facing a universal common enemy in the form of the racist, violently repressive, pro-market, and pro-oligarchic Añez government, both core and (divided) strategic organization leaders coordinated their bases to demand new elections and to support the MAS candidates Arce and Choquehuanca. The willingness to rally to support Arce at the national level to defeat the pro-market democracy opposition in the 2020 elections, despite the MAS-base tensions, suggests that what popular sector organizations want is not an end to post-neoliberal democracy, but rather a radicalization of the project which had stuttered under Morales.

While the re-emergence of the far-right in 2019–20 witnessed a re-convergence between divided popular organizations and the MAS to confront the common enemy, once the critical confrontational moment had passed, the issues regarding organizational autonomy under the MAS came to the fore again. Indeed, while the MAS emerged as a political vehicle for social movement demands to move beyond the confines of neoliberalism and remains the dominant party at the national level, simmering party-base tensions opened space for candidates to the left of the party-system at the local and regional level following Arce's election. Hence, while the linkages that were forged between the MAS and strategic organizations during the confrontations with the autonomists during the Constituent Assembly process ossified over time, the lessons learned over the duration of the Morales-led post-neoliberal process makes it unlikely that the strategic alliance to confront a common enemy in 2020 will lead to similar issues of top-down manipulation of popular organizations.

Venezuelan and Bolivian post-neoliberal (de) democratization processes in comparison

The Venezuelan and Bolivian cases examined in this book are examples of outsider-led post-neoliberal (de)democratization processes. In this section, I compare the outcomes and key historical and emergent factors which shaped the processes. I do not propose a single, universal causal mechanism capable of explaining every case of post-neoliberal democratization. Rather, I aim to highlight the broader characteristics and conjunctures of factors from the cases that impacted democratic quality. That is, the aim is to offer contingent generalizations on how variations in key historic and emergent factors influence the pathways and outcomes of post-neoliberal processes.

As Table 8.1 highlights, support for anti-neoliberal outsiders and, consequently, post-neoliberal democratization processes, is more likely to emerge in cases where labor markets are dualized and where there is a simultaneous narrowing and shallowing of democracy, leading to a legitimacy crisis and an unstable democratic equilibrium. In such scenarios, a shock such as an economic crisis or surprise austerity may push the teetering unstable democracy beyond a tipping point, leading to mass electoral and societal protests and the fracturing of the traditional mainstream party system. However, the nature that protests take—whether they are well coordinated by powerful popular organizations or whether they are ad hoc eruptions of disconnected discontent—is likely to shape the type of anti-neoliberal outsider that emerges.

As the Bolivian case demonstrates, coordinated protests organized by powerful popular movements and organizations are more likely to see a movement-based anti-neoliberal party/leader emerge whereby the outsider emerges organically from, and remains connected to, the protest movement. Conversely, as the Venezuelan case suggests, where protests are disconnected and where there is a lack of a centralized and powerful social movement or popular organization guiding the protests, the outsider that emerges, though representing the demands and concerns of myriad protesters, is likely to be somewhat separated from the protesters. That is, a vanguardist-type outsider who acts as a central hub, guiding the disconnected protesters from above, is more likely. As discussed below, the varied nature of party-base linkages (organic, vanguard) that emerge during the historical era continue to influence how popular sectors are incorporated at later stages of the process (Figure 8.1).

While the shared and varied historical factors in the cases demonstrate why (varied types of) anti-neoliberal outsiders garner support, the cases also highlight that as support for the outsider and their proposed projects grows, an opposition-bloc comprised of the traditional elite groups hardens its stance around a market model of democracy. However, given the collapse of the traditional parties who represented the interests of the dominant groups in society during this antecedent era (that is, before the elections of the anti-neoliberal outsiders), one may expect that in the post-electoral sequencing the opposition-bloc will utilize an array of tactics to oppose the outsiders (i.e., simply focusing on the use of institutionalized political party power will not capture the full range of opposition resistance).

Both cases demonstrate that to grasp the actions of newly elected anti-neoliberal governments, including willingness to engage in illiberal behaviors, and to comprehend popular sector support or rejection for government actions, it is essential to view the post-neoliberal process via a historic lens that encapsulates the market democracy era. By grasping who was incorporated and who was excluded under market democracy (political and socio-economic inclusion of middle classes and elites, exclusion of popular and

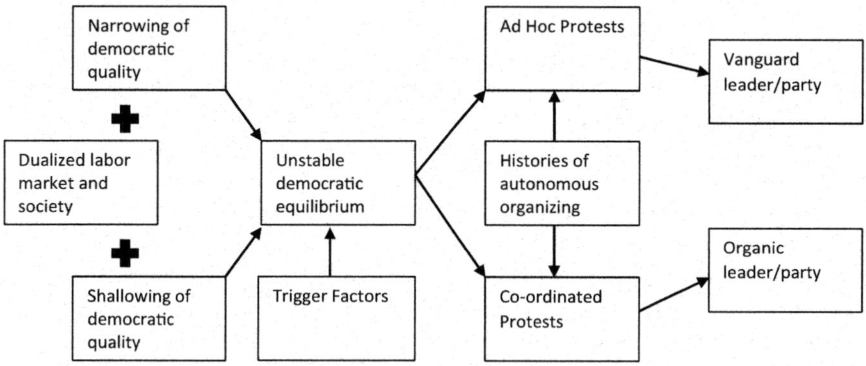

Figure 8.1 Crises of market democracy and outsider emergence (author's own elaboration).

indigenous sectors), as well as the preceding domination of ideological, economic, military, and political sources of power by a select elite bloc, we can better comprehend why governments may bend liberal norms and why they retain popular backing for doing so.

As Table 8.2 notes, the first phases of the Venezuelan and Bolivian post-neoliberal processes witnessed progressive centralization. While there was adherence to electoral norms, in both cases there was a use of executive powers in an illiberal manner. There were executive-led confrontations with private media and efforts to reform the makeup of the judiciary. In Venezuela, there were also executive-led efforts to replace senior figures in the armed forces and in the state oil company, while laws were adopted via executive decree (though these powers were granted via the National Assembly).

The quality of democracy was extended in both cases as new Constitutions were adopted which outlined that the state had a responsibility to provide a minimum standard of social citizenship to all citizens. Social spending levels increased as the state took a much more proactive role in the running of, and capturing of revenues from, the countries' hydrocarbon industries. Taxation and royalty levels increased, while state involvement in extraction also rose. However, in both cases, nationalization was partial as private companies continued to play pivotal roles in the extraction, refinement, and distribution of the countries' natural resources.

The quality of democracy was also deepened in both cases as new spaces of popular participation were created by the new governments. The newly promulgated Bolivarian Constitution in Venezuela called for a more protagonistic role for citizens who should participate directly in policymaking. The *misiones* were designed with the aim of bringing constituted power (elected officials and the executive) into a direct participatory relationship with constituent power (organized popular sectors). These state-sponsored spaces of participation sought to provide executive funding to projects designed in local participatory spaces. In addition to this dual extending-deepening role of the *misiones*, Chávez called on participants to form electoral battle units to mobilize the base to vote for him and his party. Facing a common enemy in the form of an aggressive opposition-bloc who used institutional and extra-institutional destabilization tactics to prevent the project from advancing, constituent participants engaged with top-down efforts by the executive to construct a popular base capable of mobilizing electorally and on the streets.

As in Venezuela, in the Bolivian case, participatory spaces linked organized popular sectors directly to the executive. These spaces, such as the Unity Pact, allowed organizations to direct executive policymaking and agenda-setting from below. While the executive did play a more proactive role in directing popular organization participation via the CONALCAM, as in Venezuela, constituent organizations were willing to participate in the partially top-down spaces as they were facing a common opposition-bloc enemy willing to utilize institutional and extra-institutional tactics to impede the post-neoliberal process.

However, in the Bolivian case there was a stronger bottom-up shaping of the process compared to the Venezuelan case. That is, the relationship between popular organizations and the executive in Bolivia was more heavily weighted toward the base than in Venezuela, allowing for a constituent-led, bottom-up process. Given the combination of historically well organized and powerful popular organizations guiding the anti-neoliberal protests in the antecedent era; the organic emergence of the MAS from the protest movements (particularly those in the Chapare region); in conjunction with aggressive opposition tactics which meant that the president was heavily reliant on the defensive mobilization capacities of both core and strategic constituent organizations, when new spaces of participation were opened by the executive, popular organizations were capable of, and had the leverage to guide the executive from below. Conversely, in Venezuela, given the (generally) weak nature of organized popular power, the executive sought to foster from above a constituent power from below, but in doing so inevitably played a more vanguardist role in directing the process. That is, the combination of ad hoc protests and the emergence of a vanguard-type leader in the antecedent stage, in conjunction with aggressive opposition destabilization following election, fostered a deepening of the vanguardist nature of the post-neoliberal process.

Despite the variation in the quality of democratic deepening (i.e., greater scope for bottom-up participation in Bolivia compared to the more top-down participation in Venezuela), in both cases there was an ally-type relationship between the constituent base and the executive. During this initial confrontational stage with the common opposition-bloc enemy, intensive linkages were forged as popular organization members were incorporated into the party machinery. Hence, while historic factors are key to grasping the nature of party-base relations during post-neoliberal processes, to gain richer insight into the forms that these relations take, as well as to why governments engage in illiberal behavior (with popular backing), it is vital to bring government–opposition-bloc struggles into analyses.

Examining Table 8.3, we can see that in the first stage of the processes following election to power, both anti-neoliberal governments had weak ideological power and faced hostile environments in which opposition-owned media sought to delegitimize and destabilize the governments. In the economic sphere, both governments began their terms with extremely low levels of economic power relative to the opposition. In the political sphere, power was more evenly distributed, with the ruling parties controlling the executive and with a simple majority in national assemblies, while generally pro-opposition judges staffed the judiciaries. In Bolivia, the opposition also dominated the senate and major departmental governments. In constituent assemblies, Chávez dominated the opposition, but in Bolivia, Morales and the MAS had only a simple majority. In the Venezuelan context, military power was initially split between pro-opposition and pro-Chávez wings. While in the Bolivian case transnational leverage over Morales was low, in the Venezuelan case the United States actively sought to destabilize the government.

Given such relative balances of powers, where the newly elected governments had relatively strong political power vis-à-vis the opposition bloc—though crucially, not a wholesale dominance —and where the opposition sought to utilize not only their political power but also their ideological, economic, military, and transnational powers, the likelihood that executives act in an illiberal manner was increased. In both cases, the opposition-blocs were willing to break democratic norms in order to retain the status quo.

Given their conjunctural IEMP powers, and with strong transnational backing from the United States, the Venezuelan opposition-bloc moved from political opposition to strikes to national lockdowns and ultimately to a coup. In Bolivia, the elite-led opposition encouraged violent protests and sought to divide the country, literally, by pushing for regional autonomy. Such actions gave the presidents scope to challenge liberal norms, which became a more regular feature of the processes as they advanced. That is, having been elected on anti-neoliberal mandates with large-scale popular backing (and in the case of Bolivia with powerful movements pushing the government from below), yet confronting a recalcitrant opposition-bloc, the ruling party leaderships justified bending liberal norms as necessary to weaken/overcome opposition ideological, economic, military, and political power and respond to popular demands to deepen and extend democratic quality.

Furthermore, as noted above, the nature that such democratic deepening took was influenced by both the existence of a common enemy (leading both cases to forge ally-relationships with intensive linkages) and historical factors (varied organizational histories and organic/vanguard relations leading to a more bottom-up progressive centralization in Bolivia compared to Venezuela's more top-down form). While the historical factors and the first stage outcomes in each case influenced the future pathways of the processes, they interacted with new emergent power struggles which jolted the processes in differing directions.

Following an initial progressive-centralization stage, both cases witnessed a move toward a more regressive form as tensions emerged between the ruling parties and sectors of their constituent bases. During the regressive centralization stages in each case, elections remained free, though there were examples of illiberal executive actions. In Venezuela, decree laws were used to speedily respond to the government's redistributive mandate and opposition-controlled mayors and local governments were bypassed as funding to local spaces of participation came directly from the executive. Moreover, the clashes between the Chávez government and opposition-bloc media intensified. In Bolivia, there were further efforts to reform the judiciary and remove pro-opposition judges while executive–military relations were tightened. Referring to the previous stage of opposition destabilization, the presidents argued that despite the illiberal nature of such actions, they were in fact democratizing as they helped the governments respond to popular needs while also curbing the capacity of the opposition-bloc to impede the substantive components of the post-neoliberal processes. While such appraisals of the illiberal but democratizing use of centralized executive power may be debated, in Venezuela there was also a clearly de-democratizing use of executive powers as Chávez signed many of the rejected components of a 2007 referendum into law via decree. Moreover, the new relationships between state institutions, including the military, and actors in the private sector not aligned with the opposition-bloc were steeped in corruption.

Democratic quality was extended in both cases as social spending and wages increased, while poverty and inequality decreased. In Venezuela, there was an aggressive nationalization campaign aimed at fracturing opposition-bloc structural power. In Bolivia, though there were advances regarding democratic extending, taxation remained regressive, formal sector job creation was weak, while land reform efforts were limited.

There were efforts to deepen the quality of democratic participation in both cases, though there were also regressive elements to the processes. In Venezuela, new state-sponsored spaces of participation were fostered from above and popular sectors were encouraged to organize locally and to participate in decision-making. Simultaneously, extensive and intensive linkages were forged between the participatory spaces and a newly forged leftist party and, consequently between the base and the executive who dominated the internal running of the party. While the quality of democracy for previously excluded and disorganized popular sectors was certainly boosted in the second stage of Venezuela's post-neoliberal process, informal contestatory contestation was impeded—via the use of extensive and intensive linkages—and via executive reprimands of critical voices.

In the Bolivian case, there were also advances and limitations to democratic deepening. Core-sector organization voices were incorporated into policymaking via participatory spaces, via positions within the ruling left party, and via positions in key state bodies. Moreover, core organizations could engage in successful contestatory interest intermediation if and when their demands were not respected via official channels of participation. However, as in the Venezuelan context, there were efforts from above to curb the capacity of non-core organizations to engage in contestatory mobilization via extensive and intensive linkages.

The prevailing relative balance of power between the opposition-bloc, the government, and popular organizations, the nature of transnational leverage, and historical factors shaped the outcomes (regressive-centralization) during the second stage of the post-neoliberal process in both cases. The ruling parties had moderate-strong political power, restricting the scope for the opposition-bloc to impede the process via institutionalized channels. Moreover, the boosted political power allowed the governments to attempt to restrict opposition-bloc powers (ideological, economic, military, and political). The armed forces backed the governments in each case, allowing the presidents to take such actions. While both governments continued to face a media environment dominated by pro-opposition bloc sources, earlier and continued efforts by the executives to promote alternative sources of information and to break the monopoly of pro-market democracy private media did lead to a slight rebalancing of ideological powers. Transnational leverage was low in both cases, giving the presidents scope to challenge the confines of restrictive market democracy.

Theorists examining democratic backsliding argue that once liberal norms are broken in one area, there is scope for further illiberalism. While such institutionalist analyses capture the potential for a slide toward competitive authoritarianism, it is useful to locate illiberal executive actions within a wider framework that accounts for the structural conditions in which (de) democratization processes occur. The illiberal behaviors of Chávez and Morales, though bending/breaking liberal norms, were justified—and popularly supported—as necessary to overcome the existing unequal balance in other spheres of power. Moreover, previous opposition-bloc actions, in conjunction with the nature of antecedent inclusion (middle classes, elites) and exclusion (popular sectors) under market democracy, are crucial components that help contextualize the illiberal actions by the executives. This is not to suggest that executives always utilized illiberal actions to respond to popular demands to deepen and extend democracy. As the Venezuelan case demonstrates, illiberal use of executive power to bypass a referendum outcome by utilizing decrees to adopt elements that were rejected cannot in any way be justified as advancing democracy. Moreover, as liberal institutionalists say, there is indeed a risk of initial illiberalism sliding in an authoritarian manner. The point, however, is to ask *why* such illiberalism occurs, and *what* it is used for.

Returning to the comparison of emergent power factors in the second stages of the processes in Venezuela and Bolivia, economic power continued to lay with the opposition-bloc. The more aggressive efforts to reclaim executive oversight of the oil industry—and booming oil prices—did see a greater shift in the relative balance of economic power toward the governing party in Venezuela than the Bolivian case (where a moderated nationalization occurred). In both cases, however, key sources of structural economic power, though weakened, remained unbroken. Importers of crucial goods in Venezuela and the agro-industry and transnational extraction firms in Bolivia retained capacity to restrict the agendas of the left-governments. Given the political power of the ruling parties, a strategic compromise was reached between factions of capital and the left-governments. While these pacts of non-aggression created smoother governing environments in which the processes could advance without constant capital strikes, the scope of reforms had to be moderated while room for corruption widened. Unsurprisingly, tensions between the ruling parties and sections of their constituent bases emerged as a consequence.

In Venezuela, where participation was sponsored from above by a vanguardist leader/party, where tight extensive and intensive linkages had been forged between participatory spaces and the ruling party, and with generally limited histories of autonomous popular sector organizing, popular sector critique of the corruption and undemocratic illiberal actions was limited, and when it did emerge, it was easily sidelined by the government. Conversely, given the historically powerful nature of strategic organizations in Bolivia, when the post-neoliberal project moderated in the face of economic structural limits, there was a backlash from strategic-organizations. However, precisely due to their (historically demonstrated) capacity to organize mass protests, the ruling party utilized existing linkage channels to sponsor loyal blocs within the organization leaderships, culminating in schisms and the phenomenon of parallelism. In both cases then, the executives utilized state resources to prevent contestatory mobilization from occurring.

While both cases witnessed regressive centralization during the second stage of the processes, the Venezuelan case slid toward authoritarian centralization whereas the Bolivian case avoided a similar outcome, moving instead toward undemocratic illiberalism before Morales was ousted from office. With the Maduro government having weak ideological and economic power vis-à-vis the opposition bloc, while opposition-bloc political power was dramatically boosted leading to a clash between branches of the state, and with extremely high levels of transnational leverage over Maduro by a hostile US president, Maduro utilized his key remaining source of power—military power—to entrench himself in power. Furthermore, as the process lurched further toward authoritarianism, the constituent base of the PSUV was too weak to challenge the party leadership. The forging of a vanguardist relationship at the very outset of the project had meant that extensive and intensive linkages had become real impediments to, rather than avenues for, bottom-up internal party democracy. That is, though these spaces of participation promoted popular organization, they did not foster autonomous mobilization capacity to challenge the sponsoring party. Such capacity to engage in contestatory mobilization not only ensures that a project adheres to demands from below, but, critically, is necessary to ensure that if and when an empowered executive utilizes centralized power, they do so to advance the democratization project and not to simply entrench themselves in power. Hence, in conjunction with the given balance of IEMP and transnational power, the lack of popular sector organization autonomy, and therefore, capacity to engage in sustained and massive contestatory mobilization against the PSUV leadership was a key component in understanding why the Venezuelan process drifted toward authoritarian centralization.

As in the Venezuelan context, Morales' illiberalism had always been used as a framing plank for the opposition-bloc who labeled him as a threat to democracy from the moment of his first election. Constituent organizations—both core and strategic—had backed the president, however, as they supported the logic of utilizing centralized powers to neutralize elite social forces that opposed expanding political and socioeconomic inclusion to subordinate groups. However, when Morales engaged in blatantly undemocratic illiberalism—by ignoring referendum results and utilizing loyal judges to allow him run for re-election again—he faced stern protests from formerly allied popular organizations.

Despite the top-down efforts to control contestatory mobilization, the grassroots bases of popular organizations had pushed for a reclamation of their organizational autonomy from the MAS and, in response to undemocratic illiberalism, took to the streets calling for Morales' resignation. While middle-class protesters mobilized by elite and far-right elements of society were challenging Morales, unlike the Venezuelan case, a fundamental component explaining why the police and military withdrew their backing for the president was the clear loss of his capacity to control popular sector mobilization. Whereas many popular organizations were reluctant to critique the PSUV in Venezuela for fear that the pro-market opposition-bloc would return to power, in Bolivia undemocratic actions were not supported by many popular organizations whose autonomous histories of contestatory mobilization pre-dated Morales.

Protests against Morales were not indicative of support for the opposition, as the re-election of the MAS ticket in 2020 with massive popular support demonstrates. Rather, and as the local election of non-MAS leftist candidates in local elections in 2021 suggest, the protests were indicative of the belief that the ruling party and president are there at the behest of the popular organizations. Hence, while illiberal activities may be backed where they are used to respond to popular demands, where they are not and where the party veers from demands, the leader is to be replaced. Unlike the Venezuelan case, there was a belief that popular organizations were independently strong enough to ensure that the opposition would not return to power and that under a new president the post-neoliberal process could be renewed and directed from below, even if this entailed engaging in electoral contestation and contestatory mobilization against the ruling left party. The Venezuelan and Bolivian processes are summarized in Figures 8.2 and 8.3 below.

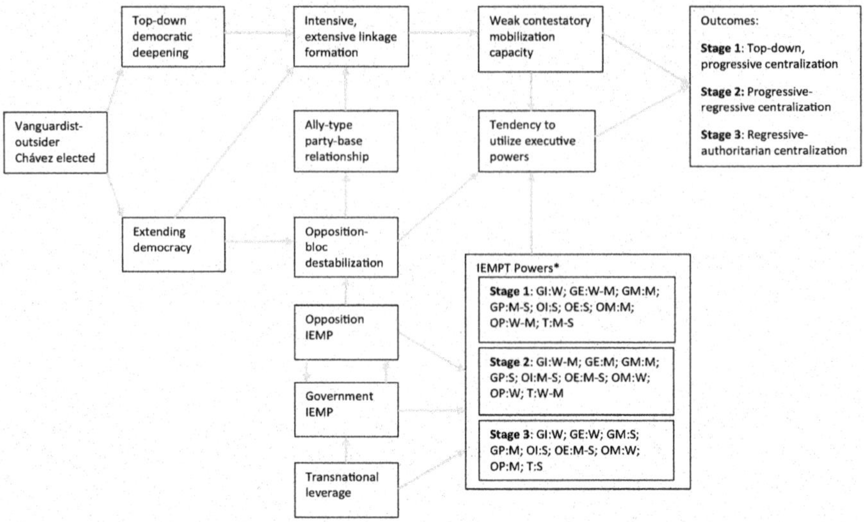

Figure 8.2 Post-neoliberal democratization in Venezuela (author's own elaboration).
**The letters G, O and T refer to "Government," "Opposition-bloc," and "Transnational leverage." The letters I, E, M, and P refer to "Ideological," "Economic," "Military," and "Political" powers. The letters W, M, and S stand for "weak," "moderate," and "strong." For example, GM:M signifies "Government military power: Moderate."*

Long-term legacies

Attempting to outline long-term legacies of any process without an extended temporal gap between assessment and the end of the process is clearly a difficult exercise. Given the recency of the processes examined in this book, in the following discussion, I outline some tentative *potential* long-term outcomes of the processes. A more nuanced appraisal ten years from now will be required to refine the following discussion.

Given the cases discussed in this book are examples of outsider-led post-neoliberal processes that emerged in response to crises of market democracy, it is useful to frame the (potential) long-term legacies by asking whether or not the processes responded to the underlying factors that fostered a crisis of legitimacy and an unstable democratic equilibrium in the first place. As such, I briefly discuss the extent to which popular sector trust in party-systems and democracy more broadly was restored and, relatedly, whether a new left-wing party with a national presence and popular legitimacy was established; whether new participatory spaces are likely to become institutionalized whereby organized popular sectors will retain access to decision-making processes regardless of what type of party is in office; whether there is cross-party (that is, across ideological lines) acceptance that guaranteeing social citizenship is a responsibility of the state; and critically, whether the processes left behind an autonomous, well-organized popular sector base capable of engaging in mobilization to protect gains achieved over the course of the

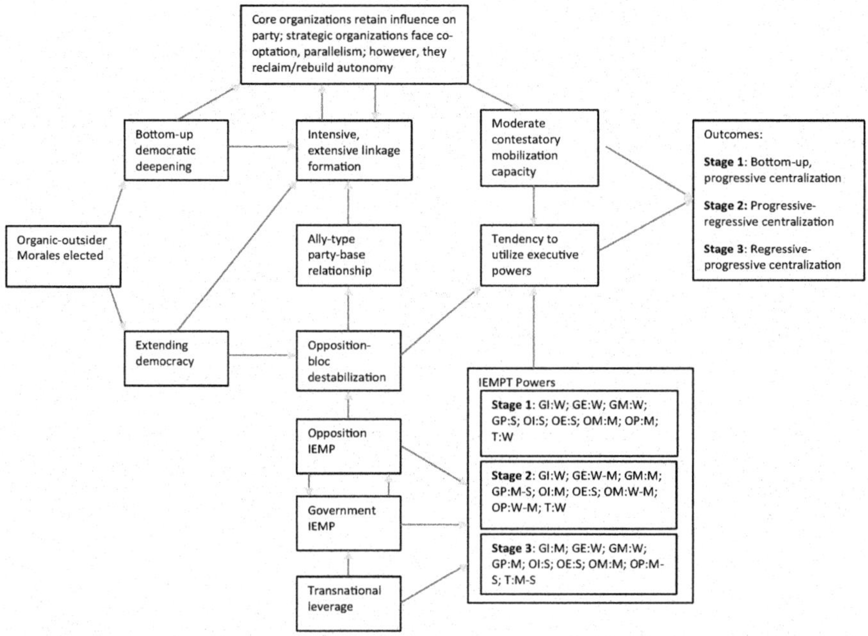

Figure 8.3 Post-neoliberal democratization in Bolivia (author's own elaboration).

processes, as well as to push for further reforms that deepen and extend democratic quality.

Long-term legacies of Venezuela's post-neoliberal process

Given the collapse of the Venezuelan case into an authoritarian impasse with an extraordinarily deep-seated socio-economic crisis, it is difficult to outline with certainty long-term legacies—that is, bar the legacies of economic collapse and entrenched authoritarianism. However, there are other outcomes which will likely persist into the future.

Though current trust in the party-system and democracy is at a base level, during the Chávez presidencies democratic legitimacy, participation levels and voter turnout, and membership of a political party all rose substantially from the preceding market democracy era. Despite the authoritarian turn, the PSUV retains the backing of a committed popular membership base across the country. While the current crisis and impasse as well as the verticalist-authoritarian shift in the PSUV certainly eroded gains regarding trust, participation, and legitimacy, the positive experiences during the Chávez years demonstrated to previously excluded Venezuelans that democratic participation can matter. While there was a politicized and well-organized popular base in pockets of the country before the election of Chávez, popular sectors more broadly did not pay attention to or participate in the country's politics.

As numerous people I met during my visits to the country's barrios told me, before Chávez they saw politics as a game played by the rich. Chávez' encouragement to read the Constitution, to participate in local level politics, and to join a party and, crucially, his successes in demonstrating that the state can in fact respond to the most pressing needs of vulnerable citizens have left an indelible legacy. Indeed, even opposition-bloc parties incorporated plans to protect the social policies of the Chavista governments in their electoral manifestos indicating acceptance across the political spectrum that the state has a responsibility to protect its citizens from the excesses of the market.

Whether the PSUV remains as the political vehicle for popular sector concerns will depend on the capacity of grassroots organizations to wrestle control from the corrupt party leadership and their military and business backers. While such a scenario looks unlikely given the bleak conditions in the country at present, notwithstanding the repressive actions by a government that jails and murders contestatory popular organizers, and despite the crippling economic crisis, anti-Maduro protests in the barrios are growing. These protests are not led by any party and are fundamentally opposed to a return of the opposition. They are autonomous protests demanding a return to the founding principles of Chavismo. As a long-time social activist and revolutionary told me,

> Not everything is lost. The people do not want a return of the right. When you talk to the campesinos, to barrio organizers, they want Chavismo. We must sow the ideas and possibilities that Chávez represented in the younger generation, teach them about their rights. The process goes on, we will continue, bit by bit we will revive the social organizations, building from below, toward real Chavismo. This is the path we are on.[23]

Indeed, the conscientization of Venezuela's popular sectors during the Chávez presidencies means that whatever pathway the country takes out of the current impasse, popular sector demands will have to be included in the plans.

Though it is highly likely that any route out of the economic crisis will see international and opposition-bloc voices advocating for deeper privatization of the oil industry and IMF loans with stringent austerity conditionalities, the popular resistance to such plans will be enormous. Unlike the ad hoc eruptions of discontent regarding the neoliberal responses to economic crises in the 1980s and 1990s, protests will be better coordinated by popular organizations capable of mobilizing politicized popular sectors under the framing banner of "Chavismo." Hence, while there were tensions given the vanguardist manner in which Chávez encouraged linkages within and between popular sector barrios and rural communities, and between popular organizations and the party, top-down efforts to encourage organization may ultimately function as a stepping-stone toward the development of an autonomous, organized popular base capable of engaging in mass contestatory mobilization. As such, while the PSUV may fracture, the collapse of the party-system which opened space for Chávez, in conjunction with the politicization of the popular sectors, means that Venezuela's future party-system will have to contain a real option that represents popular sector concerns. In sum, there is little chance of a return to the Punto Fijo era left-right party convergence around neoliberalism.

Long-term legacies of Bolivia's post-neoliberal process

The emergence of the MAS at the head of a wave of protests ultimately re-politicized politics. The party system permanently changed and become more stable. In terms of descriptive representation, "Bolivia since 2005 … experienced dramatic improvements in the political representation of traditionally disadvantaged social groups."[24] Meanwhile, MAS "significantly broadened access to the political arena for important segments of the popular sectors."[25] Moreover, in terms of non-electoral participation, Bolivia saw "important, if complex, changes in the patterns of interaction between the state and civil society organizations."[26] While tensions between the MAS and sectors of the popular base grew over the course of the project, it triumphed in national elections in 2020, a decade and a half after Morales' first election—and without Morales as a candidate. This clearly indicates that the MAS is a nationally legitimate and successful leftwing party capable of representing popular sector concerns that had been excluded during the preceding market democracy era.

As in the Venezuelan case, the post-neoliberal project in Bolivia demonstrated that a more substantive model of democracy and citizenship could be achieved if a progressive party captured state power. Despite all the frictions and the moderation of the project in the face of opposition-bloc powers, the post-neoliberal model of democracy outlined in the Constitution retains high levels of legitimacy. Spaces of participation such as the Unity Pact that brought together the leaders of major popular organizations to guide the MAS from below were reforged during the 2019–20 period of confrontation with the coup-government.

The regressive process of parallelism also left a legacy, with grassroots bases and newly elected popular organization leaderships vociferously demonstrating their rejection of a loss of autonomy when working with the MAS. Popular organizations are undergoing a process of deep introspection to evaluate the successes and shortcomings of the MAS-led post-neoliberal process. This is of fundamental importance. While in national-level elections popular sector organizations called for unity to ensure that the opposition-bloc cannot reclaim control of state powers, at local and regional levels the MAS faces progressive challengers who want to hold the ruling party to a popularly directed process.

It appears that there is no cross-party consensus that social gains achieved under MAS should be protected. Indeed, the evidence from the interim government following the coup suggests that the opposition-bloc still clamor for a wholesale return to exclusionary market democracy. The issue for the opposition-bloc, however, is they have not come to terms with the new state of affairs in Bolivia; they are the minority, and their political-economic project does not have popular legitimacy. Only by brute force can they reclaim their position at the top of Bolivian society.

While popular-indigenous organizations protested vigorously against the neoliberal reforms of the 1980s and 1990s, the actual experience of a democratization process headed by an indigenous-popular person and the incorporation of long-excluded sectors indicates that there will be no simple return to market democracy, even if the MAS lose office. There is a highly politicized and powerful organized popular bloc who have seen both the possibilities, and dangers, of a left party in office. As such, both exclusionary oligarchic market democracy and top-down crude populist democracy appear to be off the table in Bolivia.[27] Therefore, despite the shortcomings of the MAS-led process, it represents a critical juncture in the country's development.

In the Venezuelan case, the illiberal centralization in response to oligarchic pressures culminated in authoritarianism and the establishment of a new oligarchy comprised of the upper echelons of the PSUV, the military, and a new business elite. In Bolivia, the post-neoliberal process which sought to offer a more substantive model of democracy in response to the exclusionary oligarchic market democracy did careen toward dangerous illiberal centralization. However, with the help of powerful, internally democratic popular organizations, the process avoided culminating in a deeply undemocratic illiberalism. That is, the Bolivian case appears to have avoided careening from oligarchic rule to illiberal populism to oligarchic rule. Rather, the country appears to be on a path toward a consolidated post-neoliberal democracy that while challenging some liberal norms, avoids wholesale undemocratic illiberalism while simultaneously boosting the substantive and participatory elements of democracy.

Notes

1 María Pilar García-Guadilla, "Urban Land Committees: Co-optation, Autonomy and Protagonism," in David Smilde and Daniel Hellinger (eds), *Venezuela's Bolivarian Democracy: Participation, Politics, and Culture under Chávez* (Durham, NC: Duke University Press, 2011): 94–8; Matthew Rhodes-Purdy, "Participatory Populism: Theory and Evidence from Bolivarian Venezuela," *Political Research Quarterly* 68 no. 3 (2015): 415–27.

2 Kurt Weyland, "Latin America's Authoritarian Drift: The Threat from the Populist Left," *Journal of Democracy* 24, no. 3 (2013): 22.

3 Javier Corrales, "The Authoritarian Resurgence: Autocratic Legalism in Venezuela," *Journal of Democracy* 26, no. 2 (2015): 38.

4 See Gabriel Hetland, "The Promises and Perils of Radical Left Populism: The Case of Venezuela," *Journal of World-Systems Research* 24, no. 2 (2018): 277–92.

5 Jake Johnson and Sara Kozameh, "Venezuelan Economic and Social Performance under Hugo Chávez, in Graphs," 7 March (2013): Retrieved https://cepr.net/venezuelan-economic-and-social-performance-under-hugo-chavez-in-graphs/.

6 Jeffrey Webber, *The Last Day of Oppression, and the First Day of the Same* (London: Pluto, 2017): 33.
7 Johnson and Kozameh, "Venezuelan Economic and Social Performance."
8 Figures cited in Edgardo Lander, "Venezuela: Terminal Crisis of the Rentier Petro-State?" *Amsterdam Transnational Institute*, October (2014): Retrieved https://www.tni.org/en/publication/venezuela-terminal-crisis-of-the-rentier-petro-state.
9 Julia Buxton, "Continuity and Change in Venezuela's Bolivarian Revolution," *Third World Quarterly* 41, no. 8 (2020): 1381.
10 Ibid.
11 See Lander, "Venezuela: Terminal Crisis."
12 Cited in Lander, "Venezuela: Terminal Crisis."
13 Webber, *The Last Day of Oppression*, 42.
14 Julia Buxton, "Defusing Venezuela," *Section Hall Journal of Diplomacy and International Relations* 7 (2018): 19.
15 See for example Javier Corrales, "Democratic Backsliding through Electoral Irregularities: The Case of Venezuela," *European Review of Latin American and Caribbean Studies* 109 (2020): 41–65.
16 Eduardo Silva, "Reorganizing Popular Sector Incorporation: Propositions from Bolivia, Ecuador, and Venezuela," *Politics & Society* 45, no. 1 (2017): 100.
17 Omar Sánchez-Sibony, "Competitive Authoritarianism in Morales's Bolivia: Skewing Arenas of Competition," *Latin American Politics and Society* 63, no. 1 (2021): 118–44.
18 Ibid.
19 Eduardo Silva, "Conclusion: Reflections on the Second Wave of Popular Incorporation for a Post-Neoliberal Era," in Eduardo Silva and Federico Rossi (eds.), *Reshaping the Political Arena in Latin America: From Resisting Neoliberalism to the Second Incorporation* (Pittsburgh: University of Pittsburgh Press, 2018): 309-324.
20 The CSUTCB dominance of decisions regarding agrarian policy at the expense of CONAMAQ and the TIPNIS conflict are key examples of such dynamics.
21 Santiago Anria, *When Movements Become Parties: The Bolivian MAS in Comparative Perspective* (Cambridge and New York: Cambridge University Press, 2019): 143.
22 However, as discussed in Chapter 7, after the Áñez government signed off on legislation stating that police and military figures would not face any sanctions for the use of repressive force, the army killed dozens of anti-coup protesters and injured hundreds more.
23 Interview with a former member of the revolutionary Bandera Roja party, who split with the party to work with Chávez. The interviewee remains a key figure in the communes movement and helped establish one of the country's first and most successful communes in the state of Lara. Electronic interview, March 23, 2021.
24 Jonas Wolff, "Political Incorporation in Measures of Democracy: A Missing Dimension (and the Case of Bolivia)," *Democratization* 25, no. 4 (2018): 702.
25 Ibid.
26 Ibid.
27 I return to the issue and the lessons from the case studies regarding "careening" between oligarchy and populism in the concluding chapter, drawing from Dan Slater's excellent framing of contemporary democratization processes. Dan Slater, "Democratic Careening," *World Politics* 65, no. 4 (2013): 729–63.

Conclusion

Oligarchy, populisms, and pathways out of the crisis of democracy

The self-reinforcing spiral of democratic narrowing and shallowing over the course of the neoliberal era fostered a crisis of too little democracy, not only in Latin America but in Europe and the United States too. We have entered what Crouch[1] labels "post-democracy," a scenario in which democratic institutions remain, but the energy of the political system has passed into the hands of a select political and corporate elite who ensure that politics responds to their concerns. The neoliberal project has exacerbated inequalities and opened new avenues for economic power to manipulate the political system, reigniting the inherent tension within liberal democracies around equalities of citizens' votes and inequalities of economic power.

Dahl's[2] theory of polyarchy argued that if there were sufficient numbers of groups seeking to influence government, with each group influencing policy in one specific area, then no single interest could dominate. As such, issues of economic inequality and capacity for one group to shape politics in their image would be limited. In Dahl's conceptualization of democratization, democracy could be evaluated on two axes. One axis evaluates whether or not there are avenues for public contestation and political competition, while a second axis measures the breath of participation (i.e., whether all citizens have access to these channels of participation).

In the market democracy era, the notion of a functioning polyarchy whereby all groups in society have equal access to decision-makers and capacity to shape policymaking is clearly non-existent. Inequality has spiraled and the lobbying capacity of capital has increased. There is a vicious cycle as increasing wealth allows economic elites to design policies that lock in advantages to capital, thereby furthering economic inequality, and, consequently, political power inequalities. Neoliberal responses to neoliberal-fueled crises of capitalism in Latin America in the 1990s and the United States and Europe in the 2000s further eroded living standards and job quality and security for middle- and popular-classes at the same time that wealth levels of economic elites expanded. Reductions in public spending rather than increased taxation of wealth was the response to debt crises. Labor market flexibilization rather than training was the prescribed medicine that would supposedly make debtor countries more competitive on the global market. Privatization to allow for "efficient" operation and reduced state burdens went hand in hand with declining standards of public service provision—which negatively impacted the wellbeing of lower-income groups while benefitting the interests of capital. Free-floating capital, the core ideal of proponents of a market democracy—triggered competition between governments for investment via reductions in environmental, labor, and social protection standards.

The neoliberalization of democracy has shattered any illusion that unfettered capitalism and democracy go hand in hand. Democracy has been hollowed out. As parties of the center-left and center-right coalesce around neoliberal logic and technocratic governance, Madisonian concerns regarding checks and balances on elected leaders (government of the people) have come to dominate ideas of popular democracy (government by the people). Social-democratic/socialist parties and their constituent union bases have lost their ideological commitment to the economic concerns of working- and popular classes at the same time that inequality and precarity have increased. The capitalist market economy has been sealed off from democratic oversight, a sort of "Hayekian social dictatorship" in which the democratic channels for the articulation of popular-sector interests have been blocked—"either because only the same outcomes can ever emerge or because what emerges no longer makes any difference to the 'markets'."[3]

The neoliberal emphasis on low taxation and high debt from financial markets to fund state programs has meant that state managers/party leaders have become more responsive to the concerns of global financial markets than to the needs of their own citizens.[4] Neoliberal elites seek to insulate themselves from popular demands at the same time that they support strong checks and balances on elected officials to ensure there can be no deviation from market democracy. Indeed, Crouch[5] states that the preferred regime of capitalists is post-democracy

> where all forms of democracy continue, including the rule of law, but where the electorate has become passive, not engaging in disturbing activism, and not generating a civil society vibrant enough to produce awkward counter-lobbies that try to rival the quiet work of business interests in the corridors of government.

There is to be no alternative to neoliberalism. Checks on elected officials have become so severe and the breath of participation so narrow (whereby capital dictates policy, not citizens) that the agenda of politics has been set from the outset, making democratic participation seem like a futile pursuit for regular citizens.

Democracy in the neoliberal era has thus become oligarchic, not only in so-called developing democracies but in the "developed" West as well. While some theorists may resist the notion of oligarchy as relevant to examinations of contemporary democracies, it has become increasingly evident that mechanisms of representation and participation have become incapable of restraining transnationally oriented elites who work with local counterparts in the state and economy, utilizing the structural power of the global economy to reorganize state institutions and provide a more favorable set of institutions (to mobile capital, not to local citizens).[6] As Cameron[7] stresses,

> Oligarchic modes of rule are endemic wherever there are high levels of inequality and the poor are constrained in their capacity for organization and collective action. The surfacing of oligarchy in its current form is inextricably linked to the global spread of neoliberalism. By weakening the capacity of popular sector organizations to engage in the activities of citizenship and representation that would balance corporate influence, neoliberalism turns democracy, as we understand it today (to wit, democratized representative government), into something closer to representative government as it was originally understood: government by the few on behalf of the many. And since the many are excluded by the weakening of popular organizations, this formula is as oligarchic as it is democratic.

Horizontal accountability in representative democracy, essential to curb executive power, has always sought to protect the status quo.[8] Today, this status quo entails gross inequality and precarity for swathes of the population. When "people's life opportunities are systematically undermined because of factors beyond their control, they are likely to feel disillusionment and resentment."[9] At the same time, a consensus of the center whereby political parties fail to offer any redress to genuine popular grievances means that citizens vote in smaller numbers and with less partisan consistency, while party membership levels decline. As Schattschneider[10] stressed, those who decide what the game is about also decide who will get into the game.

As the interests of the rich are organized into politics while popular concerns are organized out, with party-voter distances widening, while parties of the left and right programmatically converge around neoliberalism and austerity, popular distrust of parties and politicians increases. With mainstream parties no longer offering ideological alternatives to neoliberal-infused citizenship and with union power decimated, popular sector capacity to have their concerns heard and responded to, to check elite power, has dwindled. This combination of mistrust in the oligarchic political system alongside withdrawal from participation has triggered varying forms of "populist" backlash.[11]

Slater[12] argues that democracies will careen between oligarchic forms and domineering populist forms as intense conflicts between partisan actors deploying competing visions of democratic accountability emerge. Populists will call for more substantial inclusivity or vertical accountability, while opponents will defend democracy for the constraints against excessive concentration of unaccountable power in the executive—that is, horizontal accountability. Such competing visions speak to the democratizing potentials and dangers of populism. While many theorists condemn populism as a threat to liberal democracy, Berman notes that "although it is certainly true that democracy unchecked by liberalism can slide into excessive majoritarianism or oppressive populism, liberalism unchecked by democracy can easily deteriorate into oligarchy."[13] As Cameron notes,

> without denying populism's potentially deleterious effects on democracy, the focus is partially misplaced because oligarchic modes of rule and populist mobilization are co-constitutive ... Populism is both a typical reaction to oligarchic modes of rule and an endemic feature of democratic politics in unequal societies.[14]

Foweraker[15] cogently details how oligarchic rule fosters populist responses, but he argues that populists will only achieve a readjustment between oligarchic and democratic practice, with populism tending to "reinforce bureaucratic patrimonialism, the unevenness of the rule of law, and the lack of universalistic citizenship."[16] While such concerns regarding the dangers of domineering populism are clearly legitimate, we must address why anti-neoliberal outsider responses to oligarchy tend toward a centralization of executive power, and whether such centralization can be used to advance rather than limit a (re-)democratization project.

Slater[17] states that there is "ample reason to believe that elected executives seeking to broaden substantive democratic inclusion might clash with elites who prize democracy's constraints on absolute power more than its promise to empower the many." Understanding these power struggles, between the anti-neoliberal outsiders elected to respond to oligarchic domination of democracy and the elites who seek to defend their domination of the political system, requires that democratization theorists take a broader view than a simple institutional appraisal and that the sole focus of analysis is not only on the "illiberal populist" or "competitive authoritarian," but on how anti-neoliberal outsiders interact with the oligarchic opposition. That is, elites and newly elected leaders challenging oligarchic democracy will not only utilize political power to advance their agenda or limit their opponents. As I have argued throughout this book, it is the conjunctural relative balance of ideological, economic, military, and political powers, as well as the prevailing transnational forces that will shape the directions and outcomes of processes, including whether and how executive power is used to curb opposition-elite power.

To capture the potential pitfalls and possibilities of processes headed by progressive anti-neoliberal outsiders as they encounter elite opposition, I advanced a continuum that runs from authoritarian centralization via regressive centralization to progressive centralization. While Dahl conceived of democratization entailing a dual move toward increased checks and balances on government as well as a broadening of the scope of who is invited to participate, where oligarchic opposition seek to restrict deepening and extending processes via institutional and extra-institutional means, increased executive powers to block oligarchic power may be a component of a radical-substantive democratization process. However, the inherent dangers of such a process are enormous, as the Venezuelan case study demonstrates. It is only where executive power is used to curb oligarchic powers and not to block all forms of opposition-bloc participation, and where it is simultaneously counterbalanced from below by popular power that the process may be said to be advancing democratic quality. That is, centralization may only be described as progressive where it seeks to tackle/overcome oligarchic power in order to advance an incorporation project that cumulatively deepens the scope for bottom-up inclusion in, and oversight of, decision-making processes.

Given the current legitimacy crisis facing democracy, the goal must be to re-politicize politics by limiting the scope of market forces to determine, ex-ante and ex-post, the agenda of government and to re-democratize democracy. As Streeck[18] states

> If democracy means that social justice must not be reduced to market justice, then the main task of democratic politics should be to reverse the institutional devastation wrought by four decades of neoliberal progress … Today democratization should mean building institutions through which markets can be brought back under the control of society: labour markets that leave scope for social life, product markets that do not destroy nature, credit markets that do not mass-produce unsustainable promises.

However, achieving such goals will surely trigger an oligarchic backlash, which may therefore witness the use of illiberal actions to break up oligarchic sources of power in ideological, economic, military, or political spheres.

While Levitsky and Ziblatt[19] cogently demonstrate how the erosion of the norms and liberal "guardrails" for democracy may cause democracies to "die," if the norms of democracy are set so as to provide the perfect environment for the protection of entrenched elite interests and the free mobility of capital which in turn fosters inequalities, exclusion and recurring economic and environmental crises, how can democracy be "saved"? Indeed, while Grugel and Riggirozzi's[20] question as to whether entrenched socio-economic inequality is the price that must be paid for a stable liberal democracy is pertinent, in the long run, this dichotomy must be overcome if democracy is to retain/regain popular legitimacy. Democracy is thus at a critical juncture. In an increasingly unequal world, it is only by democratizing democracy—by simultaneously deepening and extending the quality of participation—that justified popular anger with political systems can be assuaged. Not only is such democratization the best way to stymie support for xenophobic nativists who are capturing the moment of popular discontent, but more generally it is the only way to jolt democracy out of its current malaise.

As the Andean cases discussed in detail in this book attest, it is inconceivable that such a re-democratization of democracy can occur without mass popular organizing and protesting, and it is also inconceivable that the beneficiaries of exclusionary market democracy will not utilize oligarchic powers to limit reforms. That is, (re-)democratization processes will inherently entail tensions and pushback from those who have long-enjoyed dominant status. Challenging oligarchic power and bringing unelected market forces under social control will therefore push liberal democracy and respect for all liberal norms to its limits. As theorists, and as citizens, we must ask the question of what we want our democracies to be, and how we can get there. If we wish to avoid a careening back and forth between oligarchic rule and domineering illiberal populism it is essential that we set our ideals and standards high. Accepting that a deep, substantive democracy is out of reach because oligarchic elites and mobile capital will block advances is not only normatively undesirable, but it fosters the unstable democratic equilibria facing us today. Accepting unconstrained executive power and a president/government that takes decisions in the name of popular sectors without input from below is also clearly unacceptable. However, rather than throwing the baby out with the bathwater by wholeheartedly labeling all processes that challenge liberal norms as undemocratic, we must assess why liberal norms are being bent, what executive power is being used for and, critically, whether it is tethered to powerful civil society organizations capable of preventing illiberal democratization becoming authoritarian centralization.

As the Bolivian case suggests—despite its shortcomings—to try and overcome the socio-economic equality/liberal democracy zero-sum game and to prevent anti-neoliberal outsider responses to oligarchic democracy becoming anti-democratic, what we need is a deepened democracy. That is, we need progressive anti-neoliberal parties in office that are internally democratic, that foster and respond to institutionalized spaces of citizen participation, and that are also responsive to contestatory interest intermediation.

However, it is clear that when the power of oligarchic actors and mobile capital over anti-neoliberal parties in office is high, the risks of tensions emerging between the party and its constituent base are increased. Indeed, the Bolivian and Venezuelan cases suggest that such tensions will be inevitable given that the state is a social relation and that the idea of breaking oligarchic power in one quick step is unrealistic. It is therefore essential that popular movements remain/become strong in their own right since only strong movements will ensure that an anti-neoliberal party in office moves in a democratizing direction.[21] As such, managing the inherent tensions between democratic extending and deepening, between the intensive and extensive linkages that boost the quality of democracy while simultaneously opening avenues for a curbing of contestatory mobilization capacity is a key challenge for popular civil society organizations, and, consequently, for responding to the contemporary crisis of democracy.

While tensions between oligarchy/populism and horizontal constraints/vertical accountability are inherent to democracy and have been the focus of much of our theorizing over the past century, we need to bring discussions of progressive party-popular organization tensions into our frameworks. IEMP power struggles between anti-neoliberal parties and oligarchic opposition must be theorized and analyzed in relation to anti-neoliberal party-popular organization tensions—and these relations must be located within a transnational analysis that accounts for the leverage of external actors to limit the agenda of ruling progressive parties. Failure to do so leads to partial, and potentially wholly inaccurate, analyses.

To avoid careening between oligarchy and domineering populism, anti-neoliberal parties must not collapse to oligarchic demands (thereby making the project redundant in a substantive and participative sense) while resisting the temptations of regressive or authoritarian centralization (making the project redundant in a liberal-representative sense). Democracy must be representative, liberal, participative, and substantive at the same time. Achieving this balancing act may seem an impossible task, but surely this must be our target. Cases that will be best positioned to walk the tightrope and avoid sliding toward authoritarian centralization or regressing back to exclusionary market democracy will be those where a powerful, autonomous, well-organized popular society exists. Such a base must be able to engage in mass mobilization in defense of the anti-neoliberal party and its policies at times of acute confrontation with oligarchic elites, while also maintaining capacity to engage in offensive mobilization against "their" party if and when it veers from a post-neoliberal path. The neoliberal response to the "crisis of too much democracy" fostered a crisis of too little democracy today that has sparked a "populist" backlash. To counteract the rising support for xenophobic nativists and the enormous dangers this entails, the best antidote is a dose of democracy administered by an anti-neoliberal party that is guided from below by an organized popular base. Despite all the challenges and tensions inherent to such a process, what alternative do we have?

Notes

1 Colin Crouch, *Post-democracy after the Crises* (Cambridge: Polity, 2020): 4.

2 Robert Dahl, *Polyarchy: Participation and Opposition* (New Haven, CT: Yale University Press, 1971).

3 Wolfgang Streeck, *The Delayed Crisis of Democratic Capitalism: Buying Time* (London: Verso Books, 2017): 172.

4 Streeck, *The Delayed Crisis.*

5 Crouch, *Post-democracy*, 39.

6 William Robinson, "Promoting Polyarchy in Latin America: The Oxymoron of 'Market Democracy'," in Eric Hershberg and Fred Rosen (eds), *Latin America after Neoliberalism* (New York: The New Press, 2006): 102.

This phenomenon is not limited to Latin American democracies or developing states. For example, Bartels concludes that in the US the "political system seems to be functioning not as a 'democracy' but as an 'oligarchy'." Larry Bartels, *Unequal Democracy: The Political Economy of the New Gilded Age* (Princeton, NJ: Princeton University Press, 2018): 287.

7 Maxwell Cameron, "The Return of Oligarchy? Threats to Representative Democracy in Latin America," *Third World Quarterly* 42, no. 4 (2021): 786.

8 Adam Przeworski, *Crises of Democracy* (Cambridge: Cambridge University Press, 2021): 200.
9 Frederick Solt, "Economic Inequality and Democratic Political Engagement," *American Journal of Political Science* 52, no. 1 (2008): 48.
10 Elmer Eric Schattschneider, *The Semi-sovereign People: A Realist's View of Democracy in America* (Hinsdale, IL: Dryden, 1960).
11 For the remainder of this discussion my focus is on the potentials and pitfalls of anti-neoliberal outsiders, not on nativist xenophobic populists that have emerged in many northern and western European cases and in the US. For a discussion of the conjunctural factors that shaped the variation in the nature of response to the crises of market, see Brown, "Neoliberalization, De-democratization, and Populist Responses in Western Europe, the US, and Latin America," *Critical Sociology* 46, no. 7–8 (2020): 1173–87.
12 Dan Slater, "Democratic Careening," *World Politics* 65, no. 4 (2013): 729–63.
13 Sheri Berman, "The Pipe Dream of Undemocratic Liberalism," *Journal of Democracy* 28, no. 3 (2017): 30.
14 Cameron, "The Return of Oligarchy?," 786.
15 Joe Foweraker, *Polity: Demystifying Democracy in Latin America and Beyond* (Boulder, CO: Lynne Rienner, 2018).
16 Cameron, "The Return of Oligarchy," 786.
17 Slater, "Democratic Careening," 732–3.
18 Streeck, *The Delayed Crisis*, 173–4.
19 Steven Levitsky and Daniel Ziblatt, *How Democracies Die* (New York: Crown, 2018).
20 Jean Grugel and Pía Riggirozzi, "Neoliberal Disruption and Neoliberalism's Afterlife: What Is Left of Post-neoliberalism," *Critical Social Policy* 38, no. 3 (2018): 561.
21 Nicos Poulantzas, *State, Power, Socialism* (London: NLB, 1978).

Index

Note: Bold page numbers refer to tables; *italic* page numbers refer to figures.